WE WERE SPIRITUAL REFUGEES

We Were Spiritual Refugees

A Story to Help You Believe in Church

Katie Hays

WILLIAM B. EERDMANS PUBLISHING COMPANY
GRAND RAPIDS, MICHIGAN

Wm. B. Eerdmans Publishing Co.
4035 Park East Court SE, Grand Rapids, Michigan 49546
www.eerdmans.com

26 25 24 23 22 21 20   1 2 3 4 5 6 7

ISBN 978-0-8028-7778-9

Library of Congress Cataloging-in-Publication Data

Names: Hays, Katie, 1969– author.
Title: We were spiritual refugees : a story to help you believe in church /
    Katie Hays.
Description: Grand Rapids, Michigan : William B. Eerdmans Publishing Com-
    pany, 2020. | Includes bibliographical references. | Summary: "A memoir of
    Galileo Church's first five years, this is an account from its pastor, sharing
    what she learned about belonging from those who left the traditional church
    but wanted a Jesus community"—Provided by publisher.
Identifiers: LCCN 2019035982 | ISBN 9780802877789 (paperback)
Subjects: LCSH: Galileo Church (Fort Worth, Tex.)—History. | Hays, Katie, 1969–
    | Fort Worth (Tex.)—Church history.
Classification: LCC BX7331.F58 H39 2020 | DDC 280—dc23
LC record available at https://lccn.loc.gov/2019035982

The excursus "Preaching from the LGBTQ Margins" was previously published
online in *Circuit Rider* by Abingdon Press, November 2018. Used by permission.

The excursus "What Happened When Our Church Went Venmo" was previously
published in a slightly different form in *The Christian Century*, December 5, 2018,
and is used by permission.

CONTENTS

In 2004, I visited the Ring of Brodgar on the largest island in Orkney, Scotland. It is the oldest site of human habitation that we have a record of, dating back twenty thousand years. While the purpose of the stone circles (similar to Stonehenge) remains elusive, it is apparent that they were central for rites of passage connected to astronomical observation. Whatever their specific use, being there gave me a distinct impression of their lasting importance. Twenty-seven of the original sixty thirty-foot-high (and higher) stones are still visible.

I visited with a group of friends who wanted to mark our own stages of growth into adulthood. I was on this pilgrimage as a means of honoring my father, who had died a few years earlier. And I was seeking a deep connection to what it means to be living as a fatherless father myself. Others were marking their own paths of transition. We were looking for something ancient, lasting, and monumental to help us find meaning in our daily lives and a path to walk into our future.

Standing in the shadow of the large stone circle, I was taken with the fact that for centuries human beings have been forming, often at significant cost, expense, and effort, places of meaning and pathfinding.

Be it the Ring of Brodgar, a town center, a cathedral, or a fireplace in our homes, we humans make places of meaning that help us find meaning.

I have spent my adult life trying to make communities—and one community in particular, Solomon's Porch in Minneapolis—where people can find a path of human growth and spiritual life in the way of Jesus. In 1983 I was invited by friends to take on Jesus as my spiritual teacher and my Lord. For more than three decades, I have sought to understand Jesus as the Son of God as a way to see all people as the children of God. I have endeavored to join the call of all children of God to live up to Love as a way of life. One thing I know for sure: this life I've chosen, or that has chosen me, requires community. We find meaning, explore what it means to be human, with people who are trying the same. We build the Ring of Brodgar. We build churches.

That's what makes me so excited to know Katie Hays and to follow with such admiration the development of Galileo Church. What Katie will describe in the pages that follow is one story of one community of meaning. It has all the quirky particularities of one community. It is apparent that the wonderful parts of the Galileo community were made possible by the specific people who were involved in its formation. Galileo Church is not offered here as a repeatable prototype, and that is a good thing. But it remains true: what you will find in the story of these particular spiritual refugees is the universal, ancient, modern, and postmodern pursuit of a people seeking a community of belonging and path making.

What I have discovered in looking at the many ways humans have organized communities of meaning and path making is that everyone is making it up as we go. We use the tools that are available to us. Just as the ancient Scots used the stars and stones to make meaning, so we are using the internet, coffee shops, homes, bowling alleys, bars, and even a corrugated sheet metal barn to make communities today.

Not all of these experiments work in the long-term. Not all of them are particularly good ideas. But that is the very point of experimentation—to try without guarantee. It is in the risking, the trying, that we find our way. They all count, every try, every time.

I have been intrigued with the development of communities of Christian faith over the last two hundred years in the United States. I find it helpful to recognize four periods of cultural development over the last two centuries: the Agrarian Age, the Industrial Age, the Information Age, and our current period, what I call "the Inventive Age." While these ages are all built on one another, and are extensions of the previous age, they each also have their own way of thinking, value systems, appreciation of aesthetics, and useful tools. The communities that form in each age are not only products of the age, but help create the cultural norms of that age.

I have been thinking about the impacts of these changes in the communities we form now for the manifestation of our collective faith. As I was writing my Inventive Age book series (which dives deep into the implication of community, preaching, church, and evangelism in light of the Inventive Age), I engaged with people starting communities of faith around the world. It was during this time that I first met and was instantly inspired by Katie Hays and the risky project she was endeavoring. That project ultimately became the beautiful Galileo Church community.

A few weeks ago, I had the privilege to attend a gathering of Galileo Church. I was struck by how well its existence tells the story I had been seeing develop in the United States and around the world.

Galileo is not yesterday's church. Located on the edge of a sprawling urban center near a major interstate, Galileo's Big Red Barn does not resemble the Gothic cathedrals of Europe or the tightly manicured church structures of suburban Christianity. Galileo's people are as unconventional as its building. They are real. They proudly call themselves "quirky," and the label fits. Pretense is left behind here. When you walk through the doors of the Big Red Barn, you have the sense that you are entering a unique worship space, a place where people live, love, laugh, cry, curse, rejoice, and mourn as community.

Those who doubt the future of church have not seen or heard of Galileo Church. This community of spiritual refugees offers hope and healing to those near and far.

Galileo is not a perfect church (which is the entire point of it), nor is it a church that works for everyone (which is also the point of it). I see it as one clarifying lens through which to see what a church of this Inventive Age can look like. I believe it will inspire generations to come to build communities of meaning, communities of belonging, communities of path making, in Jesus's name, for their own times.

Doug Pagitt, *October 2019*

I Know Why You're Here

My name is Katie, and my pronouns are she/her/hers.

I know why you're here. You've picked up this book because you are worried and afraid and hoping for some words of comfort and courage. You intuit that the world is moving on, that things we used to know for sure are not so certain anymore, that the ones who are coming after us would hardly recognize the world that shaped our inner landscapes, nor we theirs. You go to church, but you see the ranks thinning in the pews that used to swell with eager, or at least compliant, worshipers.

You're a mom or a grandmom, a dad or a granddad, and the kid you raised through VBSs and youth groups and lock-ins and spring break mission trips has left home or hasn't left home, but either way they don't go to church now unless you raise a fuss and tell them it's important to you. You watch them during worship and pray silently that something in the familiar hymns or the usual Scripture readings or the preacher's dry sense of humor will stir some emotion in them. Your heart sinks as you read the boredom on their face; you silently seethe as they check their phone for the umpteenth time; you ache when you recognize the strong sense of *not belonging* they are experiencing. You know they will not come back, not really, not ever.

Or maybe you're that kid or grandkid, that amorphous "young adult" everybody is wringing their hands over. You remember loving church a long time ago when there was camp and friends and staying up way too late talking about stuff that really mattered. Your heart felt safe and happy at church, with the church, and you miss that feeling. You've visited a bunch of churches in the last year or two, and a couple of them have seemed okay, but mostly they just leave you feeling empty and left out. The old folks are *way* too happy to see you, and you know they would welcome you back, but maybe not if they realized who you really are, what you really believe (or don't believe), what you're really looking for, or where you were last night. You've been "spiritual but not religious" for quite a while now and maybe that's just the way it'll have to stay, but it's a lonely way to go. You know that better than anybody.

Or maybe you're a pastor, like me, faithfully meeting those Sunday morning deadlines fifty weeks a year, caring for the sick and dying, keeping aging church people busy with programming that is less and less well attended every year, recruiting volunteers to teach Sunday schools that are shadows of their former selves. And you're already overworked and underpaid, but you really wish you could figure out some way to break out of the monotony. Truth is, even *you* are a little bored with church as usual. And you're worried that the discontent you feel is obvious and contagious, and that it will keep spreading through our culture until the churches are completely empty.

Or maybe you gave Galileo Church money in the past five years, and you want to see what we did with it. Maybe you've been hoping we've got some *answers* in exchange for all your gifts.

Whoever you are, I suspect that you're worried and afraid because you are a *true believer*. That is, you're a devout disciple of Jesus, and you have entrusted your life to the God who vindicated his lovely way of life, and you love the idea that people who believe similarly could form a community of belonging in Jesus's name and help each other. You don't just love it; you've *lived* it. At some point that community of belonging in Jesus's name has saved your ass—like, spiritual salvation, for sure, but also like when your dad died or you lost your job or that guy got elected or whatever. You couldn't have gotten through that alone. You know that God doesn't need the church, but God knows we do. God knows you do.

What you can't figure out, as the church diminishes in our culture, as the next generation of adults (and the next and the next) opts out of established religious community, is whether other people just don't need it like you do, or if they just don't know they could have what you've had. Lately you've begun to suspect that people *do* need the companionship the church offers but can't get to it through all the layers of doctrine and tradition and bureaucracy and bullshit. People are hungry, but the church as we know it seems disinterested in feeding anyone. The stuff we've built or inherited—the facilities, the programs, the infrastructure of how it all fits together, the rules we run it by— it's just all in the wrong *key* somehow. The dissonance is painful, and you've been trying to sing along for a while anyway, but you're tired. And worried and afraid. And you hope for some words of comfort and courage.

I don't know if I have any words like that. What I have, though, is a testimony to what can happen when somebody risks a whole heap of their privilege and applies all their best mojo to building a new kind of community of belonging in Jesus's name. As you will see, lots of really dumb, sad, disturbing things happen. But out of all the messes I've ever made, God has managed to make something beautiful every time. I would like to tell you the truth about all of that, which is hard, because church planters lie incessantly. We tell you we're doing better than we really are, that our churches have more people than we've actually got, and that our worship service only takes an hour. You'll know soon enough if I'm credible. Trust your gut.

But please believe this: I'm writing the story I wish I could've read before I started, the story of somebody who has done this before. Not because I would have replicated what they did; we all know that congregations are contextual in the extreme these days. But I would have been grateful for the truthful testimony of any church planter whose church had not already failed, about where their ideas come from and how they know when those ideas are working and how they fix it when they're not, and what it feels like, for real, to do it.

Maybe my story can be that story for you. I'm not going to prosecute an argument here; I have no thesis other than "this is what happened." Sometimes I have the words of other people saying what was happening for them, but mostly this is about what happened in my own heart and in my own brain and in my own life. I'll include some in-the-moment writing, letters and emails and blog entries and Facebook posts that I wrote along the way. I'm not especially trying to go in a linear order, except in the broadest sense. I'll try to make sure you know if something happened in the first year or the fifth year, and here's the outline of that by what locations Galileo Church mostly used for gathering:

> Year One, 2013–2014, G-House and my Hampton Drive home
> Year Two, 2014–2015, Farr Best Theater and my Hampton Drive home
> Year Three, 2015–2016, Red's Roadhouse and my Hampton Drive home
> Years Four and Beyond, 2017–present, Big Red Barn and the Hays-Pape Homestead.

I'll try to tell the truth. You try to remember that I'm not saying how *you* should do it, just testifying to what happened—where I think God showed up—when *I* did it. Deal?

What I Hoped For

Let me be as clear as I can about what I hoped to do in starting Galileo Church: I hoped to gather people who did not have a community of belonging in Jesus's name into a community of belonging in Jesus's name. "We're a church for people who hate church," I would say to strangers I just met, "or for people who think the church hates them." I wanted Galileo to make space for the good news of God's reign to be both *good* and *news* for people who need both. Because so much of what the church has been saying lately and loudly is not really good and not really news. Conserving churches tend to mix in an awful lot of *bad* news in the form of judgment and boundaries, declaring who's in (we are!) and who's out (they are!). Liberating churches, in the interest of never offending anyone ever, tend to dull it down until God is boring as hell, bland, and sleepy, just like God's worshipers. Is that mean? Okay. I've spent a lot of years in both kinds of churches, though. I think I know what I'm talking about.

But I actually love church, and not just the idea of church but church *actual*, right on the ground, in all its human messiness. So in my imagination, before this whole thing started, Galileo Church would be like lots of churches you know. It would be a localized collection (group? gang? gaggle? flock? herd? hive?) of people who live near enough to each other to share life in the way of Jesus, offering each other safety and solace and companionship and help. I wanted Galileo Church to be able to fund its own life together, with a paid theologian in residence (me!) to guide and guard it. I wanted it to have enough infrastructure to hold together beyond my tenure. I dreamed that we would worship together, pray together, ponder biblical theology together, help the needy together, work for justice together, and raise families together.

In other words, *I wanted to make a church*. It's not dinner church or CrossFit church or house church or improv church or food truck church or intentional community church; it's just church. And that's been disappointing to some. (I'm shrugging now, in case you can't see me, shrugging in that way that means "I hear what you're saying, but we just are what we are, we do what we do, and what we do is *church*, maybe because it's all I know how to do." And anyway, some of my best friends do those other kinds of churches. They're way cooler than I am.)

I didn't just want to make another church of the kind we already know, obviously; that kind of church is failing, fading, struggling, dying, for #reasons. I wanted to make a church that would be demonstrably, radically responsive to its context in an age in which institutions of all kinds are failing to capture the hearts or serve the needs of the generations that come next. So I started dreaming about a vague idea of "Next Church," meaning whatever comes next after what we have now. The traditional, established congregations I have loved and served I call "Now Church." Now Church, Next Church. Snazzy, huh? These terms are my attempt to distinguish but not disconnect Galileo from what has come before, without limiting its development by defining it too precisely and without disparaging what has come before and already exists now. Galileo is church, like other churches, but it's *next*.

I hope this book can articulate how Galileo both is and is not like the churches you have known. Galileo Church is surprisingly orthodox in practice, meaning that we're singing hymns you already know, praying the Lord's Prayer in mostly familiar rhythms, sharing bread and cup at the Lord's table with the words of institution from 1 Corinthians 11. We're reading the Bible, *lots*, in worship and Sunday school and small groups through the week. We're teaching our kids to love Jesus and preparing for their baptisms when they are ready to make a confession of faith. We're talking about money when we have to and ignoring it when we don't. Just like church!

But there are distinctives about our life together that I'd love to show you. They go beyond questions of style and aesthetic—Galileo is *not* about cultivating a hipster vibe overlaying traditional form and content—and, I'm hoping, these distinctive are best communicated in the stories of our life together. Because, man, have I got stories to share.

Here we go.

CHAPTER 1

Before

The Making of a Church Planter

Spring Creek: I Am Not Embarrassed (Spring 2013)

It's amazing how fast our minds work when we're not thinking about thinking. "Nothing's broken" flashed forward from the back of my brain, meaning that the slip-n-fall I had just endured had not hurt me seriously. Legs splayed, skirt hiked, ridiculous shoes with little heels that were not meant for actual human propulsion hanging halfway off both feet, the tray of sliced brisket and a mountain of coleslaw coming down in a series of clatters beside me, my iced tea splashing through the air to baptize the unsuspecting diner a couple of yards away—but no broken bones. *Nothing's broken. Thanks be to God.*

And there were my clergy colleagues, all of them men, all of them pastors at churches bigger and richer than mine, all of them the exact make and model of the institutional favorites I'd been trying to win recognition from all my life, all of them now standing over me in sheer horror, their own trays still in hand, every one of them on their feet in their sturdy, sensible man shoes. And there was the restaurant manager, race-walking across the dining room panting, "Are you okay?" Every head in the place, including the poor guy dripping with my iced tea, turned toward my humiliation.

It was not the first time I had endured this exact shame. I never grew out of my adolescent clumsiness and could trip over a shred of dental floss. My mom falls too, and I've always thought it's because we're thinking too much—sometimes productively, sometimes just mentally dithering in anxiety—and not being all the way present in our beautiful bodies. But whatever. I've got a therapist for that.

So on the floor, even before I clutch at my hem to unexpose myself, that's normally the moment when my face floods with crimson heat and tears well up and over. Except this time that didn't happen. No bloom of blush, no crying. Just another rapid-fire realization, right on the heels of the unconscious assessment of my skeletal system. "Nothing's broken," came first. And then, before the next breath, "I am not embarrassed."

There have been fewer occasions than the fingers on one hand that I felt mostly certain that the Deity has spoken to me. I count this as one. Because it is not in my nature or nurture to *not* be embarrassed. Embarrassment is my baseline. Life decisions have been made, rightly or wrongly, on the basis of my internal barometer of potential shame. This is the residue of being raised in a church that required frequent and rigorous self-examination, where every church service emphasized the very near miss of God's wrath for my sinful self and God's readiness to reinstate said wrath if I couldn't keep up with doctrine's demands, and where I was the wrong gender to want to do ministry in the first place. Christianity, in the denomination of my youth, consisted of constant cycling from spiritual cleanliness to filth and back again, except that I could neither repent of nor be "forgiven" for my call to ministry. Long after I escaped the gravitational field of that upraising, my lizard brain reverted to the embarrassment-shame mind-set at every opportunity.

So: *I am not embarrassed*. Skirt straightened. Shoes on. Help from colleagues to get off the floor and to our table. A new tray of food from the manager and a sweet smile from the sticky iced-tea man. Over lunch, after somebody gave perfunctory but heartfelt thanks for the food, I took a deep breath and said to my brethren, "I am quitting my job and planting a church for spiritual refugees."

Church plants fail at an alarming rate. I had done enough research to know that you're better off Kickstarting your new Styx cover band than planting a church. And if I did what I thought it was going to take to give life to the little vision I'd been carrying around secretly for some months, my failure would be quite public. And humiliating. In front of the very people whose approval I craved. But there they were, and there I was, and I had come up off the floor with a word from the Lord. "I am not embarrassed." I could fall and fail and still live. This was the word of God for this person of God. Thanks be to God.

Fuck Me! (Fall 2011)

Everybody knew that millennials weren't coming to church. Gen-Xers started it, but there were never that many of us anyway, so it didn't hurt as much. But mainline, Protestant, North American, mostly white churches spent a ton of money on youth ministers and programming for adolescent millennials, and they didn't stick around. It felt like a betrayal. We were all kind of mad at them, tbh; our feelings seriously hurt by their disloyalty.

I was serving my second congregation of the Christian Church (Disciples of Christ), a left-leaning denomination that rescued me from my fundamentalist-evangelical (fundagelical for short; I use it a lot) upbringing, and to which I felt—still feel, most days—incredibly grateful. In the second decade since my ordination, I was taking note along with everyone else that the pews under our stained-glass windows were occupied by a dwindling number of silver-headed faithfuls and not enough of anybody else. Every time I moved to a new congregation my spouse and I were hailed as "young people" even as we got older and older, well into our forties. "This is not sustainable," I started thinking. The church I served couldn't fill its committee slots or make its budget. Its heavy infrastructure languished.

So I started reading. Robert Wuthnow, the preeminent sociologist of the American religious landscape, had been telling us for a while that things were getting bad. These next generations, he said, will re-shape the American church mainly by not being part of it. The more conserving Barna group was coming up with the same prognosis for evangelical churches: "They like Jesus, but they don't like us." The Pew Research Center delivered increasingly ominous statistics: 30 percent, 34 percent, 38 percent, every year more of these young adults claiming "none" as their religious affiliation. Lots of them believe in God—or Something—but not in the institutions that perpetuate and protect faith in Something. Many of us have to admit they have their reasons, these nones, these SBNRs, these former youth groupers who grew up swimming in suburban backyard pools and drowning in a sea of choices.

In a weird twist, liberal Protestant theology (like my own) won the day, and these numbers of nonchurchgoers prove it. After all, we told them that God is not confined to our steeple-topped churches; God is everywhere you are, unmediated by any institutional hierarchy. And we said that God isn't looking for reasons to punish you or keeping track of your rigorous religious practice; rather, God is gracious and kind and frankly disinterested in our perpetuation of religious habitu-ation. (You might even say God hates our festivals and takes no delight in our solemn assemblies. If you were Amos and rude.) We told them all of that, and they believed us and took flight from the institutions that had brought such comfort to their elders.

I read my little collection of the-church-is-dying research in my church office behind a big, executive-style desk, the same perch from which I chose hymns and studied for sermons—the serious work of ministry (she said, tongue firmly in cheek). On the other side of the wall sat the church secretary: a real live millennial, a cheerful, barely adult woman who had come to Texas from the great unchurched Left Coast United States. Her husband was a Christian convert who had followed his mentor to Texas, and she was happy enough to get away from her problematic family of origin and try something new.

At her desk she kept TV sitcoms and Broadway soundtracks streaming on her computer while she nimbly made her way through the administrative tasks I outsourced to her. We laughed at the confu-sion inevitably provoked by our names—Katie and Kaytee—and who could tell which was which when either of us answered the office phone? We cleaned up old messes left behind by previous generations of church hoarders and kvetched about the trivialities that got church ladies so riled up. Our work together was enjoyable, and the more so because she had no stake in church politics. She was not interested in Christianity, she had made that clear from the start of our working relationship, and that was okay with me. It's easier to work with a disinterested assistant.

And then one day, in a fit of frustration over something I couldn't make my laptop do, I threw a tantrum in my office. "Fuck me!" I yelled at the screen. "Come on! You can't be serious!" And as I ranted, I looked up to see Kaytee peeking around the door between our offices. "You okay, boss?" she asked. "Yeah, sorry about that," I mumbled. "I'll settle down."

"You know, boss, I've been thinking," she said, "about that baptism prep class you're advertising during Lent? You think I could sign up for that?"

God is fucking hilarious.

Baptizing Kaytee B (Winter-Spring 2012)

How do you prepare someone for baptism whose main experience of Christianity is the quite imperfect model they've seen in you and in the deeply disturbing inner workings of your church's institutional life? There were two of those someones in that spring's pastor's class: Kaytee B, the millennial church secretary, and my thirteen-year-old daughter, Lydia. Kaytee B said she always thought of Christians as people with sticks up their asses trying to pretend to be perfect so as not to displease the God they thought would punish them if they weren't. "It just never seemed worth it," she said. And who could blame her?

Something in my own, um, *expression* of faith intrigued her, though. It was probably the profanity. It seemed, she would tell me later, that I wasn't pretending anymore to play the Christian piety game. And she recognized that I was as frustrated with traditional church infrastructure as she was skeptical of it. My burnout, if that's what it was, matched her millennial distrust. Matching names, matching cynicism.

So for six Sunday afternoons that Lenten season Lydia and Kaytee and Katie talked about atheism—the God we *don't* believe in—and what it might be like to trust the God Who Is. I realized along the way that my daughter was closer in age and worldview to Kaytee B than Kaytee

B was to me. The reading I had been doing about the missing millennials was coming to life before my eyes in both of these young women I loved. I did not feel angry at either one of them for their generationally given tendency to join Jesus and unjoin the church. I felt instead how sad it would be for the church to lose them. I wondered if we could "lose" them if we never really had them. I baptized them both.

My daughter's baptism, along with my son's a couple of years later, were pinnacles in my personal and familial life. But Kaytee B's baptism changed my vocation forever. I plunged her into the water knowing that she was making a decision free from family heritage or pressure, knowing that the love of Christ alone compelled her love in return. And when I lifted her out of the water into an embrace, all I could think was, "She is never going to come to this church." I mean, there we were, looking out over a congregation of senior citizens, retired boomers, who on a bad day looked more like vampires than humans because their hunger for fresh blood to repopulate the church's infrastructure was palpable. Kaytee B, I knew for sure, had no interest in being assimilated into the institution they had built.

So I had essentially baptized her into nothing, at least IRL. No sustainable life in Christ, no life in the body of Christ, no life alongside fellow pilgrims who tread the road of life together. This was very much at odds with my own instinct and appreciation for community, my certainty that the Christian life is not an autonomous endeavor but a collaborative enterprise with people you trust and lean on when life gets truly hard, my love of the church. I had never *not* had a church. In that moment I thought Kaytee B never would.

It was the first time I had truly felt for myself, not just as a pastoral (and paid) sympathizer, the grief expressed by parents and grandparents whose kids grew up in the church but had no use for it anymore. They told me heart-wrenching stories of the young adults they raised, now existentially adrift and lonesome in their deepest hearts. "Spiritual but not religious," I now understood, is another way to say "alone but not together," trying to answer life's hardest questions all by oneself. One of the things I had given up in my own conversion from fundamentalism was the idea of church attendance as obedience, as something that God needs us to do for God's own sake. Church was, at its best, a learning lab for love, a community of beloveds who had each other's backs on the long and unpredictable path of discipleship. "God doesn't need the church," I often say, "but God knows we do." And Kaytee B, dripping wet and fired up in the power of the Spirit, didn't have one. Holy shit.

Excursus: Encountering Phyllis Tickle

Newsweek magazine, which I read (past tense!) cover to cover every single week from the time I went to college until the last issue was printed (December 31, 2012), had a feature called "We Read It So You Don't Have To." You might have read Phyllis Tickle's book *The Great Emergence: How Christianity Is Changing and Why* (2012), and you might have been lucky enough, as I was, to hear her present her thesis before her death a few years later. In case you didn't, let me make her case:

The forms that hold our religious faith (in this case, Christianity) are changing all the time, in big and small ways, in response to sociocultural changes, including scientific discoveries, literacy, communication improvements, and what people in one part of the world know about the rest of the world, and so on. But every so often—about every half-millennium, in fact—the changes are so large, so thorough, so *intense* that the Next Church is practically unrecognizable to the previous generation. And the intense changes in the forms that hold our Christian faith, broadly speaking, come about because of what Tickle called "the crisis of authority."

My own take on that crisis of authority is that the church (as the keeper of Christian faith) is in a competition, a tournament of narratives, wherein different stories strive for the privilege of naming what humanity holds most dear. What is true, what is right, what is good, what is beautiful, what is necessary? Christians (and other people of faith) might ask, "What does God *want*?" and, related, "How do we *know* what God wants?"

So, at the beginning of our story, Jesus comes on the religious scene proclaiming the reign of God, declaring that he knows better than anybody what is true, right, good, beautiful, necessary, and that if you want to know what he knows, you should come with him and enter into the life he offers. The persecution he suffers from the very religious people of his time is the result of their conflict in the tournament of narratives. Who gets to decide what God wants?

Tickle noted that there's often not a winner in tournaments like these; more often we get a split and a new normal as an alternative to what came before. So, from Jesus's Judaism, the Christian church is born. And for a while that church is underground, like the roots of a tree that will eventually grow large and leafy. The early church, persecuted and pitiful, spent several centuries hiding from the Roman Empire, hoping not to be crushed.

But in the early fourth century, Emperor Constantine's mother, Helena, converted to Christianity, and then so did the emperor himself. He sent his armies to conquer under the sign of the cross, and by the end of the century Emperor Theodosius I declared Christianity the official state religion of Rome and all its properties. The tree trunk emerged from its underground roots.

Half a millennium later, the Western, Roman-centered church found itself challenged by Eastern Christians who wanted their pope closer to home in Constantinople. If the pope mediates God's will to humanity, it's no wonder everybody wanted him nearby. In 1051 the Great Schism erupted and the tree trunk branched off, West and East, Roman Catholicism on one side and Eastern Catholicism (or Orthodoxy) on the other.

Half a millennium later, in 1517, Gutenberg's printing press made Martin Luther's Ninety-Five Theses nailable to that church door and publishable to the Christian masses. Maybe the pope didn't have all the authority after all. The challengers, the protesters or Protestants, branched off yet again, and state churches with varying forms of governance developed across western Europe, each of them a twig on the Christian family tree.

And do you see where we are now? Much has transpired in the last five hundred years or so, and here we stand on the cusp of the third millennium since the birth of the underground church. History warns that we're in for a seismic shift, Tickle contended—another crisis of authority over who gets to say what is true, right, good, beautiful, necessary. Culture, science, communication, globalization: the intensity of change in our lifetime has been almost more than many of us can bear.

What will happen, then, to any of the institutions that have a stake in the tournament of narratives, including (but not limited to) churches? Something new will branch off. Something significantly different will claim a place as at least one of the new normals in an increasingly pluralistic world. New ways of forming communities of belonging, some of them in Jesus's name, will flourish. In one sense I consider Galileo Church to be a research-and-development project in this vein. I want to know what comes next, for the sake of my kids and for the sake of the world God loves. Galileo may not be "it," but it is likely a step in the right direction—a departure from what has been toward what could be if God continues to attend to the world God still loves.

Who Are They? (Summer 2012)

The books on my desk were telling me that the institution I loved and served, the church that had raised me, was not going to sustain the nascent faith of my children or my young friend. A growing body of cultural analysis of millennials convinced me that they were done with institutions altogether and forming relationships in ways I would likely never understand. It wasn't only church that disinterested them; it was Kiwanis Clubs and PTAs and the by-now-clichéd bowling leagues too. There was some grace in that realization, you know? Maybe what was happening in my church, all the churches, the whole church, wasn't our fault. Maybe it's not the worst sin to keep doing what has worked for as long as anybody alive can remember; maybe it's not the most malicious thing to wonder what's wrong with the ones it isn't working for now. But even if it wasn't our fault, it was still our problem, wasn't it? And if I read one more essay passed around through social media about "The Millennials Who Won't Come to Church Problem," I was going to throw up. How was it helping to blame them for *being different*? And did the writers of those articles really know what they were talking about? Could an entire generation be summed up so succinctly?

(They were wrong about Gen-Xers, remember? When we were young they said we were spoiled, aimless, uncommitted, too cynical to be useful. And then we turned into these overachieving, workaholic, Whole Foods, helicopter-snowplow-monster parents. None of that brought a bunch of us back to church, but still.)

Curiosity grew in me like a pregnancy—there when I woke up in the morning, present with me all day long, not painful but so persistent: Who were the millennials in my life, really? What did they love? What did they do? What kept them awake at night? What got them out of bed in the morning? How did they live? How could I find out?

Maybe I could bribe them to tell me. So I made a list and started asking every single one of them I knew: If I made dinner some night soon and brought beer, would you tell me about your life?

I asked Malcolm, the aerospace engineering student at the nearby university who came to our traditional church faithfully but seemed more interested in running the soundboard than experiencing the liturgy. I knew, though, from one-on-one conversations with him, that Malcolm was a deep thinker and would read Buber's *I and Thou* cover to cover if I said it would help him understand human relationships (and get a girlfriend). The first time I ever asked him about church, he said he didn't really need anything different than the traditional church could offer. Boredom was his spiritual baseline, and he was okay with that. But he said yes to the offer of dinner and even said we could meet in the house he co-rented with several other engineering students.

I asked Kaytee and her spouse, Kyle. They had introduced me to Kayla and Danny, their buddies from a co-ed softball league, a few months before when their Baptist pastor wouldn't marry them because they were living together. (How does that make any sense?) Kaytee told them, "Oh, my pastor doesn't care about that stuff, she'll marry you!" which is not exactly what I would've said, but I was glad to be part of their lives.

I asked Nicole, who was a ministry intern at the traditional congregation I still served, and her spouse, Colin, himself a candidate for ordination in our denomination. They were clearly as comfortable in church as I was, but I was curious to know what they loved about it enough to base their careers on it.

I asked Erin and Joel, she a newly hired hospital chaplain and he a graduate student in theology. They were coming to the traditional church I served too, and we were forming a bond based on our common heritage in denominations that didn't ordain women and didn't appreciate our liberating leanings.

And I asked all these people to invite anyone else they thought might be interested. Freddie, Ben, Sabra, Joseph, that other girl, assorted roommates and coworkers and friends, all of us meeting in Malcolm's living room at 9 p.m. on a Thursday for dinner and beer and my investigative inquiry.

The driver of the whole effort on my part was curiosity. It's a humble virtue; I don't claim many others, but I have this one real bad. I love the story in Exodus 3 when Moses is out there just doing his job, and God sets that bush on fire, and Moses spies it with his little eye and says (to himself? to the sheep?), "I must turn aside and look at this great sight, and see why the bush is not burned up" (Exod. 3:3). How many other shepherds passed by that weird bush that day, do you think? In one way of imagining, Moses was perfect for God's job because he was the only one who felt compelled to "turn aside . . . and see." And when Jesus cryptically said to those potential disciples, "Come and see," and they did? Well, that just rings my bell. There are lots of other examples from the stories of our ancestors in faith. Don't get me started.

But here again was grace for me: this little circle of people, a couple of decades (and a half) behind me on life's journey, ready to tell me what they could see from where they stood. Mom's chili recipe is good, but it's not that good. They were doing me a favor, and even right this minute while I'm typing these words my heart is swelling again with gratitude for their openness and trust. Because here's the thing that I started to figure out in Malcolm's living room: it wasn't they who needed to change. It was me.

Malcolm's Living Room and Beyond (Summer-Fall 2012)

Malcolm's living room: the only pieces of furniture I remember with any clarity were the gigantic aquarium glowing eerily with fish gliding through cloudy water—or was it empty of fish and I just remember the aquarium?—and the hugest beanbag chair I had ever seen with a label prominently declaring it to be a LoveSac. I'm sure there were other chairs there. Maybe.

But I know for sure there were no serviceable dishes in the kitchen. No bowls or plates, utensils, glasses, napkins—if I wanted to serve a meal there, it made sense to bring everything I would need to make it work. So I packed a Crock-Pot of homemade chili into my Subaru, along with every single thing I could think of that I would need to show hospitality to these young adults in Malcolm's rented home.

Nine p.m. was way too late for me. My body clock started shutting down around that time because the alarm clock rang early in the morning to get two kids off to school. But the friends who were assembling had multiple jobs and multiple classes and multiple responsibilities. Nine p.m. on a Thursday was the only common time we could carve out. And Malcolm's roommates had generously agreed to cede us the kitchen and living room for a couple of hours at that time.

I don't remember much about that first gathering, except for how nervous I was. I was forty-four years old; these young adults could be my kids. I wanted them to trust me. I wanted them to *like* me too, if I'm being truthful. But most of all, I wanted them to talk to me.

And they did. Over chili and beer (for those who were at least twenty-one, natch), they each told me about their lives, how they paid their rent, why they were studying whatever they were studying. It felt less like an interview, though, and more like a conversation because they weren't only talking to me but to each other, in hopes, I think, of getting an acknowledging nod of someone's head, like whales sending out songs by sonar to see if there are like-minded whales in nearby waters. After a while it felt like I was overhearing them talking with one another, taking the conversation where they wanted it to go, chewing through the things that mattered to them most.

After a couple of hours we all agreed it was time to call it a night. Me, because my bed beckoned; they, because most of them still had stuff to do before morning light. Maybe that was my main takeaway from that first gathering—that these were busy people with multiple commitments (rather than the aimless slackers I had read about on BuzzFeed). I felt lucky to have had some of their time.

Before we adjourned into the night, though, I threw out a final inquiry: "Could we do this again next week, you think?" They looked at each other, at their feet, at their phones. "Would you bring dinner?" one of them ventured. "And beer?" asked another. "Sure," I said. And Malcolm agreed that we could lay claim to his LoveSac again next Thursday, and we were set.

We met in Malcolm's living room for more Thursdays than I can remember. Two, three, four months—week by week for a while, then month by month, and then someone said, "I want y'all to come to my place for dinner," and so we met at another address for a little while, and then another. One apartment was so small that we sat knee to knee, eating whatever food I brought over, barely able to shift in our allotted floor space.

It was always too late, I was always too tired, but Thursday nights rapidly became my favorite night of the week. My spouse was coming with me most weeks, and he and I spent the car rides home talking about whatever we had heard in that night's conversation. (My parents-in-law came over to our house each week to sit with our sleeping kids, God bless 'em.) I brought a question to begin each week's conversation. "Are you an ethical monotheist?" "How healthy are you right now, on a scale from 1 to 10?" "Where are you on the sliding scale between introvert and extrovert?"

One night we used Play-Doh to sculpt our biggest fears, and more than a couple of those very young adults sculpted their credit scores, already ruined by defaulted student loans or car repos. My spouse and I were shocked; we had not even known we *had* a credit score until we were nearly thirty. The burdens they were carrying were heavier than the ones we had carried at their age.

Eventually our group had moved around to all the apartments and rented houses of everybody who wanted to host, and it was my turn. "Come to my living room next month," I said, and gave them the address of our home in a suburban neighborhood in a wealthy zip code. We had *furniture*. And *dishes*. And so much *room*. The group didn't go back to Malcolm's living room or anybody else's space for a good, long while after that.

The practice of telling thirty-minute autobiographies emerged in our living room. I was learning about the inner lives of my millennial friends but didn't have the scaffolding of their life stories to hang it on. So we stole a page from the playbook of my sister's church, fundagelical but edgy in that emergent way, and started giving people an uninterrupted half-hour to narrate their own life to us in any way they chose.

Not everybody wanted to, so not everybody did. But a couple of people who went early on wanted to do theirs again after they saw how self-disclosive some of their friends were. I remember Joseph the Extremely Quiet, who it turns out is a fanatical wild-boar hunter. With a crossbow. One woman revealed her bisexuality, invisible to everyone because she is married to a dude. One man remembered his high school anorexia, induced for the sake of elite competition wrestling. Another man told us how he was homeless by age fifteen, sofa-surfing between friends, working his way through high school. Many of the stories had a common theme that I started calling "adults behaving badly"—neglectful parents, abusive teachers and pastors, bigoted extended families, exploitative employers. I was beginning to understand why they didn't want much to do with the stuff we built or the rules we played by.

I had a terrific counselor once who always signaled the end of the therapeutic hour by asking me what I had for breakfast. It was her way to ease me out of the difficult headspace of self-reflection. So I thought we would do the same with our autobiographies. At the end of the half-hour, the group would ask a nonsensical question to lighten the heaviness of whatever the person had told us. The first night I said, "I've got just one question for you, friend. Would you rather fight one horse-sized duck or a hundred duck-sized horses?" And I waited for an answer. It had been my plan to rotate through a set of silly questions in weeks to come, but five years later, Galileo-ans are still asking each other about the giant ducks and teensy horses to clear the air after autobiographies. We can raise a good argument about the right answer if we want.

Along with our location, our sense of what we were doing together was also solidifying. A few months into our time together, having finished a round of spiritual autobiographies, we were searching for our next conversation topic and someone said, "You know what we *could* do? We *could* read the Bible." A combination of shrug-nods of assent went around the room, signaling easygoing consensus. My preacher-self was ecstatic. Bible study is in my wheelhouse; I love the testimony of our ancestors in faith who tried and tried and tried to live into the heart of God. And I was so happy to hear that this gaggle (cohort? conclave? congress?) thought the Bible might have something to contribute to our rich conversations about life, the universe, and everything.

While I was jumping up and down on the inside over the prospect of Bible study, my outside was well trained in nonchalance. With a face I hoped conveyed the insouciance I definitely did not feel, I said with a shrug of my own, in my most I-don't-care voice, "Yeah, I guess we could." The next week I presented the group with a stack of Bibles, hardcover NRSVs I grabbed from a forgotten shelf in my traditional church.

I often get asked, concerning my months of listening to real-live millennials in their own words, "Well, what did you learn about them?" I would love to tell you, but then I'd have to kill you. JK. But the truth is, you should get your own—a set of people you are curious about whose lives are a mystery to you, people that you suspect might be beautiful if you could just see them a little better through your aging eyes. Cultivate your own curiosity. Make lots of chili. And maybe you'll get as lucky as I did.

Daddy, I'm at Church! (Spring 2013)

The traditional church I served while our Thursday night group was coming together was dying. The individuals in the church were mostly senior citizens, many over seventy-five, the "old old," as people well beyond retirement are sometimes called, and I had a long list of hospitalized and homebound folks to visit in a regular rotation. The congregation itself was also nearing the end of its life span, its former vitality a distant smudge in the rearview mirror. It wasn't the first time I had served such a church, but it was the first time I felt like my usual tricks (cartwheels! small groups! mission trip!) weren't going to turn the ship around.

Ministry into fading life and even unto death is really hard. Necessary and faithful work, yes, but also draining. I began to think of those late-Thursday-night gatherings as God's gift to me, a side gig as a spiritual bonus to keep me going. Those young adults gave me energy and hope; every hour we spent together was infused with the possibility that something brand-new might happen.

One night while we were reading the Bible together, straight through the Gospel of Luke over weeks and weeks, Kaytee B interrupted. "Wait a minute—did I miss something? Are you saying that *Jesus* said *that?*" I don't remember now if it was his congratulation of the financially impoverished in Luke 6, his insistence that the reign of God would come before his friends died in Luke 9, or one of the other audacious and, let's face it, irrational claims he made during his ministry. But Kaytee B couldn't go on until she got it cleared up. "If he said that, I'm calling bullshit," she said. "On Jesus?" I said, my lips suddenly dry and my breathing shallow. "Yeah," she said with a scrunch. "Can we do that?"

We could. We did. It was exhilarating. "This is the best side gig any pastor ever got," I thought. "Thanks, God."

And then one night almost a year into our gathering, someone's phone rang. Kayla slipped an impossibly tiny machine from her impossibly tiny hip pocket and answered it in a whisper. "Daddy, I can't talk right now," she rasped. "No, Daddy! Not now! I'll call you later!" Her whisper got more insistent. "Daddy! Not—no—*Daddy*! I can't talk right now! *I'm at church!*" With a flourish she pushed the button to hang up on Daddy and slid the little phone back into her jeans while I swooned with the implications. I thought I might throw up. I thought I might break into song. At the same time.

What we were doing here—the eating and drinking, the reading of Scripture, the contemplation of God's work in Jesus, the sharing and laughing and crying and praying and cussing and calling out bullshit—it was not Kayla's "side gig," nor mine. It was not a spiritual bonus awarded to me for faithful service in a dying church. How arrogant, how ridiculous! How blind I had been!

Because, obviously, we were doing *church*. We were being *church*. We were *church*. And there are some things that, once you see them, you can't unsee.

Thanks be to God.

Someone Else's Big Idea (Spring 2013)

During the time our Thursday night gathering was organically (accidentally?) becoming more and more church, I got a visit from a higher-up in my denomination. They had been looking at my town, Mansfield, or more accurately, the 76063 zip code, which was and is one of the fastest-growing areas in the country. There was no Christian Church (Disciples of Christ) congregation in 76063, but here was an ordained Disciples pastor living in it, and they had heard I was a good one. (Maybe they heard I was a young one. In my middle forties. It's all relative.)

So they sent a guy to ask me if I wanted to come on board with their plan to plant a "big-steeple First Church" in my town—their words. "Mansfield people are our demographic," he explained. "They are well educated and high earners. We'll set you up with Fortune 500 business execs who can mentor you in growth strategies. We see five hundred people in worship at First Christian Church of Mansfield within its first two years."

I can confess to feeling flattered. You already know I crave approval and recognition for my work. But I knew in my gut that I couldn't do what they were asking of me. "Big-steeple First Church of Mansfield might be a project for someone, but I'm not your girl," I said. I refrained, at least in my scrubbed memory, from sharing the scene that was flashing through my mind:

A couple of years earlier, when I had just gotten the job at my last traditional congregation, I brought my family to worship on their first Sunday morning in town. We walked into the little foyer together, separated from the sanctuary by a bank of glass windows covered with drab drapes heavy with the accumulated mustiness of decades of neglect. My nine-year-old, always prone to sensory overload, tipped his head back and sniffed at the air. With wrinkled nose but no judgement he declared, "Smells like old people."

At the time I shushed him in motherly, pastorly horror. But his words were now my go-to assessment of the big-steeple First Church idea: "Smells like the past; smells like nostalgia; smells like an institution that worked for our grandparents and our parents; smells like an institution that will not sustain the faith of our kids; smells like an idea whose time has passed." I didn't know of a single big-steeple church that was not in decline. I could not understand why we would plant more of the same just to send them on the identical, inevitable path to despair and exhaustion. I felt burned out before I even started.

A couple of days after declining the denomination's offer, my area minister (our middle judicatory level of support for pastors and congregations) called me. "You turned them down!" she exclaimed. "I sent them to you! This is your opportunity to do something big! What's the deal?"

"Honestly," I said, "I'm glad for the chance to reflect on where my passion actually is these days. I'm just not feeling it for making more traditional congregations in our image, no matter how new or shiny they are. I'm sorry to have squandered your recommendation. I'm fine over here where I am."

And, as a good area minister should, Renee said, "Then tell me: where *is* your passion actually these days?" We made an appointment to talk face-to-face. I took a deep breath and told her I had been cheating on my Sunday-morning church. I told her about the late Thursday nights, about millennials, about spiritual refugees, about reading the Bible with people who call bullshit on Jesus and each other, about the beer and the chili and the LoveSac and the *church*, and she said, "Well, then, that's what you should do. Maybe we can help."

And she asked, "What do you call it, those Thursday nights?"

"Galileo," I said. And so it was.

Why Galileo? (Spring 2013)

Galileo Galilei was a polymath—like, supersmart and working incessantly across a number of disciplines, smooshing together philosophy and science in ways that surprised and even shocked his contemporaries in the late sixteenth, early seventeenth centuries. We mainly know about him for his promotion of a heliocentric universe, against the prevailing Aristotelian geocentric assertion that everything in the universe revolves around the earth. Copernicus had said a hundred years before that it was more likely that the universe revolved around the sun (which also isn't right, but it's closer), but he couldn't prove it. So Galileo built a telescope and did the math and published his findings with a dedication to Pope Urban VIII. Because, most important to us, Galileo the scientist was a Christian. A churchgoer, even. Devout.

Until, that is, the inevitable philosophical conclusions drawn from his heliocentrism became clear. In disproving the geocentric universe, with the earth as a static and stable location from which all other heavenly bodies take direction, Galileo was saying to the church and the world that we human beings are not the center of the universe. This flew in the face of the church's understanding of humanity as the pinnacle of God's good creation, the "very good" conclusion of Genesis 1's six working days and the subject of God's ultimate concern. It was unsettling at least, enraging at most, to imagine earthlings as perpetual passengers on just another rock in a gravitationally mandated orbit around a decent-sized star. Scripture says things like, "What is the human being, that You are mindful of us? You have made us a little lower than the angels." We love to imagine ourselves as "fearfully and wonderfully made." Galileo's science was bad religion, they said.

So they kicked him out. Or, more precisely, they sent him home. In 1633, the Roman Inquisition (that is, the church) convicted Galileo as "vehemently suspect of heresy" and sentenced him to house arrest for the rest of his life. His daughter petitioned to take up his punishment of daily reading the Penitential Psalms so he would have time to keep working; Galileo wrote more science and went blind and died in confinement, all without the comfort of the church he loved.

"Happy birthday, Galileo Galilei—devout and kicked out, just like most of us!" is the tweet I send out on February 15 each year. It resonates with so many spiritual refugees, and we'll get to more on that later. But at first, I was writing "Galileo, 9 pm" on every Thursday rectangle in my extralarge Moleskine weekly planner. It was a convenience and a code; I didn't want those Thursday night gatherings to be obvious to anyone who glanced at those extralarge pages. I picked Galileo because I was becoming aware of the church's perpetuation of its own centrality in the universe—the idea that church was *us* and that our goal was always to get more people over here, in here, with *us*—and the accompanying sensation that, for me, even as a pastor, what we were doing on Sunday mornings was not any longer the anchor of the Christian faith experience. Thursdays were just better all of a sudden. We, the Sunday morning church, were not the center of the universe. Pretty soon, the Thursday night people started calling themselves "Galileo." It was good shorthand for whatever it was we were doing.

It worked for another reason too. My research into the missing millennials had turned up this sad scrap of data: young adults experience the church as antiscience. (No doubt because the loudest Christian voices in our culture make a literal six-day creation and a six-thousand-year-old universe articles of faith and decry Darwinian evolution as a socialist fairy tale and still believe Noah built a giant boat and all of earth's species survived a globally catastrophic flood on it and therefore climate change can't be real. And because progressive, thinking Christians ceded the airwaves and electrons to the fundies a long time ago, honestly it's our own damn fault.) Young adults, said the demographers, don't want to be part of an institution that asks them to check their brains at the door. Roger Moseley, a Methodist pastor who decorated his car bumper with a silver Jesus fish "kissing" a flat-footed Darwin fish, had recently published *Kissing Fish: Christianity for People Who Don't Like Christianity*, letting Schrödinger's cat out of the bag that not every church fears scientific inquiry. I got my own dual-fish bumper jewelry as soon as I read it. "Galileo Church" was meant to communicate that this is a church for thinkers, questioners, skeptics, intellectuals, nerds and geeks, and dorks and dweebs.

And finally, "Galileo Church" is eminently googleable. Go give it a try right now. You'll see.

(And no, since you asked, it's not related to the Indigo Girls song. Although that is a very good song. And it's a happy coincidence for what Galileo Church would soon become that Amy and Emily were lovers. But you have to be at least my age to appreciate them or that song, and this is a church for *young* people, remember? Give it a rest.)

So the code in my calendar became the name of our eventual church. With that code name, of course, I was also warning myself: Galileo got himself excommunicated for telling the powers that be that their worldview, the one with themselves at the center of everything, wasn't going to hold up. I was thinking the same thing, minus all the math and astronomy: there would be some among my colleagues and friends who did not want to hear that the institution we had dedicated our lives to would someday, maybe soon, no longer be the central expression of North American Christianity. My congregation, for sure, would not want to hear that I was waning in my optimism for our ongoing life together.

There's a weird factoid, verifiable on Wikipedia so it must be true, that I learned from Alice Dreger's book in defense of intellectual and academic freedom: before Galileo Galilei was buried (for the second time, long story), a few pieces of his body were removed to be displayed as relics. One of those, in fact the middle finger of his right hand, is on display even now at a museum of his accomplishments in Florence. Dreger named her book *Galileo's Middle Finger*, asserting that in the end the truth will out and make fools of anyone who stood in its way. And to me it means that our patron scientist-saint is forever flipping the bird to any institution that will not heed his counsel concerning the things we have "always" thought were true and our relative unimportance in the universe's grand scheme.

Coming around to our own smallness is hard and takes a long time. In 1992, 359 years after Galileo's ecclesial condemnation, Pope John Paul II apologized on behalf of the church and reversed the devout scientist's excommunication. Not that it mattered. The wide world had long since shoved the church's outdated antiscience to the edges. Galileo was right all along: we are not the center of the universe. *Sigh*.

So Much to Learn (April-July 2013)

It turns out that the Christian Church (Disciples of Christ) was never offering any funding for a big-steeple church plant in 76063; they were just offering the *idea* and hoping I would figure out how to do it and pay for it. But our area minister knew that the Trinity-Brazos Area (a swath of Texas Disciples churches from Wichita Falls to Waco) had a quarter-million dollars in a "new church fund." It came mainly from the closure of an earlier church planting effort—because, look, these things almost always fail—and it was just sitting there. So Renee's enthusiasm for my new passion gave me a path. It sounds small when I say it like that, but it's a Big Truth: if she hadn't caught my vision, if she hadn't been excited by my excitement, this wouldn't have worked. Every Mary needs an Elizabeth, you know? Someone who says, "Hey, good for you! This pregnancy is inconvenient, sure, but I think you just might be blessed-art-thou-amongst-women!"

Renee said, "Write a plan." So I wrote a five-year plan for growing a small but healthy church for spiritual refugees on a slow-growth model. I had a nifty mission statement to start with:

> Galileo Church exists to seek and shelter spiritual refugees; rally spiritual health for all who come; and fortify every tender soul with strength to follow Jesus into a life of world-changing service. "Spiritual refugees" are those for whom church has become boring, irrelevant, exclusive, or even painful. Millennials (born 1980–2000) are Galileo's particular focus, but all are welcome.
>
> A bruised reed [we] will not break;
> A dimly burning wick [we] will not quench;
> [We] will faithfully bring forth justice. —Isaiah 42:3

The proposal also included some language about core values and vision and form and function. Aw, hell, I'll just copy and paste the whole thing in here because I still love it. It's lovely to remember that the idea to start from scratch wasn't whimsical or sloppy; I wasn't too burned out or too cynical to dream. The work we had already done on all those Thursday nights had a shape that still makes sense to me and makes my heart sing.

Here is the thing you need to understand, though: writing a plan, articulating a vision, doesn't mean squat, and I knew deep down what I hoped nobody else could see about me: *I did not know what I was doing.* I'm saying that without adverbs or expletives so you'll know I really mean it. I didn't know how to plant anything, much less a church. I needed *so much help* to get anything like a clear idea of what one is supposed to *do* when one has this impulse. Here's where it came from.

Matt Rosine led a session at a denominational "new church" workshop on figuring out what we actually felt called by God to do for the sake of the world God still loves. I worked diligently on that in my small group even as the nerves of my back tensed and my spine compressed and a couple of disks in my upper back began to bulge. I spent much of that workshop lying on my back on the floor, groaning from the physical pain as well as from the painfully vague advice we were getting about how to do a kind of work I didn't understand how to do. I was learning how much I had to learn, but still had no idea who would teach me.

Steve Knight led a session at that same workshop on SO-shull MEE-dee-uh. Don't judge me; I really had very little idea what he was talking about. In other sessions we were literally getting advice about wearing comfortable shoes to canvas neighborhoods with printed fliers, but Steve was saying there were ways to communicate with broad or narrow swaths of people via the World . . . Wide . . . Web (say it like a middle-aged mom who's not on Facebook in 2013, please). Or, Steve said, reaching out even on our phones, but *not by making phone calls*. I didn't understand, but I was curious. I came home and asked Kaytee B to get me on That Facebook. I would Facebook for Jesus, I said. I never said I was an early adopter, okay? But I'm teachable.

I also made a timeline grid, quarter by quarter, for five years' worth of Galileo's projected life. I'm a little less proud of that one just because it shows my naivete about how hard this work is. But it was invaluable in providing direction for the first few seasons of our life together, and I wouldn't have thought to do it except for a visit I paid to some fellow church planters just outside of Chicago. Geoff Mitchell and Marissa McClure Mitchell were exhausted and broke but still so hopeful that Big Life Community Church was going to take off. They told me the truth about how impossibly hard it is to build community among people who are deeply skeptical of collective endeavors; they told me that her mom was paying their mortgage because their start-up funding had run out and their church wasn't nearly sustainable yet. And they showed me their Gigantic Chart of the Next Twelve Months—all their goals printed plainly in magic marker, so they'd know every day if they were doing it or not. It was overwhelming and so necessary.

The original "form and function" paragraphs in my plan were based largely on my belief that slow-cooked intimacy was a necessary component of this new kind of church for a new kind of people, the ones that Robert Wuthnow said found our church relationships "fakey" and "superficial." My sister was part of a church plant in her town that had built infrastructure for relationships to grow, where vulnerability was honored and friendships could flourish. I drove down to College Station to interview one of her pastors about their congregational structure and was again struck by the intentionality and specificity of the visions these church planters had.

That guy told me to read a couple of chapters in Malcolm Gladwell's book *The Tipping Point*, where the economist talks about the human mind's capacity for holding relational data. Turns out, for most of us there are only about twelve people whose death we would mourn deeply (kind of a morbid way to say we can care supermuch about a very limited number of folks), and 150 is about the maximum number of people who, if they walked into a restaurant where you happened to be eating, you'd feel comfortable saying, "Hey, come have a drink with me." Why, I mused along with both Malcolms (the pop statistician and the undergrad engineering major), would anybody want to go to church with more folks than they would enjoy having a drink with? And so I began thinking of Galileo Church as a small church (150?) made of even smaller groups (12?), where relationships would be real, where #churchfriends would be people you actually share life with. Anyway, thanks to that guy and to Dr. Gladwell.

In the summer of 2013, I signed up for the Church Planters Academy at Solomon's Porch in Minneapolis–St. Paul. I can't remember who recommended it to me—probably Steve Knight—but I'd been at another conference facilitated by the JoPa Group and knew that Doug Pagitt was doing great stuff that kinda blew my mind with regard to doing church. I can't say enough good things about that conference. The people I met, the connections we made, my dawning understanding that some of the most talented people in the world were risking everything for this idea that communities formed in Jesus's name should be the wildest, bravest, most innovative endeavors we could imagine—it was exhilarating. They were in concert with my impulse to leave traditional ecclesial infrastructure and ethos behind and sprint toward a new horizon. I was still terrified, but I had never felt so called.

In the winter of that year, I hiked to Fort Worth for a "Missional Communities" conference at Brite Divinity School, put together by Steve Knight and the Transform Network. A couple of things happened that weekend. I met Andra Moran and Suzanne Castle, who had this strange and wondrous idea that worship of our God Who Is Beautiful should itself be beautiful and inspire beauty in and elicit beauty from us. Worship that is boring or *pro forma* because "that's the way we've always done it" deserves to fade away, and the quicker the better, they said. They were generous to share not only their vision of worship but the nitty-gritty details of how they actually accomplished it fifty-plus weeks a year. I felt embarrassment creeping back into my consciousness as I kept asking questions in the "Yes, but how?" vein. But they made me feel strong and smart, and embarrassment lost its grip again.

And then there was Anthony Smith from North Carolina, a preacher and justice advocate preaching at that same Fort Worth conference. I don't know what Anthony *thought* he was doing that day, but he awakened in me a recognition that the gospel of God's reign is meant to change literally everything about the world we inhabit. He talked about Jesus coming out of the desert with the reign of God on his lips and in his heart and in his spit and leaking out from his eyes and his fingertips and his skin. He talked about how Jesus could see the secret that nobody else could: that God is in charge despite all appearances to the contrary. And then he said that if we wanted to, we could see it too. And then he said, "And when you can see it, it won't be hard to talk about it. In my experience, you won't be able to talk about anything else but the reign of God. And then like Jesus [long pause] you just spend the rest of your life riffing on that. You get out of bed every day and riff on that." Stunning. I can't do it as Anthony did it, so you may not be feeling it right now. But that talk changed me.

I'm saying all this to say that church planting, like just about everything that's worth doing, is hella hard, and there is no secret formula for doing it. But there are people who know things that we need to know and will share them if we are curious and put ourselves in the right places at the right times and deal with the shame of not already knowing everything we need to know. And yeah, you also have to deal with the heart-pounding panic that wakes you up in the middle of the night because your own life is about to be turned upside down by Jesus and his ridiculous assertion that God is in charge and actually doing stuff right now, all around you. Maybe even through you. Get out of bed and riff on that, if you dare.

Excursus: The Original Proposal

Galileo
Disciples of Christ, Mansfield, Texas
drafted February 2013

Guiding Mission
[A guiding mission should answer the question Why? Why another church, and why this church? It also makes an educated guess as to Who? Who is this church for?]

Galileo exists to shelter spiritual refugees, rally spiritual health for all who come, and fortify every tender soul with strength to follow Jesus into a life of world-changing service.

"Spiritual refugees" are any for whom "church" has become boring, irrelevant, exclusive or even painful. Millennials (born 1980–2000) are Galileo's particular focus, but all are welcome.

A bruised reed [we] will not break,

and a dimly burning wick [we] will not quench;

[we] will faithfully bring forth justice. (Isaiah 42:3, modified)

Defining Core Values
[Core values are the things a church believes in, stands for, never violates, even if the ship is sinking. No programming or budget decision is made without good alignment with the core values.]

1. Dangerous welcome.

Jesus practiced dangerous welcome when he enjoyed the company of social and religious undesirables: women, children, Gentiles, tax collectors, lepers, and all those lumped together in the category "sinners." It was dangerous because their reputation rubbed off on him and lost him the respect of his family and his religious colleagues.

Galileo practices dangerous welcome by seeking out those who have been made to feel like they don't belong in mainstream American culture or mainstream American church. We stretch our self-understandings to enjoy a thoroughly integrated group of different races and ethnicities, sexual orientations, and disabilities. We are a good spiritual home for the unsure and the unlaunched.

Warning: there may be consequences for practicing dangerous welcome. If we stretch our welcoming arms that wide, we may well get crucified.

2. Face to Face Friendship, for real.

Galileo is not a Sunday morning, get dressed up, and show up for "Hi, how are y'all? I'm fine! How're y'all?" church. Neither is it a sophisticated network of social media where you can feel super-connected even when you're sitting home alone, or sitting anonymously in a massive auditorium surrounded by people you don't know.

Actual relationships are expected. You don't have to be an extrovert, but you get a rare chance here to be real with other people who are doing the same. We're the same on Sunday as on any other day of the week. We talk and dress the same on Sunday as on Tuesday afternoon or Saturday night. When you're ready, there will be a time and place for you to share your misery, and share your bliss, as God grants.

3. Your life means something to God. Find out what.

Galileo is a laboratory for finding out what God is going to do with you and how you are part of what God wants for the world. We assume that God is working in you (individually) for the good of the world (communally).

Here we listen to the stories of people who are a little further down the road. Here we encourage you to tell your story to people who need to hear it. Here we expect the pastor to help you match your talents with the world's deep needs, but not by filling your calendar with church-y events. Don't wait for the church to program your spiritual life—we're not going to do it. Launch your life from this safe space.

4. Connecting [s]pirit to [S]pirit in worship, as best we can.

At Galileo, worship is not an event for people to watch. It's an experience for people to engage. It won't be the same every time you come. We may not hit the highest spiritual note for every worshiper every week, but we are aiming for it with our whole selves. Worship helps us love God with everything we've got—heart, soul, mind, and body. We stay flexible; we cry out for the Spirit's help; we turn on our brains; we try stuff. It's not easier this way, but it's better.

Compelling Vision

[A compelling vision is more flexible than the previous two categories. It tries to imagine what the community around the church might look like if the church plant "works." In other words, as best we can imagine, "What difference will it make?"]

We will gather a team of Jesus's disciples that looks like Mansfield's young adult population, only better, because we will do what it takes to cross each other's boundaries and get in each other's heads and hearts. In eating (and drinking!) together, in conversation, in Bible reading, in prayer, in the sharing of resources, in a commitment to worship deep but loose, we will be known as the church that takes everybody . . . seriously.

Form and Function

[Form and function outline a shape for church life—where is the center? what is actually on offer to those who are attracted to the mission/values/vision?]

Galileo exists as a network of small groups (about a dozen adults each) that meet throughout the week in homes, restaurants, office conference rooms, or any other convenient location. Small groups are the setting for the development of Christian friendship networks through which spiritual health can be nurtured and setbacks can be shared and soothed. Food may or may not be shared at these gatherings. Membership is relatively stable, with occasional additions when natural attrition makes space for newcomers.

Each small group is led by a pair of lay leaders who help set the tone and create safe space for every member to join in as they are able. Lay leaders become disciplined in the practice of prayer and help their Galileo groups pray with integrity.

Lay leaders from across all the Galileo groups form the leadership team, which meets regularly with the pastor to process the church's life and revise future plans according to the Spirit's leading. The pastor here serves as a shepherd and resident theologian for the leadership team, lending wisdom and guidance and occasional course corrections.

Galileo Worship is a weekly gathering of all the Galileo groups for a time of worship, planned by the pastor to be contextually appropriate, based on reports from the Galileo groups. Flexibility in the form and modes of worshipful experiences is key; novelty is not its own virtue but responsiveness to the Spirit's leading from week to week is highly valued. The pastor here serves as a curator of excellent worship, public theologian, and spokesperson for the ongoing mission of Galileo and the ongoing welcome for all.

Make a Video (April-May 2013)

While still working full-time at my traditional church, I presented a proposal for a new plant called Galileo to the New Church Committee of the Trinity-Brazos Area of Southwest Region of the Christian Church (Disciples of Christ). The plan included a request for four years of substantial funding, beginning with $100,000 in the first year, $85,000 in the second year, stepping down similarly for the third and fourth years, trending toward zero in the fifth year. "Wait a minute," said the committee chair, rifling through the packets I passed around the table. "How much of our fund are you asking for?"

"All of it," I said without smiling. I had read enough by then to know that church plants don't fail because their planters don't work their asses off or because people aren't hungry for a new way to imagine God and the world God still loves. Church plants fail for lack of funding. And I had rejected the idea floated by several that I should take up barista-ing or some such to keep my mortgage paid and do church planting as a passion project on the side. I had already *done* Galileo as a side project. I was ready to go all-in.

(Let's face it: I was also too old and too proud to take up a new career. I needed a salary, and I very much believe the biblical aphorism that you shouldn't muzzle the ox that treads the grain. Yes, I will be the ox in this metaphor if that means I get to eat in exchange for my education and experience and labor. I think, too, that the recommendation for me to forfeit a salary for church planting was, for some folks, rooted in the sexist assumption that my spouse's work funds our household and whatever I make is extra. I'm not making that up. People actually say that shit. Come on, people.)

So the committee recommended to the larger board that they accept my proposal, and here I met some pushback. Some of my colleagues on the board voiced concern: Why deplete the fund for one attempt? When it fails, we won't have any money to try again. Why her? She's the "wrong demographic"—a concern I would hear many more times in years to come. Not a man, not twentysomething, not a skinny-bejeaned hipster with interesting facial hair and a complicated coffee order. Just a middle-aged woman with baby-making hips and silver streaks in my hair sucking down Diet Coke like it's air. But also, in case anybody missed it, loads of education and expertise and, most importantly, a year-old gathering of spiritual refugees numbering fifteen to eighteen on any given Thursday. (I get that it's unattractive to keep saying it, but it's amazing how those qualifications can get lost behind the gender stereotypes.) The board offered a qualified "Sure." They would fund years one and two at the levels I had requested, but with a caveat to review our progress before they decided about years three and four. I was ecstatic—and terrified, as usual, as my go-to response to anything good—and ready to make my pitch to an even wider audience, the annual assembly of all the churches of the Trinity-Brazos Area, from whence funding could actually be released on the board's recommendation.

The problem was, I had already agreed to an out-of-town speaking engagement the weekend of that assembly, so I wouldn't be there to make a presentation in person. "No problem," said Renee. "Just make a video. We'll show it in your place. It'll be fine."

Those words drove an icy spike of fear into my heart. "Just make a video" was one more thing in a long list of things I didn't know how to do. How could I convert all this passion, all my Big Ideas, into a three-and-a-half-minute movie that anyone would want to watch? I reached out to a colleague at a big church with big resources, and she helpfully voluntold (such a useful word!) her "media guy" to help me; Jack Stewart knows All the Things, she said, and would be happy to help.

I wouldn't say Jack was happy, exactly. Willing, but not interested in wasting his time doing my work. (And isn't that a good lesson to learn, right there? I filed it away for future use. Thanks, Jack.) Jack was leaving for Italy in a couple of days. When he came back, he said, he would help me if (and only if!) I could present (1) a script, (2) a storyboard, and (3) legal rights to music and images we would need. I had exactly none of that and no understanding of how to get that. I got busy, asking for help as always.

I called a very creative person to help me figure out what the video should be about. Douglass-Anne Cartwright was a student at Brite Divinity School who had a reputation for organizing other people's creativity. What a good gift! She sat down with me to talk through the pictures and words that would introduce Galileo Church to the Trinity-Brazos Area assembly and to the world. "What are you envisioning?" she asked. "I have no idea," I confessed, "but can I tell you this dream I keep having?"

Dreaming the Wheat Fields (April 2013)

It was true; I kept having this dream. Some people assume I mean that metaphorically or that it's one of those preacher stories that's *mostly* true. But in my case, it was literal: a dream that returned and returned, night after night, leaving me feeling mournful in the morning.

In the dream I'm in a field of grain, golden stalks as far as my eye can see. I hear it before I see it: the tractor, the harvesting combine, rumbling through the rows, cutting and collecting the stalks. As it gets closer to me, I can see that the machine only gathers the stalks growing toward the sun. If a stalk is bent or broken, it doesn't automatically get caught in the combine. Moreover, the machine is actually rolling over some stalks, pressing them to the ground, leaving them behind.

As I recounted it to Douglass-Anne, the dream symbols became vivid and clear. Churches are like combines, grabbing and gathering people whose lives are basically upright—morally, maritally, financially—and ignoring people whose lives are bent or broken. And it seemed to me that in the cases of many of the spiritual refugees I now knew, the church it-self was responsible for their brokenness. People were suffering spiritual damage from churches that taught the exclusivism of God's love for a few who matched up to God's purported expectations. I now believed it was my *vocatio* to find those broken stalks, those broken people, gather them up, and riff like Jesus and Anthony on the reign of God's love. I wanted to say that to my friends and colleagues so they would help me get started. I wanted to say that to everybody else because it was the truest thing I knew.

By the time Jack returned from Italy, I had the script and the sto-ryboard, the images to go with it, and rights to the music that could go behind it. The music came from mobygratis.com, where the mu-sician Moby had just made available hundreds of instrumental tracks for use by nonprofit filmmakers. I chose a couple of pieces and sent in a request for use in my Galileo video. Moby said yes. Moby is my best friend. If I could have another baby, I would name the baby Moby.

Jack recorded my voiceover, put together the clips I had gathered, added the Moby music. I bought him some lunch and some beer and tried to stay out of his way. We were set. The "Broken Stalks" video de-buted at the Trinity-Brazos Area assembly in May, and Galileo Church had its funding. Thanks be to God!

"Broken Stalks" remains prominent on the church's website to this day. The production values are pretty bad—not Jack's fault, just the best we could do in a hurry—but its message still grabs people who are dis-covering that their brokenness may not be their fault and that God might actually have something different, something better, in mind for them. Galileo Church still gets emails once in a while that say, "I just saw your 'Broken Stalks' video, and I've been crying for a half-hour." Isn't that something? It's been over five years now, but so many people are still out there waiting. I think they're waiting to hear that someone has been dreaming about them.

Quitting Traditional Church (May 2013)

Have I already said that I really love church? That I love hymnals and acolytes and stained glass and preaching and funerals (more than weddings, like every pastor in the world, just ask one) and the administrative work of helping a community do what it's supposed to do in the world God still loves? I love people, truly, and I loved the people of the last traditional church I served.

But I don't love what happens to institutions over time. We've all seen the congregational life curve drawn on a marker board: the original vision and passion that propel an upward trajectory as relationships strengthen and programming solidifies, the peak years of vitality, and the inevitable decline on the other side as programming settles into the rigid tradition of "this is how we do it" or "this is what makes us a 'good church.'" Survival mode can overpower the most energetic and optimistic "young" pastor, especially if she's well into her forties and has seen this movie before.

I had been at my last traditional church for almost three years when I left to build Galileo. There was a brief period when we considered together whether this new ministry to and with young adults could be folded into the congregation's life. I consulted with colleagues; I worried myself awake at night; I talked endlessly with the Thursday night gang-gaggle-group about it. If we attached our little collective self to that established church, I would have a salary and health care and a pension. We wouldn't have to worry about money; we would have space to meet; we would have access to a copy machine. The copy machine was everything. It symbolized stability to me. The smell of fresh toner called to me.

But here's what held us back:

First, the traditional congregation expected that our Thursday night group would fold itself into the church's regularly scheduled worship life, Sunday mornings at the doctrinally correct hour of 11 a.m. We would need to put butts in pews, in other words. And pews (even though this church had moveable chairs in the sanctuary) just didn't feel like Galileo's way of being. Spiritual refugees who had experienced pain in the churches of their childhoods weren't likely to feel at home among the acolytes and choir robes; indeed, in some cases their feelings were more akin to post-traumatic stress. "Stained glass cuts are the deepest," Fred Craddock said, and I was finding that he was right.

Second, the time frames for decision making in traditional churches are so l-o-o-ong, but millennials move *thisfast*. It seemed to me that a small network of people in relationship together needed the freedom to make decisions on the fly, to try lots of things and fail quickly much of the time, to take risks before we lost our nerve. That's how we had been operating for a year—moving from one apartment to another, ditching Bible study to listen to a new person's life story, throwing impromptu parties. It felt like a time warp every time I stepped back into my traditional church, not only to a past where copy machines were more important than good Wi-Fi but to significantly slower pacing. Things . . . just . . . slowed . . . down, and it did not (could not) match my sense of urgency for this new work.

Third, the traditional church I served eschewed controversy in favor of survival. They would not acknowledge LGBTQ+ persons in their families or their church; they would not address the systemic issues around immigration and poverty in the ESL school that used their building for classes; they would not adjust their way of being to accommodate the Spanish-speaking neighbors who filled the houses around the church. I was increasingly aware that the millennials I loved were champing at the bit for a faith that would fight for something, a faith that would matter in the world God loves, even at the risk of being disagreeable. I think it came from all those months of reading together about Jesus, who was never, never, never, never concerned with whether people liked him or not.

So that's it. My last traditional church was traditionally "churchy," with churchy accoutrements and a churchy pace and the churchy niceness that precludes real engagement with the wildness of the gospel of God's reign. It wasn't a bad church, and they always treated me with kindness and respect. I remain grateful for my time with them.

But there was also this: I was discovering and coming to terms with two decades of bifurcation of my self, the compartmentalization of my way of being in the world. I had a "Reverend Katie" persona that felt very much at home in the traditional church. There's a voice, a posture, a distance, a detached professionalism required for that work. (There's even a costume, as one Galileo person called it, the first time she saw me in a robe and stole.) That persona is restrained, polite, pleasing, a perpetually nonanxious presence. But with Galileo people, I was becoming more and more *Katie*—the profanity, the jeans, the ease, the belly laughs. I couldn't imagine a way to integrate those selves; nor could I imagine switching back and forth between them if Galileo had to fit somehow inside the traditional congregation. That's it, and it's more self-centered than I wish to report: running Galileo as a ministry embedded within a traditional congregation wasn't workable for *me*.

I met with the church leaders and told them about my new project, about the energy and excitement I felt about it. I told them I was leaving to pursue this new calling. I dreaded their disappointment with me; they had been disappointed by a long string of pastors before me, and I had not intended to be another in that series. But they had learned to be gracious in disappointment, which is a difficult lesson hard won.

And I was learning too—that a church like Galileo, a calling like mine, was bound to disappoint lots more folks along the way. We would not be the church that many, even most, people expected us to be. I would not be the pastor some people wanted me to be. If we were going to sail free from the constraints of niceness, becoming bold and subversive in our declarations of God's reign of love, we would have to be ready for whatever comes in response to that.

They might kill a person for that, you know?

But another thing I was learning: this was the work I was born for. In two decades of ministry in traditional congregations, I had caught *very* rare glimpses of God's beauty, had felt God's presence a few precious times. I'm not talking about quiet moments in the woods at the edge of church camp where you sit still in hopes of inducing the emotional memory that nature is nice and God is too. I'm talking about getting sucker punched and dropped to your knees by Something so beguiling, so graceful, so *lit up* that your throat constricts and the tears are hot on your cheeks before you can fully register what is happening. I'm talking about the way God dances when God gets unboxed. I'm talking about how your eyes fly open in the morning because you can't wait to see what God will do next.

Father Richard Rohr has this book, *Falling Upward: Spirituality for the Second Half of Life*, that I didn't need until I absolutely did. Basically, he says that your life has a "before" and an "after," a first half and a second half, and you don't know where the midpoint is/was until you wake up one day and you're living the second half—you're actually doing the thing you were made for. And then you realize all of a sudden that everything you've been doing up to now has been preparatory; you couldn't have done this thing you were meant for without first doing all those other, intermediate things that were not the Thing. Galileo—a community of belonging in Jesus's name for spiritual refugees—is the Thing for me. Or I am *for* Galileo. Whichever. All I know is, I can do no other. Not anymore.

Excursus: "Spiritual Refugee Magnet" (Blog Post, September 2013)

I'm a refugee magnet. My always-expanding circle of people includes a bajillion women and men who have been tripped up, stepped on, talked about, kicked out, and left alone to the point that they don't know if they can keep going.

(If you're reading this and you're one of my friends, I'm probably not talking about you. You are the exception; you are actually fine. No worries.)

When I say "refugee" I'm not thinking of actual refugees who smuggle their babies across borders in the middle of a war-torn night. If I lived in a different part of the world, maybe. If my life were more open to the literal refugees that end up in the Dallas–Fort Worth metroplex, probably.

No, the ones who come to me are the spiritual refugees, the ones whose hearts yearn for God, whose minds cling to memories of love shared in families and churches. They are the ones who have been pushed away, pulled away, torn away from the relationships and institutions that once gave them the life they imagined God wanted for them.

They are women whose churches taught them to love God with their whole selves, their hearts and souls and minds and bodies, but then told them they had gone too far. They should not imagine that God wants them entirely, in the servant leadership of the church, because they are women, and God knows, women are not cut out for this kind of service. Serving food from the church kitchen at a potluck dinner, yes; serving the body and blood of Christ from the table in the sanctuary, no.

They are women and men whose churches cultivated the Spirit of tender-hearted love within them only to say later that such love is meant for certain ones, not same-sex ones. They should not imagine that God is the source of *that* love, the love that wanders outside the bounds of our heteronormative expectations. Suppress it, ignore it, repent of it, exorcise it—whatever it takes to banish that love from your heart. And if you can't do that, go away. We'll pray for you.

They are people whose churches didn't or couldn't make room for them in their difference, like their difference was disruptive or too big or too loud—like it was hurting the church somehow to have to live with it. They are people who at some point in the not-too-distant past believed that about themselves, that they were hurting the church they loved just by being the people they are. And so they left. And felt some relief, for a while, just being gone.

Spiritual refugees. Samaritan women minding their own business, drawing water at the well in the heat of the day. Pregnant, unmarried teenagers wondering if anyone will stand by them in their shame. Sick people with diseases so foul or fearsome that no one will touch them. Those who grieve too loudly and too long. Those without means to buy their way back in. Those without advocates to fight their way back in. Who misses them? Who wants them? Where do they go?

Not a few of them make their way to me, and now to Galileo Church, because with us they find a place to rest and consider whether God's love might still be the realest thing in the world. They find a tight-knit group of former refugees who are no longer homeless but count each other's living rooms and lives as home for their restless, hungry spirits.

I was a refugee once. I could tell you about that some time if you like. But God and the people of God have taken me in, have brought me home. And now, *mi casa es su casa*. Come on over.

CHAPTER 2

Year One

Getting Our Shit Together

#firstyear, #firsttime

One time we were taking a big group of people to Wild Goose, that leftward-leaning, hippie-dippie, Jesus-loving justice festival in North Carolina. Our musician was scheduled to play a couple of times; our church was leading worship under one of the tents; we were taking a big support team. But the main thing was, we were camping. And it turns out, our musician knew *nada* about camping. "Can you borrow a cot?" I suggested. "What's a cot?" he asked in all sincerity.

That story got repeated with much hilarity because this musician was weirdly and endearingly inexperienced in many things: a novice among some very, um, let's say, "worldly-wise" church people. One of our snarkier friends implored, "Oh, you must document this experience with photos of everything awkward that happens. And use the hashtag #Paulsfirsttime." It wasn't nice, but it was funny. So we shortened it to #firsttime and found it to be one of the most useful designations ever.

Galileo is all about #firsttimes of all kinds, for lots of us. Year one was chock-full of them. Just about everything I did that whole year was a #firsttime—not because two decades of traditional church work didn't teach me anything, but because there was so frickin' much more to learn. The world is a big place, and God has in mind that the church's imagination should sort of e-x-p-a-n-d to explore it. Doing the same things again and again, approximately fifty-two times a year, isn't all there is to ministry, as it turns out.

But it wasn't just me. I was working with some young adults who hadn't had a lot of chances to do stuff yet. Like Malcolm, Galileo's first president, who couldn't sign Galileo's papers of incorporation for the state of Texas until he turned twenty-one. Like our first treasurer, managing more money than she'd ever seen in her life and who, as it turns out, didn't know every single thing needed to write payroll and keep the IRS happy. (Do you? Don't judge.) Like the people we were asking to host small groups in their homes and apartments, in many cases their first home away from their parents' homes. (We bought thrift-store dishes and folding chairs for some of them so they could feed everyone at the same time.) Like the people we were asking to lead Bible studies or write liturgy or use their voice in worship or plan parties.

In year one we wrote our first policy ("The Big-Ass Check Fund Policy"! It was a good one!), made and canceled our first rental contract, hired and fired our first musicians, wrote and pledged our first covenant of co-conspiracy, drank our first Bible & Beer, delivered our first Cookie Evangelism. It was a big year.

But the #firsttimes more important than the mechanics of church start-up were these: the people who were coming into my life seeking something beautiful, something trustworthy, something healing. Some of them were coming out as LGBTQ+ for the first time. Some of them were out everywhere *but* church and wondering whether church could really be a place for their whole selves. Some of them were moving away from painful pasts, painful churches, painful families, hoping to find softness for this present moment and hope for the next moments. Some of them were families, 'rents and sibs, of LGBTQ+ people who were no longer willing to be part of anything that excluded their beloveds. "I just want to be part of a church where my son could come if he ever decides to come home," one woman told me.

Some of them were trying on new identities for the #firsttime in the safety of this shelter we were building together. Nathan brought a duffel bag to worship every week for months, going into the bathroom to change into the femme clothes he-becoming-she loved most, existing in that genderqueer space for ninety minutes of worship, then going back to the bathroom, changing back to "regular" clothes before going home to her campus. Lesbian and gay couples who were ultra-careful not to show public affection to their partner or spouse (because in Texas that can get you hurt) were experiencing their first opportunities to hold hands and snuggle—in church! One of my favorite pre-worship activities is to watch the entrance door from a distance, just close enough to see people's neck and shoulders relax when they come in the door and realize that here they are safe and seen and loved for their whole selves, many of them for the #firsttime.

Galileo has given a lot of people their #firsttime feeling like God's love is the realest thing in the world despite all appearances to the contrary.

There were #firsttimes happening in my life too. One day in October 2013 I encountered my husband in the dual-sink, heteronormative master bathroom of our neat suburban home. (Come on, one sink was several inches lower than the other. It stereotypically screamed male and female.) It was the morning of the #firsttime Galileo was going to be a part of Tarrant County Pride—we were going to walk in the Pride parade and host a booth at the Pride festival and just be as Pride as we could be. I had even ordered a cheap, nylon, rainbow-striped flag for someone to carry and wave in swoopy figure-eights like those French revolutionaries in *Les Mis* ("Can you hear the people sing?" How are you not singing right now?). I had never been to any kind of Pride anything. I didn't know what to Pride expect.

Lance (husband, twenty-seven years as of this writing, most of which we're proud of) was brushing his teeth at his sink, and I at my slightly lower one, both of us wearing brightly colored Galileo T-shirts, both of us contemplative about what we were about to do. Our eyes caught each other's in the mirror. "Oh, honey," my reflection said to his, "we are not where we started." (Keep in mind we both grew up in fundagelical Christianity. We didn't know from gay.) "No, we are not," he agreed. *Brush, brush, brush, spit.* "Thanks be to God?" I asked his reflection, searching. And God bless him, my spouse nodded his head with all the seriousness the question required. "Thanks be to God," he confirmed.

You never forget your #firsttime.

Excursus: Our First-Ever Policy

Policy for receiving large, non-repeating, financial gifts
aka "Big Ass Check Fund"
Galileo Church • approved by Leadership Team • September 2014

Because the people of our generous God can be extraordinarily generous, Galileo Church occasionally receives large financial gifts. The leadership team has discerned that such gifts can be reserved for our future life together, according to the following guidelines:

1. Financial gifts that are large and non-repeating will be routed into a Big Ass Check Fund.

a. A "large" financial gift is a single gift that totals more than 2% of our operating budget in the year in which we receive it. (That means gifts over $3,200 for 2014–15.)

b. "Non-repeating" means that we're mostly certain that the gift won't reoccur as a regular or semi-regular tithe or offering.

c. The Big Ass Check Fund is not a separate bank account; but it is delineated in our accounting software so this money will not automatically be absorbed into our operating fund. It does not seem wise at this point to tie up money in ways that would make it unusable for our day-to-day operations.

d. We intend to spend gifts to the Big Ass Check Fund within about a year of their receipt, for the ongoing life of Galileo Church. If this changes, i.e., if we think it seems wise to invest for a longer term, we'll let everybody know.

2. We intend to tithe from any offering for the Big Ass Check Fund into our Helping Hands Fund.

a. "Tithe" means 10% of any large, non-repeating gift.

b. The Helping Hands Fund is a separate fund in our accounting software that is designated to help Galileo co-conspirators and friends with financial emergencies.

c. Gifts to the Helping Hands Fund are always welcome; it is not necessary to make a large gift to the Big Ass Check Fund to designate a smaller offering for Helping Hands. And if you need help from Helping Hands, please speak to the pastor.

Things We Didn't Want to Do (June 2013)

I preached my last sermon at my traditional church on June 2, 2013. I woke up on Monday, June 3, as the official church planter of Galileo Church. I had no fracking clue what to do next. I can't express how terrifying that was. There were no events to plan, meetings to chair, sermons to prepare, complaints to field, or crises to manage. What is left of one's pastoral identity if all those things are taken away?

One of the notorious traps for church planters and other entrepreneurs who work from home is the Pajama Pitfall. You wake up with good but vague intentions, open your laptop while you sip the first Diet Coke of the day, and suddenly it's noon-thirty and you still smell like last night. Even worse, you're sleepy again. Don't ask me how I know this.

So pretty soon I made a checklist—I make killer lists and accomplish an extraordinary quantity of work by using them—titled "Every Damn Day." It was simple, just five things:

1. Every damn day, get all the way dressed, including shoes.
2. Every damn day, leave the house.
3. Every damn day, communicate with someone you know about Galileo Church.
4. Every damn day, introduce Galileo Church for the first time to someone you don't know.
5. Every damn day, read something that helps you figure out what to do next.

I actually remember showing this list to my start-up team. They were underwhelmed and probably thinking, "Is it really that bad? Holy crap, we thought she knew what she was doing." But it saved my life by giving it some daily direction (outward! onward!), and little by little, piece by piece, I actually did figure out what to do next.

Next, we needed to get legal. We couldn't actually accept any money until we were a 501(c)3, and the Christian Church (Disciples of Christ) wouldn't share that with us until we did a little work to make things official. We got a lawyer to help with that, free, through our middle judicatory office. Thanks be to God.

We needed a bank account, which requires a surprising amount of paperwork; see "lawyer," above. Thanks be to God.

We needed a logo and a website. Our website would be a mostly static placeholder in the dubya-dubya-dubya that would tell the world what we thought God was doing with us, and our social media would point to that. Our first budget included $5,000 for graphic and web design, which at the time sounded like such a *huge* amount of money. (Actually, it still does. I would do a lot of things for $5,000 if it was for Galileo.) I had experience with the way churches usually do it: the cousin of one of your members knows HTML and they'll "do" a website free, eventually. And you'll wait for months and it will look like crap and the tiniest edits will be impossibly complicated. If all those snarky online essays about the millennial generation had taught me nothing else, I had at least absorbed the fact that they have little patience for shitty design, especially online.

I googled around and found the Fowler Group in Fort Worth, a design firm whose stuff was edgy, funny with a dash of irony, cooler than thou but without the smug. I got an appointment with one of their designers and told her the whole story: the BBQ restaurant slip-n-fall, the stained-glass cuts, the accidental church, the devout-and-kicked-out mathematician. She told it back to me, but better, because that's her job. "When people see the amazing stuff we're going to make for you," she asked, "what's the one reaction you hope they have about Galileo Church?"

That was easy. "Curiosity," I said. Our stuff didn't need to be ordinary and overlookable; it needed to provoke people to investigate further, like a burning bush, like a come-and-see Messiah. Plus, we didn't yet have enough solidity to be really clear—like, where we would meet or when or what we would do together when we did. We hadn't figured all that out yet. We wanted people who came on board to have a voice in what it would be like. Rather than saying, "Here's our church, here's how we do stuff, and you can come do the stuff we do with us," we wanted to say, "Here's a vessel for holding our thoughts and inclinations about what God might do with us all together, and don't you want to come help us figure that out?"

In a couple of days Dacia the Designer called me with a proposal: her firm could do everything we were asking for, for the low, low cost of $40,000. I'm proud to report that I did not burst into tears on the phone. She sweetly said, "We have some freelancers we work with who can probably help you within your price range. I'll send you some contacts." I said, "Thanks," not quite as sweetly.

A couple of days later she called again. "We had our weekly partners meeting," she said. "I told them about your church, about what you hope for, about what you need. They decided to take up your project for $4,400, which will get you a logo, a website, and those curio cards to give away—everything you need for now. Can you swing that?" Oh. My. Dear. Jehovah-Jireh ("the Lord will provide"). There was much rejoicing in the tents of the righteous. Pretty soon we had Galileo Galilei's actual signature (cribbed from Wikipedia by Dacia's millennial assistant) scrawled across a bright orange circle and a website that popped with funky, edgy excitement. And best of all, a pastor trained by the patient web designers to edit the thing!

Dacia's millennial assistant was concerned about my word choice for the place on the website where sermon recordings would go. "That's What She Said" is the title I picked, and I think he thought maybe I didn't understand what that meant. Similarly, one of our curio cards announces:

> We are searching for you / queer / doubtful / tattooed / blue / raw / ungainfully employed / sciency / philosophical / THIRSTY / And maybe you wonder whether God cares about any of that stuff when there are bigger things on God's plate, like how to get earthlings to make love not war and be nicer to the whole, gorgeous planet. / Come search for us. / galileochurch.org

Dacia's millennial assistant wanted to make sure I knew that *sciency* was not a word, that *queer* could be offensive, that *blue* means more than one thing, that THIRSTY would mean something different by 2018 than it did in 2013. And I kept saying, "Yeah, I know, except for what THIRSTY will mean in 2018. We're aiming for 'mildly transgressive' here, in the tradition of Jesus who was himself mildly transgressive when the situation called for it. Just print it." We have given out thousands of those cards. Thousands and thousands. I like to imagine them held by magnets to refrigerators all over DFW.

There was one more preparatory step we needed to take, and it was the hardest of all. Since announcing that Galileo was going to become "a real church," our group had slimmed down to twelve adults, two of whom were my spouse and me. And while twelve is a terrific size for a small group of people doing life together, it does not leave any room for newcomers. We had spent every Thursday night together for so long, but now we needed to divide up to make space "for the people who aren't here yet," as we often said. Cellular mitosis in service of anticipated growth, see? We aimed for half-and-half, but our six-and-six plan didn't work out exactly right, and pretty soon we were more like eight-and-four, one group meeting at Kayla and Danny's house and one group in my living room. But that website went up, and Google did its magic, and it wasn't too long before both groups were full again. People were hungry, and we had food. People were curious, and we were findable.

Seek and Ye Shall Find, Online Edition (Summer 2013)

How do spiritual refugees find a church they're willing to take a chance on? How does a risk-worthy church make itself findable? I've got two words for you: *The. Internet.* But then I've got two more words for you: *go. outside.* Turns out, it's a delicious cocktail of virtual presence and IRL.

Here's what Galileo Church did: We paid good money for a fabulous website that we crammed with clues to our ethos. We maniacally Facebooked for Jesus (and added Twitter and Instagram when the time was right). And we did church in public as much as we could. Why am I using past tense verbs? We still do all those things.

First, virtually.

Our website is up-to-date but stays mostly static with long-term descriptions of our way of being together. It answers the question, What kind of church is Galileo? and demonstrates our commitment to transparency by including links to job descriptions, annual budgets, and policy documents. Eventually we added recordings of every sermon preached in our Sunday worship, even the really terrible ones (hey, Sundays whiz by like telephone poles on the interstate, and not every sermon can be the GOAT), and later a dedicated Galileo-an started work on a searchable sermon index. The goal remains the same: to give the most wounded and reluctant spiritual refugees a fulsome opportunity to investigate who we are and what we're committed to *being* before they have to take the risk of showing up in person. I cannot exaggerate the number of times first-time worshipers have told me, "I've spent the last six weeks (or six months) reading every single thing on your website." Photos of people and places are important; newcomers often recognize our servant leaders before being formally introduced and know the layout of our worship space before they walk in the door.

Our social media presence is punchy and pervasive. We announce what we're going to do across several platforms, then live-tweet and post photos *while* we're doing it, and then post photos to show what *already* happened. It's a little hit-and-miss, but that's our goal. We encourage lots of sharing, retweeting, whatever. We're careful *not* to tag people in photos, because not everybody is out (as LGBTQ+ or as a Christian!) to all their social-media friends. We're snarky and self-critical, not too polished, not very cool. We're trying to be as real as we can be in an arena that mostly celebrates life's greatest hits and most polarizing opinions. We pass along resources (i.e., share links, repost, retweet) that are relevant to our missional priorities, which means we leave a lot of stuff out. I know there are people who check in to our Facebook page on the regular because they want to know what Galileo is thinking about, not just what we're doing locally.

It remains true that whenever a person walks in the door of the church, their friends and family, coworkers and neighbors, people who populate their lives that you have yet to meet are trailing invisibly behind them. But it's even more true that whenever a person "likes" or shares a Galileo Church post or tweet or photo, there's a galaxy of connections forming in microseconds. And all that goodness we're putting out into the world is available whenever the Spirit moves some sad soul to click around online—in the middle of the night, on a Saturday afternoon, times that the church and its pastor are usually not available for quizzing.

Indeed, the round-the-clock nature of online communication was the best and the worst thing that ever happened to this pastor and this church. I'll tell you the worst part soon enough. But trust me when I say

Galileo Church would not exist today without a strong online presence. "Where are all the young adults?" I hear traditional churchgoers worrying. The answer is not hard: they are online. Get in there, church.

Postscript: While I'm writing this section, here in 2018, I'm watching a conversation unfold in Galileo Church's Facebook group, where anybody who has been admitted to the group can post and comment. It's a space for lively conversation, silly jokes, prayer requests. We have a few guidelines for how to have appropriate conversations pinned to the top, and people mostly pay attention to those.

A woman we don't know at all has commented on an article I shared in the Facebook group this morning about a fundagelical pastor who has denounced "social justice" preaching as "evil." It's so ridiculous that it's funny, and sometimes it feels good to laugh with relief about where we came from, celebrating our great escape from the bondage of mean, small-minded religiosity. This stranger has commented, "Preachers like him are why I will NEVER go to church again." My heart sinks. Who is this person? What is she doing in this Facebook group? I let it lie.

In a couple minutes, a relative newcomer to Galileo, whose spouse happens to be a distant cousin of this stranger, replies, "Hey M, I didn't know you were in this group! How are you?" And she continues:

> If you'll allow me a moment of complete honesty, preachers like this are EXACTLY why I needed to find a group of people that were the antitheses of those beliefs. Because on one hand, my cynicism is completely in the "let's throw out all religion" camp, and on the other hand, I see a group of people coming together and doing good work. Whether people are coming together to do good work in the name of Jesus or Allah or Humanism or whatever, doesn't matter to me. I need to be around people doing good together.
>
> This group, this church, this body of believers is essential for me to not drown in a pool of my own cynicism. This is essential for me to learn HOW to fight the good fight and hopefully learn to be a positive and constructive voice in the world.
>
> I'm never going to change a law or debate one of these guys or make a huge difference in the world, but because of this group of peo-

ple who love justice and also love Jesus, I've been able to have some really sweet and amazing and heartfelt conversations lately. People who were in the same boat as me, asked the same questions, felt the same discontent. And I can tell them, hey, they're not all like that.

And it's giving me a little more hope in the world.

The stranger doesn't miss a beat:

Hi K. I'm doing ok. I do agree that what I've seen so far of this group is a lot more tolerant than what I've experienced during my church going days. These days, I see so much intolerance and victim blaming going on in the religious world. It's hard to explain in a public forum why I'm so distrusting of religious leaders and churches, as there are people who would be hurt deeply by what I have to say. Let's just say that the church I was raised in burned me and others so badly, that I am afraid to trust. That being said, what I have seen of this group is something different. Perhaps with time, trust will grow. I do like the fact that they are not anti-LGBTQ. That means something to me.

And our friend replies, "I'm still relatively new to Galileo, but from what I've seen so far, many of us would find your distrust and fear completely rational and many have experienced the same. I hope you find this group as refreshing as I do. [heart emoji]"

And the stranger says, "I hope so too."

I can see it happening, in real time, right down to the bouncing dot-dot-dot that means someone is typing. It fills me with wonder, this medium that allows vulnerable and potentially life-changing conversations to flourish. The G-person responding to her husband's cousin would never call herself an evangelist; she as much as says she's barely Christian herself. But she is a trustworthy witness for the reign of God that we preach and embody together. I stop to pray that the stranger who has trusted us to overhear that conversation will find her way to a community of belonging in Jesus's name. Might as well tell the truth—I hope she comes to Galileo. Like, soon. We definitely need her. Maybe she needs us too.

Get Out There, Church (Fall 2013)

Online presence, though, doesn't work by itself. Or maybe it could, but that's not what we did. We remembered that for much of the twentieth century, the mainline church's evangelistic method boiled down to "We will be as nice as possible so that people will come to us, in here, and stay." That church isn't working in the twenty-first century, though, so we figured we'd try something different. What if *we* go to *them*?

In short order we found that we needed—like you didn't already guess it—a float. As in, a mobile expression of our ethos that we could tow behind my Subaru in parades. Galileo Church joyfully walks/rides/waves a rainbow flag in two parades a year, every year, without fail. I think we just walked in a clump, with posters and handouts, in the local, small-town Pickle Palooza festival parade that first year, as well as in the Tarrant County LGBTQ Pride parade. But soon thereafter we started commissioning float design and construction from among our own dedicated membership.

Let's just say the results were mixed. Our first float was comically craptastic, a hand-painted, blood-red sun with snaky voodoo rays on a painter's canvas affixed to some recycled PVC pipe. Let the reader understand: I/we adore the True Francine who made it pretty much by herself during an incredibly busy season. But when the parade marshal announced, "And here comes Galileo Church, quirky church for spiritual refugees, with their float, and isn't that, um, *interesting!*" I fell to the asphalt in a spasm of laughter. That did not stop us from using it again, though. A float is *so much better* than no float, and the True Francine gave us one. Thanks, Francine! Mwah!

The next year another friend took up the challenge. With some power tools and one of those stencil-cutting things, plus some actual money (an advantage over Francine's situation, for sure), she made something a little more presentable.

Third time is the charm. Mark and Ryan reinvested in new PVC; added spray paint, fabric, and plastic curtains of colorful ribbons. David G. bought a Bluetooth speaker that blasts our LGBTQ+ soundtrack on repeat (Aretha's "Say a Little Prayer for You," Tomboy's "It's OK to Be Gay," etc.). The current iteration of Galileo's parade float still looks homemade because it is; it still says we have a sense of humor about ourselves and the silliness of parading down Main Street to say that we love Jesus and Jesus loves everybody.

Our three-phase float development is like a lot of things at Galileo and a lot of things in life: you have to try a lot of things you don't know how to do yet to learn how to do it better. So much of our life together has a story like this, of iterations that get progressively better, never perfect, always room for another bigger, better try. It's like the apostle somewhere says: "All of us . . . are being transformed . . . from one degree of glory to another" (2 Cor. 3:18). I'm sure the apostle didn't have parade floats in mind when he said it, and I doubt that *glorious* is the best adjective for describing even our latest efforts, but mostly we keep getting better at the stuff we keep trying.

Alongside our float, we also developed a set of stuff for setting up a booth wherever people would have us. Beginning with my card table and one of those trifold, science-fair cardboard displays, we rented space on college campuses and in town festivals. We have handed out approximately thirty-eight kazillion Starburst and Milky Way candies (get it? because we're Galileo? Astronomy!) along with the afore-described cards that say, "We are searching for you" with our URL at the bottom. We do our best to pick up the candy wrappers and discarded cards when we're finished at the end of those days. We discover that some of us are able to withstand the constant rejection, the inevitable homophobic/transphobic resistance, and the heat that come with booth-babe work, and some of us are not, and that's okay.

But here are a couple of reasons why we do it. First reason: Melissa. Second reason: Amber.

Melissa had just moved to Texas, a retired schoolteacher, divorced from a dude, two kids, barely out to herself as a lesbian, closeted everywhere else. Oh, and a devout Christian, so devout that she stayed with the abusive husband much longer than was rational on the advice of her fundagelical pastor. On her third or fourth day in our state, she attended her first ever Pride event and saw our float. (Iteration 2, I believe.) She came by our booth at the postparade festival and asked if we were really truly Christians. I said yes, we were sure trying. I asked if we could add her to our email list. She said no, thank you.

But later, in line for a beer, she saw a couple of our folks in their Galileo T-shirts that say on the back, "We are not the center of the universe." She asked about that. They were married, Caroline and Michala, and they introduced Melissa to Jill and Tricia, also married. She hung out with them for a little while that afternoon. That was Saturday.

On Sunday at 5 p.m., Melissa showed up for worship. "I met y'all at Pride yesterday," she said. We were a little skeptical and completely delighted because it doesn't usually work that quickly. But here she stays, and now we can't remember life without her. I cannot imagine my life without her. These days we call her "Lady Justice" because she keeps our church aware of policy issues and election seasons.

More often, it works like Amber. We plant our booth at the Student Activities Fair at the University of Texas at Arlington every fall and every spring, paying for that 10 × 10 space so we can set up our stuff (which, like our float situation, has improved vastly over time). One winter Amber showed up for worship and said, when I introduced myself, "Oh, I met you at the fair at UTA." I apologized profusely for not remembering; the fair was the week before and I had met so many students and my late-forties brain does not hold names and faces like it used to. (That's a lie; I've never been great with names and faces.)

And she said, "Oh, not last week. Back in the . . . let's see . . . spring, I think, a couple of years ago? Remember, I said . . ."

It came back to me in a flood. "You said how done you were with the church, how badly it had hurt you, how hypocritical and mean it was, how useless and harmful it had been in your life. And I held your hands because you were crying, and then I was crying too, and I said how very sorry I was for all that hurt and how you had every right to be pissed off, even mad as hell, and how much our church would like to try to ease that pain, and you said no, thank you, and you ran off."

"Yeah," she said, shyly. "And I saw you there a few more times, last year, this year, and y'all just keep coming back. So I figured you were serious." And so, here is Amber, who helps on our ministry finance team with her almost-a-bachelor's degree in accounting. Recently, she posted a reflection in our Facebook group:

Hey, church. Today is my 4 year anniversary of the day I came out, and I am kind of astonished at the contrast in who I am today versus the person I was on this day four years ago. I was so unsure of myself and what I believed and who I was.

But you changed that.

Galileo has become my home, my family, and my heart. I have learned so much, met so many wonderful people, and gained so much confidence in myself since that troubling time in my life. The day I saw that big rainbow sign at the UTA Activities Fair that said "Gay and Christian? YAAAS!" my life was changed for the better.

But I didn't come to church right away. Then I even came a few times and talked a lot with Katie, and then didn't come back for a long time. But you were patient. And you were always willing to accept me for who I am, even the noncommittal parts of myself.

It was your love and acceptance that taught me to love those who have a hard time accepting me. After church last Sunday, I was able to have a real talk with my dad for the first time in a very long time. Even though we still disagree on so much, the door is now open because you gave me the courage to open it.

I just want to thank every single person here for just being you. I'm not sure I would've made it without you, and that thought drives me every day to make sure others make it here, too. You are my heart, and I am so grateful to have you in my life.

Thanks for everything,

Amber

My point being, there are some spiritual refugees who have the gumption to do Sunday-by-Sunday church search until they find the exact right place, the exact right mixture of kindness and devotion and intellectual integrity to feed their spirit. Worry less about them; if they're meant to find you, they will come. But there are many, many more spiritual refugees who are drifting, drowning, weary and wary. They very well may not come to you for good reasons of their own. How far are you willing to go to get to them? And when you find them, or they you, will they trust that yours is a safe place to reveal their comically craptastic selves? And will they find sufficient help and patience to try out new iterations, new degrees of glory, the transformation that the Spirit of the living Christ can work? To the point: *Can people tell by your parade float the truth of that gospel?*

Bible, Beer, Integration, and Holding the Space (Fall 2013)

Look, I know it's played. Theology on Tap, Hymns and Libations, Bible and Beer—You're rolling your eyes. It's justified.

But we're living down here on the blessed buckle of the Bible Belt, okay? And there is a strong tradition among Christians down here of tucking your Saturday night self down deep in your purse or your pocket on Sunday morning. It's quite possible that you drink beer *and* go to church, but you have to keep those identities separate from each other and one of them secret from the other. There's an old joke: Why do you always invite two Baptists fishing? Because if you invite just one, she'll drink all your beer. Replace "Baptists" with the fundagelicals of your upbringing and it'll be funnier.

A fast-casual, honky-tonk taco place was opening a franchise in our town—Fuzzy's, for the locally initiated—and during their first week, I went to introduce myself to the manager. "Can my group meet here on Tuesdays?" I asked. "Sure," he said, smiling. "Can we put up signs that say who we are, a church group drinking beer and doing Bible study?" "Sure," he said, smiling more. I think he thought I was not serious. But we started in September 2013, Tuesday nights, 8–10 p.m., with little table-top signs that say "Bible & Beer—Galileo Church—come join us!" We took off for Christmas Eve 2013. Then we didn't miss a week for 246 consecutive Tuesdays after that. We brought homemade cookies to all the waitstaff, kitchen workers, and bartenders, none of whom had been there as long as Galileo Church was. There are actually photos of Galileo Church people tacked up in the Fuzzy's kitchen from the Christmas cards (and cookies) we have delivered there over the years. Bible & Beer recently moved to a more northerly location of a different taco restaurant; it remains to be seen if we'll feel at home there as we did at Fuzzy's. Or if their beer is as cheap on Tuesday nights as it is at Fuzzy's.

Here's how Bible & Beer works. I print *next* Sunday's Scripture on a half-sheet of paper and write questions on the other side. The questions are in the reader-response vein. If we're reading about Cain and Abel, for example, I'll ask, "Do you have a sibling? Do you get along?" Or "Have you ever been so mad at someone that you wanted to do violence to them?" Or "What do you think was up with God and the plants versus animals thing? Does that seem fair to you? What would it mean about God if it wasn't fair?" The studies don't really aim toward a point; they just help readers critically and carefully engage a text they may never have read for themselves. I might also include a couple of clarifying details to help inexperienced readers: "A *Pharisee* is a devoutly religious person, a leader in Jesus's Jewish community, tasked with protecting community boundaries," for example. Or "*The Son of Man* is a nickname Jesus uses for himself, borrowed from the Hebrew prophets. It means 'the very human being' or 'the representation of all humanity.'"

The last question on every week's study is the same: "What's your takeaway tonight, a word of good news that you've heard from Scripture or from someone else at the table or from your own heart? Write it down; keep it close." Yeah, I bring pencils.

The study is designed to work without a theologically trained leader, but it works best if there's a facilitator to help keep the conversation flowing. At Bible & Beer we often divide the whole group into little groups of three to four people. Each group reads the Scripture out loud, paragraph by paragraph, with a caveat for those who don't want to read ("Just say 'pass'; it's not a big deal"). It changes Scripture when we read it out loud in that noisy, sticky, crowded environment with '80s rock or country music blaring and several TVs showing sports. And it definitely changes my reading of it to engage with readers from my church (and strangers, once in a while). I can't imagine preaching now without having dug through the text for points of contact with people whose lives are so different from mine.

But before the study, the beer and the conversation. Here's where I need to make a confession that is slightly embarrassing: we don't actually drink that much beer. A pitcher or two at most, for five, six, or seven people who want a glass. Everybody else drinks Dr Pepper or water, yawn. The church buys the beer; B&Bers buy their own tacos. Or Dr Pepper. Or water. Galileo folks just aren't interested in beer the way the *HuffPo* articles about millennial hipsters say they should be. (We hate IPAs. We're not too proud to say so.)

(And we don't really do drunkenness, not usually. There was that time I did shots at the Fuzzy's bar with the son or nephew or something of the woman from whom we were desperately trying to rent a place for worship, and Ryan and Kyle M. had to drive me home. But that's it. Mostly.)

The conversation, on the other hand, flows freely at Fuzzy's. We call Bible & Beer "gateway Galileo" because it boasts the lowest barrier to entry of all our gatherings; you just show up on the patio and talk about your day. We do that for a whole hour. Sometimes a newcomer will lean over at 8:45 and whisper, "When does this thing get started? The website said 8." And I whisper back, "Yeah, we started at 8. We're actually doing it right now. You didn't recognize it because you're not used to the church nurturing infrastructure for the facilitation of healthy human interaction." Actually, I don't say that last part. But I could.

Bible & Beer is about the integration of selves—the Saturday-night self with the Sunday-morning self, the beer-drinking self with the Bible-reading self, and the decompressing-from-the-day's-stresses self with the incrementally-questing-to-know-God-better self. Around those sticky tables we practice the art of putting our fragmented selves back together in front of people we trust. It's one of the most beautiful things I've ever seen.

And while I would say now, five years later, that Bible & Beer is so quintessentially Galileo that we wouldn't be "us" without it, you should know that it *almost* didn't work. The first few times we did it, the same few people came who were also coming to everything else—G-groups, planning meetings, parties. One by one they bowed out of the additional weekly commitment of B&B, till it was down to Chris and me.

It's hard to put into words what Chris has meant to Galileo over the years. In some ways he is not a spiritual refugee; he's got lots of congregational experience and deep denominational roots and tons of local church friends. He has always thought of himself as a helper for

Galileo Church, and while I have resisted his self-appointment as my colleague in this work, the truth is, Chris has been helpful in ways we didn't even know to ask for.

I did ask him, though, if he would keep meeting me for Bible & Beer if no one else came for a while. "The thing is," I said, "we can't *have* Bible & Beer if we don't *have* Bible & Beer. It takes a group to make a group, you know?" He generously agreed with this weird logic, and we kept meeting. It must have looked strange—a woman in her mid-forties and a man in his early thirties meeting up every Tuesday at 8 p.m., clinking glasses, shooting the shit, arguing about politics, and leaving to go home in separate cars. We called it "the ministry of holding the space." We didn't want to squander the manager's good will or the consistency we had built up over the weeks or the Tuesday evening placement on our collective church calendar. We wanted to be present *in case* anybody ever decided to come to Bible & Beer. Which they eventually did and still do. Some weeks we have six. Twelve. Twenty. I can't account for the fluctuation, but I figure the people who need to be there are there.

One Tuesday night a noisy group of slightly drunk folks at another table kept looking toward our table, obviously eavesdropping on our conversation. Upon leaving the bar, one of them got brave. "Hey, can I take a picture of your sign?" he asked, already pointing his phone at it. "Sure," I said. "Just don't be a hater."

Once in a while people stop to lecture us about how sacrilegious it is to have the Bible in close proximity to beer. My response is always the same: I stand up and stick out my hand. "I'm the pastor and I bought the beer tonight. Would you like to talk about it some more over at another table? And would you like a glass?" I want to draw the fire away from those who have been brave enough to come. And I want to heap burning coals on our detractors' heads (that's from the Bible). So if this guy was going to post a photo of our sign with his condemnatory, fundagelical POV, I didn't want to give permission for that. Since he asked.

The photo-taking guy said, "Naw, I'm not a hater. I'm gonna text this to my pastor and see if we can do it at my church. That's fuckin' brilliant, pastor. I don't know why all churches don't do it."

Neither do I, slightly intoxicated man. Neither do I.

Excursus: "You Just Love" (Blog Post, September 2013)

So here's how I thought the "Bible" part would go at Bible & Beer last Tuesday:

1. Read the Ten Commandments from Exodus 20, note how simple they are. Black and white. Don't do this, don't do that, and you're good. So graciously clear.

2. Read Romans 13:8-10, where Paul says, "All the commandments—don't kill each other, don't lie to each other, yada yada yada—are summed up in this word: Love your neighbor as yourself." Note how complicated that is. Love is more than "mind your own business." Love is not black and white; it's murky gray decision-making space, obscuring a rainbow of confusing beauty and trouble. It requires more from me than the Big Ten. I can't just ignore my neighbor (or that stranger or even my enemy). I have to love them. Lord have mercy.

3. Everybody agrees with these conclusions; we finish our beer; we go home.

But here's how it actually went.

First we read Exodus 20 and noted the simplicity of the Ten. "Yes, exactly," I affirmed.

Then we read Romans 13 and talked about love, and the obligation to love, and the complication of being *told* to love, and so on and on and on. We were on the right track, headed directly to the preplanned destination station of my imagining.

And then she spoke up, the young woman who hadn't made much noise all night. Here's what she said, best I can remember:

"I don't know if it's so hard. I was raised to believe the Ten Commandments, you know, in a religious school, and we memorized them. And the whole time I was there, one of the adults there was molesting me, and the other adults knew about it, I'm pretty sure, and they were the ones teaching me the Ten Commandments. And I would have probably killed them if I could. That was complicated, you know?

"But it's been a while since then, and what I've finally figured out is that when you don't have anything else, when you can't do anything else, you can always love. Love is simple. It's not that hard. You just love, you find a way to love from your heart, and that's all you need. That's all there is. Just the love."

She took a sip of her beer and looked at her hands in her lap.

Nobody breathed for a long time. We probably should have finished our beers in that holy silence and gone home, but of course there are always more words. Words of comfort and confirmation, though she was asking for neither.

Words of conclusion and wrapping-it-all-up, though they fell far short. And, after a little while, words that drifted back to our present; a return to the beautiful, breezy night on the taco bar patio with the Bible. And with her, reminding us that it's not supposed to be that hard. You just love.

Cookie Evangelism (Fall 2013)

Before the cookies, Jennie, and her ever-lovin' curiosity about *every*-thing. (I said curiosity is a virtue, right? Well, if that's true, Jennie is eligible for sainthood.) She stalked us online for a couple of weeks, sent a message, and we met up for a beer before Bible & Beer. I think it's safe to say that we clicked—we find each other to be hilarious and smart, which is nice for both of us—and she was ours. But oh! The questions! The urgency! So many urgent questions, our Jennie. About God, about the universe, about everything.

So I suggested we start reading together, choosing some books that would give us a common vocabulary and framework for working through stuff, maybe even providing better questions, which is the best possible outcome for study, right? And we decided together we could invite other people to join us, and thus G-Study was born. Galileo buys the books. You bring your brain.

Many of those books were deeply influential in Galileo's understanding of the gospel—someday maybe I'll write essays on each one, recounting our collective sense of wonder and hope expanding as we unfolded all these new ways of thinking about old things. Probably my fave of all time was Walter Brueggemann's *The Bible Makes Sense*. But this is the one that got us to the cookies: Rob Bell's *What We Talk About When We Talk About God*.

I had resisted Surfer Rob for a while; I don't like people who are that much cooler than I. But he was so far ahead of me in figuring out how hungry people are for new categories, new metaphors, new language (and therefore the possibility for new thoughts) about the Deity of the universe. And while I have approached each of his books with real skepticism *(What have you to say to me, het-cis white man, looking so smug in your super-skinny jeans?)*, he never fails to take my breath away with his dazzling clarity about the most important things in the world.

(I should probably also confess to having been in his presence one time for a surprise appearance he made at a conference I was attending, and from the moment he materialized into sight to the moment he vaporized in a puff of smoke [not really, but if you've seen him you know what I mean], I couldn't take my eyes off him. He is mesmerizing and extremely gifted. As you know.)

So in *What We Talk About*, Rob says that, among other things, God is *ahead*. Just a little ahead of us, beckoning us to come along with God, like a patient human companion (that's God) for a new puppy (that's us), moving a little bit further each time we get near so as to help us make incremental progress toward the *telos* God has in mind for everybody and everything God has made. God also sometimes interrupts the incremental, day-by-day progress with something shocking and new that jolts us into a better understanding, a better place. Like Jesus, for example. This, Rob says, is the gospel of the God Who Is Ahead of Us: today is not the same as yesterday, and tomorrow will be different still. Christianity is, or could be, a stay against the deathly hallows of monotony.

And so, in G-Study one day we asked each other, "What would it be like if the church took up a ministry of 'piercing the monotony'? What does that look like on the ground?" I hope that feels as electric to you as it still does to me: the Next Church imagining together over coffee and donuts what might be entailed in pulling God's best ideas, including one *we just heard for the first time*, into this present moment, with the intent to *make something happen*. It's completely *contra* Now Church's investment in preserving the status quo or even retreating into nostalgia; it's against the grain of the church's apparent vested interest in lamenting "this present darkness" and revering stuff that happened a long time ago in a Galilee far, far away. (I didn't make that up, but I'm stealing it because it's funny *and* true, no?)

We wondered where, among our neighbors, we could see the soul-crushing effect of monotony. It wasn't hard to discern. It was at Chipotle, and all similar assembly-line burrito restaurants, where the workers stand in place and say, repeatedly, "Flour or corn? Black beans or refried? Pork or chicken? Do you want guacamole for an extra two-twenty-nine?" What would it look like to pierce *that* monotony, specifically?

We had heard about Nadia Bolz-Weber's church in Denver assembling gourmet Thanksgiving to-go meals for bus drivers and other workers who don't get the holiday off. We weren't quite up to gourmet anything, and there's no public transit where we are, but we had low-wage workers all around us and several bakers on board—Aisling! Susan! Who else? How to find out?

And so, #cookieevangelism was born. It wasn't "evangelism" in the sense of "getting people to come to our church" but in the pure sense that we've actually got some good news—"Today is not the same as yesterday! Tomorrow will be different still!"—that we are actually excited to share with people who might not have heard yet. We picked Labor Day for our #firsttime, a day originally meant to give workers a break, now a day for low-wage workers to work even harder while rich people (like me) take a day off to shop and eat out. We asked people to participate in one, two, or three ways: bake, pack, or deliver.

We collected batches of cookies that people baked at home. We gathered at my house to assemble nine-inch pie boxes with cellophane windows, nestling a selection of cookies and a couple of cards about Galileo Church in bright tissue paper and taping a note to the top of each box: "You're working today. That sucks. Have a cookie." And of course, our dubya-dubya-dubya addy.

Notice that this brilliant (if I do say so myself) plan required no previous sign up, no prior commitment from anyone. We would only pack as many cookies as were baked. We would only deliver as many boxes as we packed. Some people would bake and pack but not deliver; some couldn't bake but were happy to drive. I had already figured out that if our life together required RSVPs for the church's programming—if *my* comfort in planning events required that I know in advance how many people would show up—it wouldn't work. Galileo's gig-economy folks, which was just about all of them, were often not apprised of their work schedules until days or hours before. Their lives were fluid and uncertain. Plan making was destined to disappoint.

For cookie delivery, we made a list of retail and fast-food places in proximity to our primary meeting place—actually in a circumference around my house because that's where most of our life together happened. We sent people out with cookie-stuffed boxes and a list of places to go and these instructions: "When you go in, stand in line if you need to. Don't interrupt the flow of business or otherwise draw attention. When it's your turn and the employee says, 'How can I help you?' or 'What can I get you?' just say, 'I don't need anything from you today. I brought you and your coworkers some homemade cookies.' And then get the hell out—don't wait around for a thank you; don't take a selfie; don't order food. In the name of Jesus and for Christ's actual sake, reverse the expectation! Now go forth and pierce the monotony!"

And with that charge, we went forth with cookies for burrito assemblers, haircutters, grocery clerks, dishwashers, pizza bakers, and ER nurses. That first Labor Day we sent out thirty boxes of cookies. On Christmas Eve it was sixty. For Valentine's Day, eighty. Memorial Day. First day of summer. Any excuse we could think of to commiserate with working people and pierce their monotony. We became known as "the cookie church" when we went to the same places again and again. We thought the best possible outcome might be someone going home after a long shift and saying to their beloveds, "You'll never believe what happened today." That would be the word of God for the people of God, wouldn't it? *Thanks be to God.*

But we were wrong. The *best* thing that happened was Andrea and her spouse D.J. and their BFF Ryan. Andrea was at work, got the card that came with the cookies, took it home, shared the weirdness of it with D.J., who shared it with Ryan; together they made plans to check out Galileo. (Andrea would tell me later she had seen Galileo's cards before the cookie evangelists made it to the salon, but there's something to be said for the cookie *emphasis*.) They looked us up online first, of course. "You had me at Bible & Beer," D.J. would say later. But really, we had them at their individual griefs over a faith that didn't respect Andrea's hard existential questions, didn't give D.J. anything but platitudes when his dad died, and rejected Ryan when he told the truth about being gay.

Ryan showed up in person before his friends did, exhibiting unbelievable courage to walk into our dingy, low-ceiling worship space alone. He sat by himself near the back, which is hard in a room with only forty chairs or so. He was polite but guarded. When we all got up for communion, he didn't. In the hubbub of liturgy, a couple of our steadfast worshipers were gossiping in the row behind him. "Oh, sorry," they said to him when he glanced around. "We're the snarky Christians here." Sold.

Six weeks later Ryan was swathing our dingy worship space in yards of billowy white fabric for Easter—like the resurrected Jesus had unwrapped himself from one hundred yards of shroud. We had heard he worked in wedding planning, and we needed help. "You can use my credit card," I said, having met him two weeks before. "Buy something pretty." It was a good gamble. Ryan has been making beauty in our space for our God Who Is Beautiful ever since, except for that year we sent him to California for a vocational discernment internship. He came back and went to work as our "evangelist for youngsters and public provocation" and has been commissioned for ministry by our denomination, so we could call him Rev. Ryan if we wanted to. He would love it.

Cookies, y'all. Go forth. For the love of God and the world God still loves, go forth and pierce the monotony.

Don't Fuck This Up (Summer-Fall 2013)

Picture Kyle M. noodling around on his laptop in his bedroom in his parents' house, procrastinating his nursing-school homework, queueing up Lorde tracks on YouTube and wondering if anybody in the universe is as gay and Christian as he is. Google eventually gets him to Galileo Church, right there in his room. He finds us on Facebook and Twitter and reads his way backwards for all the weeks (!) we've been alive. Sends me a message in July 2013—"Are you for real?" is the gist. Ignores my earnest reply. But he's still around, "liking" some stuff, commenting a couple of times, beginning to think maybe it *is* for real. Maybe *we* are for real.

I reach out at the end of August, again through Facebook, saying that I hope his summer semester is going well. He ignores that message too. In October I ask him (and all my FB friends) to "like" Galileo on

Facebook, something I had apparently just learned to do. This time he writes back: "When I received your request this morning for me to add Galileo to my timeline, it made me smile to know that I had been thought about. And then as I was getting ready this morning and listening to music, Amy Grant's song 'Galileo' came on. I think that's a sign that I need to find time to finally make it out to a gathering. I love what you've started and can't wait to be a part of it myself!" I send back the times and addresses of all our stuff. Does he show up?

Nah.

One day in December I catch him skulking around Galileo on-line (you can see it, sometimes, with clicks and likes) and send him a quick message before I can change my mind: "Kyle, get your ass to church, dude! But don't blow off work to do it. But I want to meet you in person! But I know you have responsibilities. Ahh, you see, I'm torn. Peace—Katie."

And so. Six months into our . . . relationship(?) (in the middle of Advent, fittingly) Kyle came to church.

A few weeks later, we threw one of our epic parties, which we do at the rate of about five a year. We had decided not to cram a celebration into the Thanksgiving-Christmas frenzy; with a bunch of students and retail workers (and plenty of student-retail workers) among us, that's a wildly busy time. Plus, it was dawning on me that family-themed holidays were super-stressful for my LGBTQ+ friends. They very often went home to, or stayed away from, their FOO (family of origin, but we just say "foo") that was stuck in the specious "we love you, but . . ." category. Holidays felt less holy and more dangerous for your average G-person. So instead we bottled up our good cheer and saved it for our We Survived the Holidays party in early January. We've been partying heartily around the first weekend of the new year ever since.

I mention it here because when Kyle M. showed up for our very first When the Shit Hit the Fan party, he brought friends. Caroline, someone he knew from a previous job working the front desk at a downtown hair salon, and her partner, Michala, were a little thrown off by our intergenerational good cheer, complete with karaoke and cheap red wine and lots of chances to make fools of ourselves in front of people we were learning to trust. They didn't trust us, not yet, but like a lot of folks in the years to come, they found something compelling about a church that partied like Jesus on Friday and came back together on Sunday to worship in Spirit and truth. There was a long time when, if you asked Galileo for a show of hands of people who came to one of our parties before they came to anything else, we would look like Pentecostals at prayer.

I always invite newcomers to have coffee or get a beer so we can swap stories about "what God has been up to in our lives, and what we think God might be doing next," as I type and retype in all the emails. Michala and Caroline didn't really want a meeting, though. What I knew about them, I learned by going to dinner after worship and staying around long enough to catch their stories. Michala told us how much she loved church as a kid and how it had hurt her when they kicked her out of her youth group leadership when she came out. Caroline said she wasn't raised religious and didn't think much about it. "I don't really think about God," she said, "because I don't think God has thought very much about me." Isn't that the saddest thing you've ever heard? "Yeah, Caroline , that's on us," I thought. But I kept my mouth shut; she wasn't really inviting a conversation.

A few weeks after the When the Shit Hit the Fan party, after Michala and Caroline had been to worship with Kyle a few times, my phone rang, and the screen said it was Michala. I answered in a panic because millennials don't actually use the phone to *call* unless someone is on fire. "I need to meet with you," she said. "It's important."

I got to the coffee shop as fast as I could, bought us both something to drink from Galileo's generous Jesus-ate-and-drank-with-everybody-all-the-damn-time-so-we-should-too budget. I started in on my spiel about Galileo as a start-up, not fully formed yet but looking for people who wanted to invest their energy to help us build something beautiful. But Michala wasn't really responding to that; she was bouncing her knee up and down like you do when you're nervous or impatient or both. Finally, I stopped talking. Sometimes it takes me a minute.

"Michala, what's on your mind?" I asked. She leaned forward, looking right into my eyes. With her teeth clenched and her lips tight, she said, *"Don't fuck this up."* Not your usual pastoral session outpouring.

She said, "Caroline has never wanted to go to church with me, so I haven't been to church in forever. But I miss it so much. I miss God. I miss Jesus. I miss the people and the songs and the Bible. Caroline says she can keep coming to Galileo until y'all do something stupid or mean, which she knows you will. So I'm telling you, seriously: *Don't fuck this up.*"

I have never taken any (ahem) "request" so seriously.

Michala and Caroline quickly became people we couldn't imagine life without. They came to Bible & Beer, contributing generously to the conversation. Reading the Bible with Caroline, who had never heard most of its stories before, remains one of my favorite experiences ever. Within a few months, they were serving on a worship-planning creative team, planning a baby shower for our first congregational baby, buying supplies for our next party (with my credit card, natch; that card got a lot of play that first couple of years, sometimes passing from G-person to G-person without getting back to me in between). They were integrated into the life of the church in every conceivable way.

And then one day, during fall 2014, the phone rings: Caroline! OMG! Someone's on fire! And sure enough, when I say hello, I can hear her crying. "Katie, I don't know what to do," she says. "Is anybody hurt? Have you called 9-1-1?" I ask. "No, we're fine," she says. "But remember when we first met, and I told you I didn't think about God because God doesn't think about me?"

"Oh, yeah, you sweet soul, I definitely remember that. It still stings. I'm still so sorry."

"Well, now I don't know what to do," Caroline says, "because since I started coming around Galileo, I'm thinking about Jesus all the time. I think I love him." Sob, gulp, sniffle.

"Oh, honey," I say, reverting to my *amma*-theologian self, "I know what to do! If you love Jesus, you gotta get with him. We'll baptize you. The whole rest of your life starts now."

The Gift of the Homeless Church (Fall 2013)

After I tell people I'm a pastor, in the dentist's office or the grocery-store line or wherever, the very next question is always, "Where's your church?" That was an easy question before—my church was on Sugarloaf Parkway in Lawrenceville or North Davis Drive in Arlington, and the asker could mentally map it. (Not that the asker ever really intended to *come* to my church, but we humans like to file stuff like that in our brains.)

With Galileo, there has never been an easy answer to "Where's your church?" "We move a lot," I used to say with a grin or a sigh, depending on the day. Or, if I were feeling theologically provocative, I would look dramatically at my watch and say, "I don't know, what time is it? Wednesday at 10:30 a.m.? I believe my church is currently at AB Coffee in Mansfield, eating donuts and discussing parables." And then I would explain to the poor bug who was now trapped in my ecclesial web that Galileo doesn't own any property, so the church just *is* wherever the people of it *are*.

Let's be clear: Galileo doesn't own property because Galileo doesn't have any money. I've already told you some stuff about our finances—namely, our start-up funds for two years areat exactly $185,000. You don't buy property with that. But we have pretty good reasons for thinking that's okay with us. Here are some:

1. Property management is a drag. I've done the part of pastoring that is more like being an on-site building manager, and I've seen whole churches consumed by it, and it's awful. It's not just money the church spends maintaining its building and grounds; it's hours and hours of energy poured into that work by people who participate in a collective delusion that weeding the flower beds and discussing bids for a new roof and replacing the boiler *is* ministry, rather than equipping the church that occupies the building *for* ministry. How depressing is it to imagine that Jesus died for the sake of building maintenance? But churches do it, all the time.

2. Most of the refugees Galileo seeks and shelters don't own property. Or at least the start-up team didn't. They were renters or living at home with their parents. They went to school part-time, worked full-time for hourly wages, and drove Uber on the weekends to make ends meet. It was hard to imagine they were going to be enthusiastic about our church taking on a bunch of debt. (Almost as hard as imagining anyone would actually lend us money. Let's be real.)

3. We didn't know for sure where we would land geographically. We were committed to staying in the politically/socially/religiously conservative suburbs of the Dallas–Fort Worth–Arlington metroplex, but there's a lot of fluidity out here. People live in one municipality, work in another, shop and eat out somewhere else. It became clear to us pretty early that Galileo wasn't going to be a neighborhood church; it was going to be what we called a "special interest church" (read "quirky and queer"), meaning that people would drive long distances to get "there," wherever "there" turned out to be. We've never printed our address on anything, including my business card. We wanted (and want) to stay light on our feet.

4. We didn't want to "nest" in the facilities of an established church because the people we hoped would come were people who likely had negative associations with traditional church spaces. That whole integration-of-selves project that Bible & Beer represented meant we needed to avoid "churchy spaces." We needed a place where we could pray *and* party, sometimes on the same night. (That's not exactly about property ownership, but "nesting" is usually an intermediate step toward "going out on your own," right? You borrow somebody's fellowship hall or family-life center as a holdover, till your baby church gets a room of its own.)

But here's the main gift we continue to get out of being renters (and the gift we're so far inclined to hang onto): when none of us owns the space where the church meets, the categories of "host" and "guest" get all mixed up. "We" (myself as the pastor, the lay leaders, and anybody who's been around for more than two weeks) can't really welcome "them," those newcomers, whoever "they" are, as if the space belongs more to us than them. We are all guests in the rented space with all its contingencies, including the AC that can't cool more than twenty degrees when it's 106° outside and the toilets that run sometimes. None of us really belongs here, except that God has welcomed us here and we have paid somebody some rent. It's an equalizer, I'm saying, this homeless way of doing church.

That feels essential to Galileo's evangelistic identity—that none of us are more or less needful of God's mercy, none of us more or less deserving of God's love, none of us more or less grateful for God's welcome. We're all here, wherever "here" is at the moment, on equal terms, hoping for hospitality, arriving in the open arms and open heart of God and finding our true belonging there, with God and with each other, rather than the space we happen to be in.

And, dear bug, because you are trapped in my ecclesial web, let me say one more thing about that. For most of our church's life, we have set up and torn down the entire worship aesthetic every single Sunday. We arrive in the bar or the coffee shop or the pizza place patio or the theater, and we put it all together. We move chairs and tables, set up the prayer wall and the communion table, hang the lights, wire the sound, drape the rainbow flags, light the candles, arrange the toddler corral, lower the screen, set out our signs with giant arrows pointing to the entrance, and the people come, and suddenly there is a church where there was no church before.

A few hours later, after we've sung and played and prayed and preached and laughed and cursed and held each other tight and kept the faith, we take it all apart. Flags and candles and communion dishes go back into storage. Chairs get moved back into place for the regular customers. We shut the lights and lock the doors and call out one more time to make sure we haven't left anyone in the bathroom. The parking lot empties; the church scatters; we each carry a little bit of Jesus in our bodies back into the world God still loves.

"Where is your church?"

I don't know. They're all over the place. Where's yours?

Now Is the Time to Man Up (Spring 2014)

Back to Caroline. The problem was, we didn't have a baptistery. By this time we had moved from G-House (our first rented home) to the Farr Best Theatre in downtown Mansfield. This old, historic theater with a deep stage and red velvet seats bolted to the floor was not equipped for Disciples-style baptism, which requires full immersion for believers—in other words, grown-ass people have to get their whole self completely under water.

A friend at another Disciples start-up told me they bought a three-hundred-gallon cattle trough that did the job just fine. I could find it at Tractor Supply not far from my house, but it was going to cost $450, and that felt like a *lot*. I was scrolling through the Tractor Supply website one morning in algebra class (more on that later!) and D.J. reminded me to check Craig's List for a used one. *Voila!* The very trough we wanted, on a ranch east of Dallas, $150 cash if you come get it before the weekend. (The lady we met out there was divorcing her husband, and I think she was selling all his stuff before he got back into town. Kinda shady, but good for us.)

But I didn't have a truck, and my hatchback was too narrow. I posted in the church's Facebook group, where Galileo people can post prayer requests or knock-knock jokes or whatever: "Anybody got a full-size truck I can drive to Dallas?" The only person who responded in the affirmative was S.

S was a teenaged kid who lived with their grandparents and sometimes got a ride to Galileo worship, after which I would give S a ride home. The first time I met S he was "Sam," a boy (we didn't know to ask for pronouns back then). But the next time S came around she was "Sarah," a girl. (Those aren't the real names S used, for S's privacy.) She told us that her grandparents kicked her out whenever she insisted on being Sam, so she was intermittently homeless. Additionally, there were parents and stepparents coming in and out of S's life, separately and unannounced, and an older brother who abused S every chance he got. S was surviving a hellish adolescence, and I felt glad that Galileo could be a little oasis of safety and friendship. (Yes, there were also issues of reporting the endangerment of a minor, which I worked on, but this is a story about how S and Galileo connected.)

S said they had a truck we could borrow. I said great. We made an appointment for Wednesday afternoon. Then S texted to say that the truck wasn't actually S's, but S's granddad's. I said fine, tell Granddad thanks. S texted several hours later to say that S him/herself didn't have a driver's license, so I'd have to drive. I said terrific. Then S texted to say that Granddad wasn't going to let a stranger drive his truck, so Granddad would drive and I could follow behind in my car.

I had pledged gas and toll money for this trip, and it was going to be pricey, so I asked if I could just ride in the truck with Granddad and S. A few hours later: okay. So I show up at their house on Wednesday, ready to go. Granddad comes out and kicks the tires (of his own truck!), checks the oil, starts it up. Then he goes back in the house with S. A full ten minutes go by, and S comes out grinning. "Granddad says he likes you, and you can drive the truck. He's staying home."

So I clambered up into that beast, a dually Ford F-650 or something huge like that, and adjusted the seat. It was 4:30 p.m. We were headed straight into rush hour. Sam, who it turns out was being Sam that day, said, "It doesn't go very fast," as I tried to get it up to sixty-five on the interstate. With the pedal to the metal, it never got above fifty. Dallas commuters whizzed around us, shooting blessings with their middle fingers.

But the time was not wasted; on the way, Sam told me his life story, all fifteen or sixteen years of it. The divorces, the abuses, the homelessness, the gender dysphoria that made him feel insane and deeply sad. There was theft and drugs and sex for money; there was such pain that I blinked back tears and tried my best to keep the giant truck on the road. Sam kept talking, pushing his voice into the lowest register he could find in his slight chest, until the story was all the way finished, right up to present day: finding Galileo Church on the Internet, making friends with me, cajoling Granddad into sharing the truck. Then Sam was quiet for a long time. So was I. After a minute I thanked Sam for trusting me with his story, with his one wild and precious life.

A few more minutes went by.

Sam said, "There's one more thing I didn't tell you. I can't believe I forgot."

I said, "Hit me."

Sam said, "It's big."

I said, "I can take it."

Sam said, "Also, I'm Mexican."

I don't know why it struck me as funny. I guess because alongside all the tragic disclosures of the day, Sam's Mexican American heritage was just so ordinary. But he delivered that news with heavy seriousness, and I tried to match his weighty delivery with a pastoral nod, furrowed brow. But there we were, on the east side of Dallas now, tooling along in this gigantic truck with cars racing by, and I started to laugh.

Like, the kind of hysterical laughter that turns to crying real fast, and then there's snot and snorting and apologies through the tears. "Sam, I'm sorry," I laugh-cried. "Your story is so important to me. I just didn't expect 'Mexican' to be one of the things you felt you needed to share."

Then Sam started laughing too. And we laughed together all the way to that lady's ranch, until she pointed to the pasture in the distance and told us to go for it. There was no one around to help us load that trough, and Sam was not five feet tall on his tallest day. This was going to be fun.

When we managed to get one end of the filthy, weathered trough leaning against the open truck bed, I said, "Sam, we'll have to do this part together. On the count of three, we'll both lift and push this thing up and forward into the truck, okay? One . . . two . . . three!" And I lifted and pushed, and nothing happened. I peered across the trough at Sam, looking small and stricken. "I can't," he moaned. "I've got little girl hands. I'm too weak."

We were now two hours into this excursion, with at least two hours to go, and I'd already handed over $150 cash to the Craig's lister. I said, "Sam, there are moments when we have to summon strength beyond ourselves. Moments we have to muster every bit of power we've ever imagined having. Sam, I'm telling you, now is the time to *man up*. One . . . two . . . *three!*"

Judge me if you want; I judge myself all the time. I realize it's inappropriate to tell a young trans kid to "man up." It may be inappropriate to tell anyone, ever, to "man up." All I know is, I needed that trough. Caroline was in love with Jesus, remember?

That conversation with S, and my whole relationship with S, exemplifies how Galileo Church became a safe place to transgress the bounds of propriety, occasionally, for the sake of relationship. Sharing laughter around S's pronouns and "little girl hands" and completely unexpected "confession" of Mexican heritage—and equal laughter around my awkwardness with the granddad, and how I could barely reach the pedals of that humongous truck, and the truly filthy cattle trough in which we were going to baptize Caroline into her brand-new life—it was how we were building trust, forming community, learning how to love each other.

We have developed an ethos of care with language—us cisgender folks naming our pronouns, for example, whenever we go to the mic in worship, so that everyone feels free to name their pronouns—but not so much care that we stop laughing at our mistakes and peculiarities. If Wanda, who is trans, not in the expensive body-altering Caitlin Jenner way but in the "Now that I'm fifty-five I'll wear sundresses and take estrogen if I want to" way, takes off her wig during a summer worship service when the AC isn't working, revealing her male pattern baldness, and proceeds to *fan herself with the wig*, it's okay to laugh. Nobody, including Wanda, is trying to pretend that's not funny, all this working out of identity and language and practice and just *being human*. Humans are fucking hilarious. We take after God that way.

I wish I didn't have to report that Galileo's relationship with S didn't end all that well. S was one of those people who pushes everybody's buttons, saying mean things on social media, asking for stuff we didn't have to give and becoming furious when we didn't give it, spreading their misery around. I stuck with S for a long time, enjoying one last long afternoon together on an Ash Wednesday, burning last year's palm branches in my driveway to make ashes for the service that night. We laughed a lot that afternoon, remembering the truck and the trough and me laughing so hard I snorted Diet Coke out of my nose.

But soon S turned on us again, in a middle-of-the-night Facebook rant, warning people to stay away from @GalileoChurch because we were dangerous. I no longer remember the specific accusations, but I remember confessing shamefacedly to the church leaders that I was not going to pursue S anymore. I was disengaging, online and IRL, after months of exhausting dysfunction between S and the church, between S and me. "Oh, thank God," one of them said. "You were the last person left who actually liked S."

Which was exactly true. I did like S and strangely still do. If S showed up right now, I'd ask what name they're going by and which pronouns, and if they need something to eat and if they need a ride home, if there's a home these days. I trust God is still looking after that one wild and precious life, just like God looks after mine.

Oh, and we got a killer baptistery out of that deal. Cheap.

Frankenstein Baptistery (Spring 2014)

D.J. calls it the Frankenstein baptistery. Here's what we've got:

- one Rubbermaid Structural Foam Stock Tank, three-hundred-gallon capacity
- one tankless water heater, propane powered, intended for wall mount in a fishing cabin or some such
- two long water hoses
- two big pieces of pink foam board insulation
- one electric pump of the kind for emptying your *huge* aquarium or clearing the water out of your basement after a mild flood.

At first, the "stock tank" lived in my backyard, killing the grass under it in a five-foot diameter circle. We could haul it to the theater in a borrowed truck and put it outside, behind the theater on a little concrete patio just off the street. We hooked up one hose to a spigot around the corner and ran it to the tankless water heater, which we attached with bungee cords to a little metal fence. The propane tank fueled the heater, which ran water through its warm coils before spilling it, through the second hose, into the baptistery. It took several hours to fill this way. If we put the foam board over it like a lid, the water would stay warm for a couple of hours. After a baptism, we could drain much of the water into the street and use the pump to empty the trough completely. Not exactly efficient but quite serviceable.

For Caroline's baptism on Easter Day 2014, D.J. was in charge of that whole operation. He hooked it all up, sat on the theater's back patio consuming cold beverages, and watched the water rise. We worshiped inside at 5 p.m., raising our alleluias and singing exultant songs. At the appointed time, everybody got up from their red-velvet seats, climbed the stairs to the stage, scrambled through the heavy velvet curtains to the cluttered backstage, and spilled out the back door. Caroline wore shorts over her bathing suit. Michala and I rolled up our pant legs and sat on opposite edges of the trough with our feet and shins in the water, with Caroline sitting down in the water between us.

I don't remember exactly what I said that day, but over time the baptismal formula at Galileo Church has evolved to this:

Do you confess that Jesus was the embodiment of God's logic (logos) among us, and that through his life and death and resurrection, God's own will for the salvation of the world God loves, and your salvation, too, has been accomplished? [Yes.]

We baptize you for the forgiveness of self-interest and self-reliance past,
> and for the empowerment of God's Spirit for your future,
> and into the worldwide family of God in the present,
> in the name of our Mother-Father God
> and our Brother-Savior Jesus
> and the Spirit of the living Christ.

And then—splash! whoosh! Caroline lies down under the warm water, then does a heroic sit-up with our help, and a child of God is reborn to beautiful, abundant, ongoing life. Everybody cheers. We laugh. We sing a song. We go back inside. We share communion like it's the #firsttime all over again.

That gigantic plastic trough is now encased in weathered-fence wood, thanks to Mark and my spouse, the people who build most of our stuff out of trash and somehow make it look like we did it on purpose. It looks kind of like a sacred hot tub, honestly. Wanda inherited D.J.'s job as resident hose runner and water watcher. After we burned up the one heater and Wanda soldered it back together, we splurged on an electric gizmo that is as slow as Christmas but less of a fire hazard. Our Frankenstein baptistery lives at the front of the Big Red Barn now, in plain sight, waiting for the next time somebody falls in love with Jesus and doesn't know what to do.

Finding Our Place (Summer 2014)

One summer at the Wild Goose festival in Hot Springs, North Carolina, the general minister and president of the Christian Church (Disciples of Christ), Rev. Sharon Watkins, was a featured speaker. It rained the entire weekend, and we were camping with two thousand of our best friends in mud up to our ankles. I spied Rev. Watkins stepping out of a Porta-Potty one morning into a particularly juicy puddle and I thought, "Here is a true servant of the church."

A few minutes before her slot on the main stage, the clouds broke open with yet another steady downpour. Our little group, ponchoed and soggy, huddled under a couple of umbrellas and cheered hopefully across the mostly empty field where the audience should be. Rev. Watkins gave a mercifully abbreviated talk about what she observed was happening at Wild Goose—not the rain or the alt-gospel bands or the social justice shot in the arm we all craved, but what she called the "redenominating" of the American church.

"A time is coming," she said, "and coming soon, when no one will care if you're Presbyterian or Baptist or a capital-D-Disciple or maybe even Catholic. Those labels won't communicate very much in terms of how you think about your faith and what your faith compels you to do. But perhaps in the future if you say, 'I am a Wild Goose Christian,' it will matter. You'll find points of connection in these new affiliations, and those connections will become fuel for the change the world is waiting for, the difference that Christianity is supposed to make."

Galileo is absolutely caught up in the redenominating of the North American church. The "Where's your church?" conversation can mean "Where do you meet for worship?" but it can go in a whole nother direction too, though I probably think about this one more than most Galileo-ans. It's not geographical, except metaphorically; it's the ongoing exercise concerning where exactly Galileo fits on the big theological and sociological map of North American, Protestant, mostly white Christianity.

(It feels important to name "mostly white" because while not all people at Galileo are white, the way we do church is born out of a tradition that assumes itself to be *mainstream* but is deeply influenced by white supremacist, melting-pot culture. If we were doing church from the American black church experience, we would need to name that, right? So I'm trying not to let "white" be the default where we say nothing and assume everybody knows.)

If Galileo isn't actually sure where we fit, we're in good company. The denomination we're part of seems similarly sociologically disoriented, sometimes. The Christian Church (Disciples of Christ) has some marks of liberal (mainline) Christianity (professionalized clergy; use of the Revised Common Lectionary [RCL] along with the liturgical calendar; ecumenical and interfaith relationships; educated appreciation and deep respect for the Bible as sufficient testimony, but not infallible or inerrant historical report). At the same time, Disciples churches manifest characteristics of evangelical Christianity (emphasis on personal relationship with Jesus, individual piety as a grateful response for salvific atonement achieved through his death, freedom in liturgy for congregationally created expressions of worship). Galileo has camped out on the leftmost end of our denominational spectrum, and overall Disciples as a whole land pretty leftward on the North American denominational spectrum. So we're classically liberal, right?

Except that we have this wild idea that God does actually intend to save the world through the Jesus event, the whole Jesus enchilada; and we have an equally wild idea that the Spirit of the living Christ is present here, now, actually *doing* stuff; and we have an outrageous idea that the Bible, as the testimony of our ancestors who similarly believed that God is busy on our behalf, can be trusted to show us things we wouldn't discern on our own. So we read the Bible a *lot*. And we pray *hard*. And we sing it like we *mean* it. And we keep telling people we've just met that the stuff we've found out might actually save their lives too. In some ways, our form of life looks kind of like rehabilitated, repurposed evangelicalism.

Many, even most, of the people who come to Galileo and stay are former fundagelicals who loved the feeling that God was on their side and busy on their behalf, and they loved the hymns and the praying and the Bible and the family feeling of Church Before—before they came out or before their kid came out or before they had eyes to see how mean and stingy that expression of church could be. Coming to Galileo gives them back so much of what they had before minus the meanness, and they don't mind the strangeness of Advent and Lent and the other quirks of mainline church practice. Many, many Galileo people love the thrill of riding the huge wave of books by former (or progressive) evangelicals like Brian McLaren and Rob Bell and Rachel Held Evans. The theological rehabilitation we're doing together draws heavily from their insights as we plot out the movement we're all making from there to here, from one form of Christian faith that starved our spirits to another in which our tables are laden and our cups runneth over.

Over the years that means we have hung out in a number of places where the fit is a little uneasy for me but kinda perfect for most of the people in my church. Progressive and former and disenfranchised evangelicals really know how to throw a conference, and we have enjoyed many of them: Wild Goose, the Gay Christian Network (now Q Christian Fellowship), the Reformation Project, C21, OPEN (now W/), Evolving Faith, and more. Many times Galileo has supplemented the cost of travel to these conferences so the people who went could come back and tell us what they discovered out there. They return to us energized, spiritually speaking, and that energy is rooted in relief from the realization that Galileo is not a singularity, that we are not alone in our reimagining of what a community of belonging in Jesus's name, aka church, could look like. And, very importantly, that we are not the only Christians in the world who believe that LGBTQ+ identity is God's idea, fully embraced in God's heart. Being "the only ones" would be lonely. And not very hopeful. So we reach out and connect wherever we can.

It remains important also that we stay connected to our denomination. Galileo tries hard to be a team player with Disciples infrastructure at every level, even when our form of life seems different from most of the congregations we're friends with. We partner up to do stuff we couldn't do by ourselves, like build Habitat for Humanity houses. I stay connected with clergy colleagues and do my bit to serve the wider church. We initiated a program to partner with nearby traditional congregations to sponsor the ordination of several people who asked for Galileo's support on that journey. It felt weird and wrong to ordain ministers whose only consistent experience of our denomination would have been us, because we're, uh, *atypical*, so we asked for help and we got it.

And we keep looking for ways to connect. One of the first things we did in the summer of 2013 is register with gaychurch.org, going through their vetting process to make sure we were truly inclusive of LGBTQ+ people. We made a little movie to post on notalllikethat.org. We're happy to be graded "clear, affirming" by churchclarity.com. Not only are those ways for people who aren't here yet to find us, but they're also reminders to ourselves that we belong, that we have companions on this journey.

Here's my point (and I do usually have one): Next Church churches are probably not going to fit neatly on the sociological-theological map, at least not the way it's been drawn for the last couple hundred years. But that doesn't mean Next Church churches have to live in isolation from the wider Christian world. Stand-alone, breakaway congregations make me sad, just like "spiritual but not religious" people make me sad. Because it's hard enough, this Jesus-following life; it doesn't have to also be *lonely*. Redenominating is more work, but it's worth it. Rev. Watkins used a Porta-Potty in a muddy field to tell us that. Insights like that don't come cheap.

G-House, the Beginning (Winter 2013-2014)

Okay, but for real, some people *do* actually want to come to our church, and they need to know where to find us. It's tricky. We've been in five worship spaces in five years, not counting the first place we rented for the Most Awful Worship Service Ever—more on that later, I promise.

First was G-House. I found that by befriending Mansfield's city planner, Felix, who knew just about everybody and every block in our town. He told me about the Seventh-day Adventist church that bought several acres of farmland, including the low-slung ranch-style house the farmer built. The Adventists renovated that house for their worship when they first started; then they built a traditional sanctuary on the property and moved across the parking lot, leaving the house ready for renters. They, of course, didn't call it G-House, but we soon did. It was ours on Sundays from 3 p.m. to whenever, and again on Thursdays from 5 p.m. to whenever.

G-House had a big front room with lots of windows that held about forty chairs, plus a piano we never used. We covered the windows with black sheers and draped twinkly lights around the ceiling. We hung a TV at the front and ran a long cable to the back so we could shoot slides of Scripture and song lyrics directly from our laptop. We bought junky end tables from thrift stores to intersperse with the chairs. We emptied the nearby thrift stores, actually, of end tables and anything else we could use for church—funky bowls and pitchers and plates that would work for communion, lanterns and candle holders to go on the tables, other weird stuff we thought might look pretty.

G-House had additional rooms: a kitchen and dining space where we held an early iteration of a weeknight G-group, and a bedroom we turned into the G-Kids room where our kids could have their own share-pray-study space. There was another bedroom in the very back where we never went, but more than once the Adventists allowed people to live back there, so sometimes when we came for worship we found strangers hanging out in their pajamas, their towels and toothbrushes dripping in the bathrooms we were meant to use. It was a little weird.

Weirder yet was the "roommate church," the second church that the Adventist church rented to, which met on Sunday mornings. We were happy to share, except that the roommate church hated our black sheers, our twinkly lights, our rainbow flag, our end tables. They actually hated pretty much everything about our aesthetic. So we were constantly putting it all up, taking it all down, and getting in trouble for the beer we accidentally left in the fridge.

The Adventists had another building on that property, though, that had struck my fancy. ("Struck my fancy"? Really?) The farmer had left a barn, a big, red barn with a loft, that was now filled with junk but was equipped with plumbing and electricity—we checked—and might have been perfect for a growing start-up church to renovate. I really wanted that barn. I hoped the landlord church would like us enough to want to keep us around. We could do the renovation in exchange for rent, I imagined.

So I started meeting with Landlord Pastor to think about how Galileo might cooperate with the Adventists in ministry. He agreed with me that it could be mutually beneficial; his church wanted to develop the land they owned, but they were mostly older folks and couldn't do the heavy lifting. We were "just like our country / young, scrappy, and hungry" (oh, just let me have it), and excited to think about earning our keep with something other than cash money. Landlord Pastor and I thought the inaugural project might be a garden, both churches working to prepare the land and grow something lovely together. If that went well, the barn could be next.

We plotted. We planned. We prayed. We thought for sure it was the right way to go. Or maybe that was just me, thinking for sure it was the right way to go. And a more salient question: when have I ever been more wrong?

G-House, the End (Spring-Summer 2014)

I don't know what made me call my friend Melinda, the executive director of Tarrant [County] Churches Together, our local branch of the World Council of Churches. I definitely was not consciously thinking, "We're potentially making a huge mistake here that I cannot see, and maybe Melinda can save our ass before it gets handed to us." Maybe the Holy Spirit was consciously thinking that and nudged me toward getting coffee with Melinda. Anyway.

I told her about the Adventists and the possibility of cooperating with them in the project of reclaiming their land and renovating their barn, and how good it felt to have a potential ministry partner so early in our church's life. Melinda listened patiently and then asked one question: "Does Landlord Pastor know what kind of church Galileo is?" What she meant was, "Does Landlord Pastor know how queer Galileo is?" But that's back when we weren't sure whether *queer* was a good word or a bad word. So she didn't say that. She did urge me to get a meeting with Landlord Pastor and be completely clear about our church's theology. "Don't start up a partnership until you've got transparency," she said. "Talk some more. Take your time."

Yeeaahh . . . about that. It's so hard to "talk some more" and "take your time" when your church is brand-new and every day feels like the make-or-break day. The sine waves of highs and lows, successes and failures, are so compressed. I'd been at Now Churches where the waves of vitality and decline stretched over decades; I knew that developing a new idea in a context like that could take months, seasons, years. But Next Church is fast, did I mention? And my self-diagnosed ADD brain really likes moving fast. Melinda's advice seemed out of time, old school, old church.

But I called Landlord Pastor and asked if we could meet for lunch. This is normal practice for most clergy I interact with; we enjoy getting away from our offices (back when I had an office) and mingling work with personal conversation over tacos and iced tea. But this Adventist pastor would not meet me for lunch alone because I am [spoiler alert] a *woman*. So he suggested that we invite our spouses along; that would be good in the long run for our churches' partnership, right?

Oh, please. I could write a whole nother book about what it has done to my marriage that I have sometimes needed to drag my spouse into my work for the sake of appearances and other people's expectations. It's so unfair to him and to me. Ridiculous. But I really wanted what I wanted, okay? And my beloved spouse was doing his dead-level best to support this venture. So we went.

Over lunch we chatted, getting to know each other's spouses, talking about our kids. And then I said, "Landlord Pastor, I need to tell you something about Galileo Church that I assumed you knew, but now I'm thinking maybe you don't." My heart was pounding. My palms were sweaty. My voice sounded weird in my own ears. "I mean, we're the same church we've always been, but there's something about us that's different from most churches. It's not just the curtains and the candles. It's deeper than that. It's who we are."

Seriously, I was struggling for the words. "I'm hoping when I tell you this, it won't affect our friendship or our churches' partnership. I'm hoping we can go ahead with our plans, just the same. I'm hoping you'll accept us as we are."

You see what's happening here, right? I, a het-cis person married for twenty-odd years, with two kids and a Labrador retriever, was *coming out*. I don't mean to co-opt anybody's narrative; I don't pretend to have experienced the same level of identity-development trauma as many of my LGBTQ+ fellow humans. But I needed this colleague to know my church's identity, and taken all together, we were queer as fuck.

I said, "Our church welcomes lesbian and gay and bisexual and trans people. We consider all people to be made in the image of God, just the same."

In my mind's eye I can see Landlord Pastor with a forkful of healthy vegetables (Adventist!) halfway to his mouth, frozen in place, mouth open. He lowers the fork slowly. He says, "You welcome these people because you are trying to help them, yes?"

I say, "How do you mean, 'help'? We believe God's love helps people, yes. We want to share it with everybody, just the same."

He says, "You keep saying 'just the same.' What do you mean by that?"

I say, "I mean that my church believes that God loves everyone without distinction. I mean that the gay people [it seemed prudent to shorten it] in my church are Christians."

He says, "So they are learning to change?"

I say, "What do you mean by 'change'? Do you mean, not be gay? Then no, they are not learning to change. Not at my church. They are already Christian. And they are gay. That's it. We don't want to change that. We don't believe God wants them to change that."

He says, and this is *verbatim* because I will never forget it, "I have never heard of such a thing."

I believe him. I think his ecclesial world was insular and small. I think everything he knew about LGBTQ+ people he learned from the teachers of conserving church doctrine. Galileo was truly a new animal to him. He pressed a bit more. If we cooperated on a garden, he wondered, could I ask the gay persons in my church to not *show* it when his church members were around? "No," I said. "It doesn't work like that. They are who they are, and even if they pretend when they are at work or elsewhere, they are fully themselves when they are with our church. And some of these people are married. To each other. They have children. They are families."

Again with the frozen fork. "I have never heard of such a thing," he says again.

So we didn't make a garden together, and I didn't get to renovate the Adventists' barn. Indeed, when Landlord Pastor told his church leaders about our conversation, they sent him back to me with a message: we could finish out our one-year lease at G-House, but it would not be renewed for the following year. If we could leave sooner, it would be appreciated. And that rainbow flag needed to disappear for good, now that they understood what it meant.

I felt like I finally understood what it meant too. It means that when God makes a promise, you have to trust that promise, even if you're packing your communion dishes and candles into boxes and have nowhere else to go.

We counted this as our first eviction. It would not be our last.

Thus ended our first year.

CHAPTER 3

Finding Our Voice for Worship

Everything Is Architected

What It Isn't Is Easier Than What It Is (Summer-Fall 2013)

There's some conventional church-planting wisdom about not starting worship until your start-up group has been meeting and praying together for a year or more, and until it's *big*. One fear is that your group will get into worship habits that are terrific for twenty people but not scalable to two hundred people. Another is that you don't yet share a common imagination about the Deity, so how can you collaborate in a common worship experience?

But the Galileo gang (company? band? cabal?), which had been eating and drinking and Bible reading and loving each other for such a long time already, was *starved* for worship. We were well practiced at saying what we did *not* want that worship to look like; we just couldn't figure out what we thought it *should* look like. So we started investigating.

Over four months our start-up team set out to join the worship service of any nearby expression of Next Church, which to us meant that their theology was progressive, even liberating, and that their infrastructure reflected our new, Next Church context. We did not care whether their aesthetic was traditional or nontraditional. We seriously did not want to visit churches, mainline or evangelical, that were experimenting with "contemporary" or "emergent" worship styles laid over conserving doctrine and traditional infrastructure. We wanted to go where people were being set free by the gospel, where women's voices were prominent, where black and brown people brightened the room, where queer people were normalized. There were more of those in the Dallas–Fort Worth metroplex than you might imagine.

For our visits, we often carpooled, four or six or eight of us making our way on Saturday night, Sunday morning, or Sunday night to addresses we found online. I drove and navigated and talked and listened all at the same time; the rest of the crew clenched their teeth and held their breath. "I've never lost anybody yet," I chastened them, the cowards. "Ye of little faith."

We kept a collaborative worship journal in Dropbox, which each of us could add our learnings and observations to after each visit. The journal had two main questions: "In that worship service, when did you feel your heart drawn near to the heart of God?" and "In that worship service, when did you feel your attention jerked away from the Transcendent, your communion with God interrupted?" We were trying to stay away from the language of preference. It wasn't about what you liked or didn't like; it was about being in the very presence of Very God.

June through September we worshiped and talked with thirteen churches all over DFW and then traveled to Nashville to join two more. Sometimes we went to two in one day. Always processing, always writing our notes, always building a dream in our heads of what Galileo's worship might look like someday soon. These are the ideas that took shape during that exploration and are still relevant for Galileo's worship five years later.

Worship Must Be Excellent

Honestly, we saw a lot of crappy worship. That is, we saw gatherings of people who obviously loved God and each other but had not given a lot of thought to how they would come before God together and speak words of good news to and with each other. We called one church to say we were coming (because we had traveled extra-far to another that decided not to meet that Sunday but didn't bother to tell the Interwebs), and the pastor-planter said, "Terrific! Do you think you could bring some bread and grape juice for communion? We forgot to pick any up."

We heard mumbled prayers and amateur musicians, people who were doubtless doing their best but whose leadership did not inspire much followship, if you catch my drift.

We also saw some lovely, well-crafted, well-rehearsed worship in which we could relax and trust that the worship leaders would take us somewhere good. We developed a strong sense that God loves beautiful things and that we could make something beautiful with our words and songs and whatever else if we tried. We wanted our worship to always reflect the reality that we *tried*. Really, really hard.

Worship Should Be Scalable

We experienced a lot of worship practices that work well for ten to twelve people, but would never be practicable for, say, the 150 we were aiming for someday. Like, asking people to say prayer requests out loud is not scalable. People won't share vulnerably, from the heart, in a big group, and some people will never speak out loud at all.

If we wanted to pray for each other, and we did, we would need a scalable, maximally participatory way to do it. From that conviction we built our prayer wall. (Rather, my spouse built it; in those days we often said "we built" when really we meant "Lance built.") We liberated some wooden grocery pallets from the alley behind Kroger, took them apart to sand and stain them, put them back together to create *über*-pallets and hung them on the wall. People write their prayers on cards we provide and tuck them into the pallet slats, making their prayers visible or invisible, whichever they choose. We kneel (or don't) on thrift store pillows to pray at the wall. Prayer cards come home with me each week. We archive them, and recently we strung hundreds of them on twine like little prayer flags, repraying years' worth of our community's yearnings.

The prayer wall has been configured differently as we've changed locations, but it remains a central feature of our worship space. When we've done visioning exercises where we ask people to name things about Galileo that are indispensable features of our life together, people say things like "love" and "trust" and "safety" and "prayer wall."

And that's just one example of scalability in worship and in our life together. We ask that question all the time about everything—if we design a practice or move a piece of furniture or schedule an event, does it work for who we are now as well as for the people who are not here yet?

Worship Is Better with Preaching

This is one of the most controversial things I ever say about Next Church worship. Tons of people preach (oh the irony) that the model of a monological preacher who commands the attention of the room for an extended time, purporting to say something authoritative about what God wants, is passing away and must pass away, sooner rather than later.

I get it. I was prepared to give up preaching for Galileo because I'd read and heard that Next Church churches don't really do that. (Evangelical, rapid-growth, attraction-based, wannabe megachurches do because they're built on the superstar quality of their pastor and his [always *his*] trustworthiness to tell you the correct answers to all life's hardest questions. But that's not something we wanted to replicate, obviously.) In our travels we witnessed several versions of conversational sermons in which the pastor offered some opening remarks and invited anyone to jump in for a whole-room discussion. For one thing, it didn't seem scalable—like, how do you have a whole-room conversation when the room has more than ten people in it?

And for another thing, my all-millennial start-up team bemoaned the conversational sermons we endured. Who wants to listen to a half-hour of the chaotic brain farts that most of us produce when we have thought not at all about the subject at hand, have no serious biblical-theological education, possess only the vocabulary and syntax of faith given to us by the fundagelical churches that spit us out, and have little practice in actually listening to each other in curiosity and humility? *Conversation* implies that people listen to each other, and honestly, most people just like to hear themselves talk. I'm a people; I should know. Sermons, though, aren't just more talking, by one or by many. At their best they are the report of an exploration of God's intentions as mediated through our ancestors in faith, not in service of a foregone conclusion but in hopes of discovering something new about our ever-changing, always-up-to-something God. The best sermons make people *curious*. And get people *all riled up*. Sometimes even *cranky*. Galileo's start-up team wanted to hear that kind of preaching, and so they made me do it. I'll say more later about the preaching voice they helped me discover.

Worship Requires Architecture

Remember that time Kanye jumped up on a table in the commons room at Harvard University's school of architecture and gave an off-the-cuff but cogent speech about how "everything is architected"? (This is back when Kanye was cogent.) Well, you should google it. He basically said that the human experience is about changing the environments we move through to make them beautiful or fair or soothing or whatever. Passivity or thoughtlessness about our surroundings and our experiences is simply bad architecture.

We saw examples of good and bad architecture in our worship exploration. Here's a pretty awful one: we worshiped with a little start-up church in a barn for showing animals at an unused fair grounds. We sat on metal folding chairs. I'm not complaining about the chairs or the barn. But I'm complaining about how, just as the last "amen" was exhaled from the mouth of the musician, the person in charge of cleanup jumped up and yelled in a desperate voice, "Everybody please grab your chair and help us get everything in the shed!" The architecture of the moment was against lingering, conversating, resting in the peace and presence of God's people. Our team wanted to be aware, always, of how the moments we were stringing together for worship would be architected for good or for ill, for transcendence or leadenness, for community flourishing or against it.

That's a lot of *should*s in a row, but please don't misunderstand. I'm not saying all expressions of Next Church should do all those things for worship, only that our team was intentional about how our worship scheme developed. We were ready to get started, but not so hasty that we didn't take our sweet time figuring out how to do it right, for *us*.

We took all that we saw and heard, processed it carefully and prayerfully, and then we planned and executed the most horrible worship service any of us had ever suffered through.

The Most Horrible Worship Service Ever (October 2013)

We thought we knew what we were doing. Oh, sweet Jesus, were we wrong.

Kayla and Danny were at a country-rock-something concert, something loud, and during intermission they met the guys sitting in the next row down, one of whom played the double bass. Kayla said, "Oh, our church is looking for musicians," and he said, "Terrific, I'd love to." Pretty soon we had hired him and his buddy on keys to help us put together our inaugural worship service. "Do either of you sing?" I asked hopefully. "Sorta," they both said with twin winces. That should've been a sign.

We needed space to rent in Mansfield, our hometown. Mansfield was a cattle town of sixty-five hundred until well into the twenty-first century, when it exploded in suburban growth and started building new everything. So there were just a few super-old buildings and a few more super-new buildings, and I swear I looked at every single one of them to find a place we could affordably rent for a Sunday night service. (There is a surprising amount of real-estate hunting involved in church planting; who knew?) The new activities center was available for cheap, so I paid for a reservation that included the use of chairs. Perfect.

Well, perfect except that the activities center was all bright white, with white walls and white floors and bright, fluorescent lights. We were pretty sure we wanted a dim atmosphere with candlelight and soft shadows. But at the activities center, candles weren't allowed. Lights could be on or off, nothing in-between. We thought we could curtain the windows and drape the walls with fabric, but that wasn't allowed either. *So much was not allowed.*

Undeterred, we (Lance!) built a giant backdrop out of white PVC pipe, hung with sheer black curtain panels from IKEA. If you were involved in an evangelical puppet ministry circa 1975–1985, you know the structure. Heavy and huge, and not altogether stable. And the white pipe glared through the sheer curtains. But never mind. With the lights completely out, no one would be the wiser.

But with the lights out, how would anybody be able to see anything? And how could anyone read lyrics for a song or join a responsive reading of Scripture? We had no projector, no screen. We were printing little programs on my laserjet. So we ordered several dozen little party-favor flashlights and batteries to go with them. Every worshiper would have one! And plastic floor lamps from Walmart for the worship leaders up front! For the low, low price of . . . never mind.

The day of the service we paid extra money for several hours of setup time, and we used every single minute of it, schlepping in carloads of stuff we had collected to pull off a multisensory service with refreshments. There is a photographic record of our collective stress. But it is also a record of our extremely high hopes; it is not a small thing to imagine that with this stuff, and the liturgy it would eventually contain, we could lead people into the presence of the Deity. We were taking this responsibility seriously. It was not *casual*.

That night, we had about thirty people in attendance. Okay, twenty-seven. Some were actually interested in Galileo Church; others were supportive friends who just wanted to see it work. There might have been one or two there who would be secretly pleased if we couldn't pull it off. There were flashlights and little programs. And there were those two sweet boys with their keyboard and their double bass, who could sing "sorta"—and wow. Just wow.

Here's my honest assessment: the musicians were awful, the space was awfuller, the worship architecture was even awfuller, and *I* was the awfullest of all. Nervous. Adrenalized. Jittery. Barely able to remember my own name. Goofy-happy to see everybody; stomach-churningly anxious to do it right. We did not do it right.

When people help lead Galileo's worship now and they make a mistake or feel incredibly anxious about the potential to make a mistake, I always say, "We do our best. And no matter what, God is glorified." And I mean that in my heart.

But the night of that awful worship, I think God had God's head in God's hands, wishing we would hurry up and *stahp*.

The next day, Monday, I did not get out of bed. I mean that in the most literal way possible. Except to pee. And refill my iced tea. And pee again. Repeat.

The next day, Tuesday, I called the community center and canceled our reservations for all the Sundays to come. I called the musicians and said, "Thanks for your help. You're lovely people, and you're both fired. Your checks are in the mail." And against any rationale the universe can offer, I announced on the socials that Galileo Church's weekly worship services would begin with Advent One, first Sunday in December, six weeks away, location t.b.d., musicians t.b.a. And we started all over again.

Musicians Wanted (October 2013)

This announcement for a worship musician is one of the best things I've ever written, sincere and specific, optimistic and practical:

The Most Interesting Church Gig You'll Ever Get

Galileo Church seeks Musicians
for Sunday evening worship beginning in Mansfield, 12.1.2013.

We're a church starting completely from scratch, built on the idea that everybody—

everybody, truly, even the skeptical and the bruised and the queer and the science-y

and the unemployed and the underemployed and the not-sure-I-believe-any-of-that-stuff-anymore—is welcome in God's heart.

We need musicians who:
- Play beautiful, singable, reverent music that does not sound churchy
- while coaxing sometimes reluctant congregants to sing along with joy
- and who love the idea of employing many different kinds of music for an eclectic inspiring mix—old-timey hymns, Taizé meditations, honky-tonk psalms, Top 40 hits recycled for worship, alt-rock soliloquys aimed at the heavens . . . and more.

We're looking for an unusual mix of 2, 3, or 4 instruments. An upright bass, a violin, an electric piano, and a cajon drum walk into a bar . . . or something like that. We're flexible. Just no drum sets, please. It's too loud for us. Please.

We need a singer—maybe with a guitar, maybe without: someone who can bridge the distance between the musicians and the congregation, helping all who gather to lift their voices in poetic reverence.

We need collaborators who can help us develop musical themes for each worship service.

We need musicians a little cooler than us, but not too much. Actually, geeky losers are quite welcome.

We're prepared to pay actual money. To be negotiated.

Check out the church at www.galileochurch.org, or FB Galileo Church. Audition alone, or get some friends together. Either way, **let me know** you're ready to give it a try: katie@galileochurch.org, 817-773-XXXX.

www.galileochurch.org

We put it on Facebook. A guy who was following Galileo with interest (thanks, Brian!), himself a musician who worked elsewhere, sent it to a guy he had heard play at some youth event the year before. That guy called me. "This sounds like a good job for me," he said, with what I would come to know as his typical understated confidence.

"Can you sing?" I said.

"Yep," he said. "I'm doing a coffee-shop gig for my church on Friday. I'm Presbyterian. You could come. And I'm singing covers at a sushi place on Saturday. You could come then too."

Lance and I drove across the metroplex to the youth annex of a traditional Presbyterian Church (USA) to hear Paul Demer open for another band. He was not much older than our kids, and he was small of stature, with the kind of geeky-cool hair and clothes and shoes that whispered "hipster, but not on purpose." He played the guitar with such facility that you could kind of forget how hard he was working to spin a song out of rhythm and chords. He sang sweet songs in a kind of sad voice, clear and easy, standing mostly still, feet planted. He sang songs of longing: longing for God, longing for love, longing for his own real life to begin someday.

And then he sang a song that he said he had written when he was in high school. (I think up to that point he had written all his songs in high school. He was barely *out* of high school.) It was addressed to God about whether God keeps God's promises, whether God can be trusted when your life has gone to hell. It incorporated all four texts from the lectionary, he said, from an Easter Sunday a few years back. (Eek! He knew what the RCL was!) The lyrics were smart and theologically sound. It had a hook that was really just "woah-OHH-ohh" strung across a catchy melody. When he got to that part, he sang it once and then leaned into the microphone, looked right at us, unblinking, and said softly, "Can y'all do that?" And just like that, we were all "woah-OHH-ohh"-ing, joining our voices to express the beauty of shredded faith that is still holding on to hope. That was it, for me.

After the show I went to introduce myself. "I want to talk to you about what it will take to get you to Galileo Church," I said. "We want you to do there just what you did here."

"Okay," he said, understated as usual. "Yeah. I'd like to try that."

The next night, our leadership team ate sushi we could not afford at the restaurant where Paul was covering James Taylor in the corner. He joined us during his ten-minute break to wolf down the free sushi that was part of his compensation. There's no way you could call it an audition, but it was clear to all of us: we had found our worship architect. All we needed to do was hire him. We scheduled a meeting to do that and thus set the stage for the strangest dinner I have ever shared.

Bronies and the New Sincerity (November 2013)

Getting hired at Galileo Church must be a strange experience. I myself am not very good at the personnel management stuff, and for several years our leadership team didn't have anybody on it with human resources experience. Shoot, we didn't have anybody over twenty-five on it. We tend toward a conversational approach to interviewing, which is a phrase I just made up to name our practice of having conversations with people who want to work with us and seeing where the conversations go and how they feel.

To "interview" Paul we decided to meet for dinner near his school and home at a Lebanese restaurant inhabiting an old Sonic where we could sit outdoors and take our time. And because we practice radical transparency in church operations, we announced via our Facebook group that anybody who wanted to could come.

Kaytee B met us there, and then our new friend Paul S. showed up. Paul S. was a grad student in computer science at UTA, the local university where Paul D. was an English major. I think he came because of the prospect of free dinner and his curiosity about our weird church. So if you're counting, now we've got two Katies (or Kaytees) and two Pauls, and Kaytee and I know each other but everyone else is just getting acquainted. We're waiting for Joel, to break up the name game if nothing else, and I take the opportunity to get to know the Pauls. "What'd you do over the weekend?" I ask them both. Paul D. gives an answer I don't remember because then Paul S. says: "I spent the weekend at a My Little Pony convention. Got back late last night."

"Ha! Good one!" I chortle, slapping my leg at the hilarity. "But for real?"

Paul S. is not laughing, though he has a pleasant smile on his face. His eyes are clear as he looks directly into mine. "That is what I did," he says. "Friendship is magic."

"You're hilarious, Paul!" I hoot. "Were you babysitting? Nieces, maybe? Or did you lose an ill-advised bet?"

Paul S. says, "I am a brony. The national MLP convention is the highlight of my year."

Approximately thirty more times I try to appreciate what is obviously, to me, a ruse. I try to communicate that I get it, it's a funny joke, and it's time to move on. This man is in his *twenties*. He is working on a *PhD*! I have never heard of bronies, so how can that be a thing? Approximately thirty more times Paul S. tells me that he is serious, his brony-bros are serious, the MLP convention is serious, it's all real. Irony wears him out, he says. Cynicism is played. There is too much multilayered passive aggression in the world. What he loves about the Ponies, he says, is that they are *sincere*. Not once in the conversation does he become frustrated with me; every single time I broadcast my ignorance (and, let's face it, a brand of bigotry I didn't even know I had) he responds with patient kindness.

And here is real hilarity in that falafel-and-baba-ghanoush-fueled conversation: out of Paul S.'s strange-to-me hobby, and his clear-eyed willingness to share it against what he recognized as a cultural tide of condescension and contempt, emerged a critical distinction that Galileo Church has maintained to this day. We pour out buckets of irony on just about every aspect of our lives together; our karaoke efforts are *not* sincere. We swim in cynicism about religion, school, parents, het-cis people, whiteness, capitalism, government, the entertainment industry, the commercialization of Christmas, Starbucks. I poke fun at everything, mostly myself; having a sense of humor about oneself seems critical to maintaining Galileo's "We are not the center of the universe" slogan.

But, and this is a Big But, *Galileo Church does not do irony in worship*. Worship is not a joke. Worship requires vulnerability and hopefulness, an absurdly clear-eyed positioning of self in the presence of God whose prerogative it is to show up or not. (Right, not unlike Linus in the most sincere pumpkin patch waiting for the Great Pumpkin: "Maybe next year.") Worship at Galileo Church, we agreed at Prince Lebanese Grill that night, must be *sincere*.

Paul S. named it for us, and by the end of dinner Paul D. had agreed to help us do it. For his entire tenure as our worship architect he would be the unblinking foil to my sarcastic self, Galileo's token straight man (in more ways than one, heh heh).

Go look up "new sincerity" on Wikipedia and follow that rabbit trail to David Foster Wallace, Arcade Fire, Wes Anderson, and yes, bronies—you won't be disappointed. I mean that sincerely.

Planning Our Not-Casual Worship

There's a thing people sometimes say when they're describing Galileo Church to someone who's never been to one of our services of worship: "It's *casual*," they say with a lackadaisical lilt, intending a compliment, meaning that we don't stand on formal ceremony, that we're not uptight about "getting it right," that you can wear your flip-flops.

It's true; you *can* wear your flip-flops, and no one will care. Not all that long ago Corina, our congregation's president at the time, showed up for worship in a unicorn onesie. Like, with a sparkly horn protruding from her forehead. Like, that's what she was actually wearing that day. Your flip-flops bore me.

But it's a thousand percent *un*true that Galileo's worship is "casual." We have an order of worship that's planned down to the minute—literally—and we start on time, every time (actually at 5:01 p.m., with a five-minute countdown on the screen at 4:56 to help people know it's time to get in a chair), and finish on time, every time (by 6:30 p.m., and no one has ever complained that the service was too long. Maybe those who want the fifty-nine-minute mainline Protestant service just don't come back). In the eighty-nine minutes we've got, none of it is wasted, and none of it is carelessly executed. A preaching book I read in seminary said when you get in the pulpit, you should take a second to look out at the congregation and think to yourself, "At least half of these people almost didn't come." That's how you keep from preaching pablum that doesn't matter a whit. And if that's true in Now Church, how much more true in Next Church where everybody out there identifies as a spiritual refugee, skeptically but hopefully giving God and God's people *one last chance*?

It turns out to be a delicious truth that, when the church elevates the voices of people who normally would not be heard—too young, too female, too gay, too gender diverse, too nonneurotypical, too potty-mouthed, too unorthodox—those people take the responsibility very effing seriously. They *write* the prayers they lead, having prayed them through the long week preceding. They *plan* the welcome they extend, checking notes on their phones to make sure they've remembered everything. They *practice* their Scripture readings, not because they're scared of "messing up" but because they are honored to have been asked. They *rehearse* the breaking of bread and pouring of cup while reciting the words of institution from 1 Corinthians 11:23–26, which is so much harder than it looks.

And I feel honored to have a voice here too—honored that these skittish souls trust me enough to speak some good news into the world in their hearing. So I labor over sermons (and every other word I'll speak on a Sunday night) like a woman giving birth. Having done it a couple of times for real, I can tell you that sometimes the baby/sermon cooperates with your pushing and sweating and grunting and comes out with a swoosh of water and blood, and sometimes you have to get a scalpel and cut her loose. That's graphic, I know, but this is real life, y'all. I don't sleep well on Saturday nights. My stomach does flips. A preaching mentor once cautioned, "Never trust a preacher who didn't have gastro-intestinal distress the night before."

Here's the process we use for making our beautiful, intentional, surprisingly orthodox, Spirit-led worship.

First, I consult with the Revised Common Lectionary and think about what Galileo needs next. Then I write a six-to-eight-week worship series, maybe with the RCL, maybe not. Usually we read longer sections of Scripture than the RCL prescribes because we aren't assuming everybody in our church knows the context. And context matters hugely. The worship series demarcates primary and secondary texts for each Sunday and has a name and a graphic so we can announce what's coming. Some favorites include "Pray It Like You Stole It: Great Prayers of the Hebrew Bible," "Jesus H. Christ! The Messiah in Mark's Gospel," and "Monsters in the Dark: The Ugly Psalms."

The worship series notes go to a creative team assembled from whoever (whomever?) wants to help, is available at the time we're meeting this go-round, and wasn't on the last creative team. We get together for one long-ass meeting (three-plus hours, usually) to talk through all the Sundays—what those Scriptures sound like, look like, taste like, smell like. What they raise up in us. What they call forth from us. How they scare us. How they piss us off. How they contain the gospel—if we can find it. We brainstorm how to help the whole church engage the theme, reflect on the Scriptures, let the Spirit change them through worship. That team never meets again in exactly that configuration. We do nine creative teams a year, for nine liturgical seasons: Advent/Christmas, Epiphany, Lent, the Holiest Week, Eastertide, Pentecost 1, Pentecost 2, Pentecost 3, and, you guessed it, Pentecost 4.

The week before the new series begins, somebody changes the visual aesthetic of the stage and communion setup. Textiles, colors, dishes, branches, lanterns, crates, bricks, ribbons, pipes, lumber—we have tons of that stuff collected from yard sales and curbs and thrift stores and our own closets. It gets combined and recombined in the most amazing ways. It's not slick, it didn't cost much, and it's beautiful.

Some parts of the worship space stay mostly the same. The communion table is made of reclaimed fence wood and metal electrical conduit piping. The prayer wall I described earlier where worshipers can write prayers on index cards is mounted in a corner. And there's a giving station in the back; more on that later.

In the week leading up to Sunday, the worship architect (musician) and I work by email to design a cohesive worship service that follows a plot from open to close centered on the theme presented by the week's Scripture. The creative team and I have already imagined a "reflection station," which is a simple, hands-on way for worshipers to engage the Sunday theme; during the week I get supplies and put that together or ask someone else for help. I recruit people to help lead worship. Between the setup and cleanup crew, the audio-video tech, the person making slides for Scriptures and lyrics, the kid who rings the bell at the top of worship to clear the air and clear our minds, and the folks who pilot the giving station, along with all the other participants who will speak and sing and read and pray, there are a couple dozen worship leaders every week. None of them, trust me, is *casual* about their responsibility for what's going to happen.

In the first church I served several eons ago, I kept begging the music leader to teach an old congregation new songs. He was trying, really trying, but felt the pressure to make it better, bouncier, more uptempo, more contemporary. (I feel so differently now and always ask the worship architect to s-l-o-w down those old hymns and give them the sobriety they deserve. But it was the nineties, okay?) In a leadership meeting, enduring yet another conversation about our lackluster worship, his face got redder and redder until he exploded: "I'm trying as hard as I can! I'm trying so hard, I've got sweat running down my butt crack!"

I would say at Galileo's weekly worship, there are lots of people who have sweat running down their butt cracks and smiles on their faces as we labor together to make something beautiful for our God Who Is Beautiful. Sweat down the butt crack, *soli Deo gloria*.

Excursus: "It's Not Casual" (Blog Post, November 2013)

"Yeah, my church sounds just like yours," he says with an affirming nod. He's a good guy, a local businessperson, helping me complete one of the eight thousand tasks on my list to get Galileo Church a worship space. "We're real casual too."

I suppress the urge to growl like a threatened animal and murmur instead, "Can you say more about that?" It's my go-to response when I need some time to process. Plus, it's honest. I really would like to know what he means by "casual church" and if that's a good description for Galileo.

"Well, you know," he says, "we wear whatever we want; if there are some Sundays we can't go, it's okay; there's nobody breathing down our neck if we take a break for a while. That's what we're all about. It's, you know, casual."

Nope. Galileo Church is not casual.

I mean, sure, you can wear whatever you want at Galileo, and if there are some Sundays (or Tuesdays or Thursdays) you can't go, it's okay, and there's nobody breathing down your neck if you take a break for a while. But that's not what we're all about. Those are not the first three things to say about the way we are learning to be with each other. Those don't even make the top ten thousand.

Witness: later that same night, one of our G-groups is sitting in a Mansfield living room still as statues, holding our breath all together while a young woman curls up and sobs and her young spouse wraps himself around her. We have been praying for their comfort after terrible news—a miscarriage, another one, and the decreasing likelihood of a healthy pregnancy in their future. We have joined our hearts with God's heart and enlisted ourselves in their grief as best we can.

How many times have we prayed for each other in the weeks past? How many times have we bowed before God's throne together, just six or seven or eight of us, in the dim light of a friend's living room lamps? Long before this bad news: all the practice, all the care we have taken to cultivate trust and share life together.

We will sit here for a few minutes more while she pours out her flood of sadness. We will squeeze his shoulders and kiss her hair and whisper our love and pray God's comfort. This is not casual. We are not casual.

Our Preacher Says "Fuck"

Preaching is a huge part of what I do with and for Galileo Church. It is the main vehicle for the theological rehabilitation we all engage in together. In sermons I model how to read an ancient, sacred text, how to navigate the alternative world the Bible projects, how to trust the promises it makes, how to argue strenuously against its obscenities and still love it and the deeply flawed ancestors who wrote it. It's a weekly exercise in starting from scratch—questioning basic assumptions about how God *is* and how this world *is* and filling in a framework of what *could be* if God really gets God's way and what that might mean for the people with eyes to see, namely, *us*, right here, right now. It's a *big project*, is what I'm saying.

Galileo Church has given me the room to do that in a way I never had permission for before. My spouse, who teaches homiletics, sometimes says, "Churches get the preaching they deserve." A nicer way to say it is that preaching is a mutual arrangement, an agreement between preacher and congregation, and the preacher cannot consistently preach what her church will not hear. When the church is as thirsty for good news as Galileo is, and as exhausted of all the clichés and diminished, diminishing interpretations of Scripture as Galileo is, the preacher finds herself liberated, suddenly, to read the Bible like it's brand new and to express what she finds there in the most vivid colors she can paint.

Let me say it another way: if the sin of the conserving church is that they asked us to believe too much (pull out the Jenga block of the virgin birth, and the whole doctrinal tower comes tumbling down!), the sin of the liberating (North American, Protestant, mostly white) church is that they made God boring as hell. Boring, in the polite orderliness of liturgy, in the stayed hymns of sameness, and, yes, in the deathly tedium of the preaching. "God is really nice, and you should be too" is one way to sum up the kind of preaching a lot of us have endured. (And by "us" I mean to include those of us who actually wrote and delivered those sermons.)

At Galileo, there's such a sense of *urgency* about God, about what God is doing in the world, doing with us. The preaching reflects that urgency and becomes—vibrant? I don't want to sound braggy. I just mean to say the church is asking me to do the really hard work of saying how this gospel saves lives, including theirs, including mine, every Sunday of the world. It's not boring. Boring, in this context, would be a death sentence.

That means I will do basically anything to preach with the urgency the gospel demands, including embarrass myself. For example, early in our life together I was preaching through Exodus, exploring the serious theological rehabilitation that the Israelites endured as they learned the liberating nature of the God of their ancestors. "For freedom Christ has set us free" from Galatians 5:1 was the series theme. For the last sermon, we moved from Exodus into Galatians with the intent of showing that God's liberating nature obliterates the mental-spiritual enslavement of imagining that God needs us to get certain things right before God can love us. Galatians is about the religious requirement of circumcision and whether gentile converts are required to keep kosher in order to be "in," so I began the sermon like this: "Church, I haven't known you all that long, but I feel in this short time we have traveled a great distance together. And so the time has come. I need to talk to you about your penis." What I mainly remember about that night is that Travis's parents were visiting Galileo for the first time. Before worship began, I whispered to Travis, "For what I am about to do, I am really sorry." He said, "Whatever it is, if it's good for the church, it's going to be fine."

What I'm trying to say is, preaching at Galileo both allows and requires that the preacher get completely real about the possibility that any of this is *true*—that God is in charge, despite all appearances to the contrary, and ultimately gets everything God wants—and in the conveyance of that possibility, the preacher makes use of whatever language she has at her disposal.

That includes, for me, a smattering of four-letter words whenever they're needed. Not every Sunday, not every text, but sometimes nothing but *fuck* will carry the intensity that the gospel requires. It's not cursing for the sake of cursing but considered usage that carries weight when it comes. It's the *exact same way* I use that language when I'm *not* preaching. It's an integration of selves that feels essential for Galileo's preacher to live and demonstrate, whoever she may be.

The Sunday evening profanity can be problematic for parents whose kids are old enough to pay attention but not old enough to use words like that themselves. "What are we supposed to say to our children about how you talk?" is a question I get a lot. To which I have a trio of answers. First, aren't you thrilled that your kids are listening? If they lean forward into the preaching moment hoping to hear the pastor say a dirty word instead of zoning out and hoping it will end soon, isn't that a good thing?

Second, isn't this how you want your kids to learn about God, in a context where people can be themselves, where nobody's pretending on Sunday to be other than they are on any day of the week? You could go to a church where nobody cusses when they're in church and everybody follows a different behavioral standard elsewhere. But isn't that what we're trying to get away from around here?

And finally, does it have to matter so much that it's the *preacher* using those words? Your kids hear those words everywhere, all the time, maybe even from you. One thing we're trying to do at Galileo is let the preacher be a human being, one with a potty mouth and a terrible sense of humor. So we put up with her bad language and her dumb jokes because she's got some terrific things to say about God and the world God loves. "And if I hear you using language like hers, my child, you're grounded, and grounded hard. Understand?"

I think kids can understand—and do. So far there has been no outbreak of the f-bomb among the children of Galileo, and we hope to keep it that way. From my filthy mouth to God's ear.

Excursus: Preaching from the LGBTQ Margins

For almost two decades I served small, traditional congregations where heteronormativity was the unspoken rule. In those churches we were attentive to our ethic of hospitality: *How can* we *be more welcoming to* them, *the people who are our guests?* We ran "hospitality audits" that resulted in better signage, cleaner bathrooms, greeters at the front door, and the Lord's Prayer text printed in every bulletin. We sought ways to help "them" fit in with "us"—as a gesture of Christian friendliness but also to preserve and prolong *our* way of being.

In my new iteration as the planter of an explicitly LGBTQ-inclusive church, I find that the roles of host and guest have gotten upended. The upset is made concrete in the spaces we rent for worship—five addresses in five years—where none of us is the host but rather all of us are guests in a space we don't own and can't monopolize. It's an equalizer when everybody has to help set up the chairs, find the candles, arrange all the accoutrements that help us remember the sacredness of any place where God is.

Over these years we have set up weekly communion on a literal bar, pushing the tequila and rum bottles to the side. We have imposed ashes at a coffee shop, with the espresso machine chirring behind us. We have mopped up beer spills from last night's party so our shoes (and our kids) won't get so sticky. We have learned to stash the kneeling pillows off the floor so when the rain seeps in under the barn walls, they won't get soaked.

Moreover, in all these places and more (Easter sunrise huddled under a park pavilion for which we didn't have a permit, in a rainstorm that pounded the metal roof, making us sing louder and louder and louder!), I have preached, bringing news of such urgent goodness that all of us, together, become breathless with the possibilities of what God might do next. I'm not saying my preaching does it, but when I stand in these weird places, on the margins with my LGBTQ+ friends, these beautiful people made in the image of God but pushed beyond the edges of their families of origin, their schools, the churches of their youth, the whole Texas-red culture, I find myself panting along with them for the justice the prophets promised. I find myself squinting toward the horizon that Jesus forever points to, where the reign of God is "at hand." We are—all of us, all together—leaning hard into the future that is God's, wherein God gets everything God wants. We are—all of us together—believing hard that what God wants is us. All of us, together.

In the traditional churches I served, where mostly everybody was straight, cisgender, white, and upper-middle class, there was another us-them dynamic at work in my preaching. I often sided with the Bible against the congregation. If Jesus condemned wealth, I pointed out the congregation's affluence. If the prophets spoke up for homeless refugees, I shamed the congregants for their bigotry. This kind of preaching is when the preacher says to her church, "Last week the Bible and I got together and talked about you." I confess it; it's ugly. But the Bible sides relentlessly with the marginalized against the oppressors, so if your church looks more like the latter than the former, what's a preacher to do?

The gentler form of that preaching is something like "The Bible is nice to people who are lower than we are, so we should be nice too." That way the preacher and the church can be together in dreaming up ministries that help *us* help *them*. In better seasons, I did that too. Then I could say to the poor of our community, "The church and I got together and decided to do something nice for you." It's a different triangulation, more benevolent, but still ugly at its core. *Us* and *them* remain firmly fixed categories, and the hierarchy is preserved.

Now imagine Galileo Church, which for this season meets in a corrugated sheet-metal barn with inadequate air conditioning tucked under Interstate 20. People walk in the door to find low lights, flickering candles, mismatched chairs clustered around thrift-store end tables. There's no pulpit—just a wobbly music stand. No organ—just a solo guitar, spare and lovely. At fifteen minutes till 5:00 we're still running around, making sure the communion table is set with clean dishes and fresh bread.

Couples come in—two women here, two men there—who are hesitant to show affection to each other anywhere public except here in this cozy space. Families are here—moms, dads, kids, in more configurations than I can count, including some straight couples who found us after their kid came out and their old church kicked them out. Single people are here, wondering who will love their gender-fluid, ever-evolving self, finding friends who are wondering the same. Trans people are the most dressed up people here, enjoying the compliments, feeling strong and beautiful. Everybody who comes in blinks a little, letting their eyes adjust from the bright sun outside. Everybody who comes in releases the tension in their shoulders—I can see it happen—and begins to breathe a little easier.

And I have the enormous honor to stand up in front of them all and say, "This is the word of God for the people of God." For you! For me! For all of us, together! And in the preaching event we are truly together, they and I, exploring the testimony of our ancestors in faith, listening to Jesus with great anticipation, hoping beyond hope that we will find *gospel* here, the best possible news: that we are all of us loved, the same.

> Once we were not a people,
>> but now we are God's people!
> Once we had not received mercy,
>> but now we have received mercy! (1 Peter 2:10)

All of us, together. Amen.

Excursus: "Why We Play Cards against Humanity"
(Blog Post, April 2014)

"Cards against Humanity: A Party Game for Horrible People" really is an awful game. I've heard it described as "Apples to Apples, but filthy." A player draws a card and reads the incomplete sentence found on it. Other players submit cards with their suggestions for filling in the blank. They're mostly R-rated or worse. Hilarity ensues.

We love this game. At least, some of us do. Some of us really just love the thrill of playing it with (gasp!) church friends. At (gasp!) church functions.

I've been trying to figure out why, and here's my best guess: Galileo Church doesn't have a ritual of confession of sins. But humans need to confess their sins, and CAH fills the gap.

In some churches, the people confess their sins every single Sunday. For example, in the Book of Common Prayer, used by several mainline Protestant churches, this ritual is repeated each week:

The Deacon or Celebrant says:
Let us confess our sins against God and our neighbor.

(Silence may be kept.)

Minister and People:
Most merciful God,
>   we confess that we have sinned against you
>   in thought, word, and deed,
>   by what we have done,
>   and by what we have left undone.
>   We have not loved you with our whole heart;
>   we have not loved our neighbors as ourselves.
>   We are truly sorry and we humbly repent.
>   For the sake of your Son Jesus Christ,
>   have mercy on us and forgive us;
>   that we may delight in your will,
>   and walk in your ways,
>   to the glory of your Name. Amen.

The Bishop, when present, or the Priest, stands and says:
Almighty God have mercy on you, forgive you all your sins
  through our Lord Jesus Christ, strengthen you in all goodness,
  and by the power of the Holy Spirit keep you in eternal life. Amen.

In Disciples churches like ours, weekly communion can be used as a ritual-ized confession and absolution. People are regularly asked to think about sins they've committed during the communion meditation and to thank God for forgiveness through Jesus, whom we remember at the Lord's table.

We don't really do that at Galileo. We could. But our pastor (that's me) is a little suspect of the power dynamic in such an exchange—making people think about the embarrassingly small and large ways they have not been the persons of God's imagining, *right this minute*, as if by thinking about it *now* we can induce God's forgiveness *in just a second*, a transaction that needs our initiative to set it in motion. I don't believe that. "Forgiven" is a state of being. I'm swimming in it. It has already happened, and it's happening right now, and it keeps happening. I don't have to do anything to get it.

(I should say that I grew up in a church where a weekly "invitation" was offered for people to walk to the front of the church and confess their sins out loud. People did it. I did it. It was shaming and terrifying and just awful. I could say more about that, but my therapist knows all about it, so I don't have to.)

So, there's no point in Galileo's weekly liturgy where people are explicitly given the opportunity to tell this particular truth about ourselves: that we are broken, that we think ugly thoughts, that we do selfish things, that we ignore all kinds of heartaches that should grab our attention, that we participate in systems that are themselves broken and perpetuating more brokenness. That we are kind of bigoted. And a little bit homophobic. And ridiculously sure that we're right most of the time. And often jealous. And usually frightened. And daily willing to hurt other people with our words. And rarely willing to take real hits for our beliefs because most of the time we believe we can't afford it.

And consequently there's no point in Galileo's weekly liturgy where some-one says out loud, "It's okay. You are forgiven. Yes, you. Yes, we're sure. Thanks be to God."

And I think that's why we play Cards against Humanity with such relish. Because in that game, we are confessing the truth. That we sometimes laugh at people who are different from ourselves. That we know lots of words for sexual (not necessarily sexy) things. That some body parts get us into trouble. That we know way too much about certain celebrities. And when I play my card, and when I win the round so everybody knows it was mine, and they all laugh while I am blushing in triumphant titillation, I feel absolved. I feel like these people of God are saying, "It's okay. You are forgiven. Yes, you. Yes, we're sure. Thanks be to God."

Maybe now I've ruined the game for you. Or maybe now you'll want to play it more. I don't know. But if you get it going, call me up. I'm there, my whole, real, gross, embarrassed, forgiven self.

G-Kids: A Word from the Lord

When I was a little kid, we went to church every time the doors were open. Mom washed and set our hair in rollers (hers, mine, my sister's) on Saturday night while Dad polished everyone's shoes. At church we were on our best behavior. We were hoisted into pews from which our feet would not touch the floor for years. We were quiet and still, still and quiet, as if God honored those two virtues above all others. We got pinched on the leg if we blew it, or pinched on the tender part of the back of the arm if we *really* blew it.

I love and hate that upbringing. I hate that going to church was a source of stress for my parents and thus for me; I hate that we were taught to imagine God as a fussy, prim schoolmaster who demanded silent submission for an hour a week. But I love that it was the expectation of my family and my church that little kids and big kids would be present in church, like we were part of the church or at least learning how to be. They figured we could do it if we tried. So we did.

Fast-forward to my career as a pastor in small, struggling Now Churches, each of them trying to figure out how to solve the "kid problem." Either there are too many of them in here with us, making too much noise and keeping us from the serious business of worship, or there are not enough of them to justify the weekly get-em-outta-here programming sometimes called "children's church."

It was a problem I wanted to solve before Galileo Church even had any little kids. Rather, I didn't want it to be perceived as a problem at all.

There are so many things the church tries to do where the What Would Jesus Do? question doesn't help us at all, because Jesus knew little about the dilemmas of two thousand years after his moment. But here is one, I say, one situation where we have an *actual word from the Lord*. In exactly this situation, where noisy, snot-nosed, pee-soaked little kids were brought by their parents seeking some relief from the exertions of child rearing, he said, "Let them come." He got hot at anybody who tried to shoo them away or program them away. "Let them come."

So in every space where we've held worship, Galileo has incorporated an actual space within a space where kids and their caregivers can hang out together. The "toddler corral" is our favorite iteration, once we had room for it: two sets of big plastic baby safety fencing hooked together to form a giant, well, corral. We are in Texas. It's the only word that will do.

At Red's Roadhouse, a party room in the back of a bar, the acoustics and the growth of Galileo's families meant that every sound our babies made reverberated through the room. There was a little grumbling from folks who sat near the back, to which I usually replied, "Move up front. You can hardly hear them from up there." That or I pretended I just couldn't hear the grumbling, a tactic I don't recommend but which works as long as you don't use it too often. At the Big Red Barn the corral is bigger and encircles a recycled pew from another church. Hand-me-down toys are stowed under the pew. Little chairs and a little table make snacks and art possible. The caregivers who use it most keep it mostly clean.

Some families keep their kids by their side for worship, never even stepping foot in the toddler corral, which is okay too. We've got marker boards and dry erase markers if anybody wants to scribble during worship—not just kids but anybody.

I have to admit, this aspect of Galileo Church is a turnoff for families who are seeking church programming that will free them from childcare for an hour or two each Sunday. It's an FAQ, for sure: "What kind of stuff do you have for kids during worship?" But—and this is gonna sound harsh—if the criterion by which you're deciding your next church move is whether the church has the demographically optimal programming for your fam, it's probably not Galileo Church you're looking for, you know? We're not competing (as if church competition was a thing!) with churches that can do all that stuff. We're just not in that game at all.

We're here on the fringe, in this barn tucked under the interstate, for people who are so hungry for the good news that God is *for* them, for themselves and possibly also for their quirky kids, that it's not even really occurring to them to ask whether we can make sure the children's church snacks are locally sourced organic free-range fair-trade. (Sorry. That is sounding meaner than it should, but I'm leaving it because it signifies.)

What Galileo's people want is for their kids to grow up *belonging*, no matter who they turn out to be. What they want is a space where their kids are recognized as *beautiful*, no matter how neuro-atypical they are, no matter what. They're feeling rather desperate, actually, that their kids *not* become spiritual refugees in the future. So more and more we're working it out so Galileo is a place where every kid can be appreciated as a quirky, interesting, difficult, beloved child of God entitled to a worship experience along with the rest of us. Let them come. Our arms are open because Jesus said so.

Prayers on a Wall

From time to time we ask the church to do a little identity work, a little visioning, a little examen of the *why* of Galileo Church. Like, what are we doing? And how does it feel? Are we being true to our calling, our gifts? Are we doing what God meant for us to do? And how's it working? We take our pulse. We look around from where we are standing and see what we can see all together. We've got lots of exercises for doing this work, using LEGO pieces or Post-Its or marker boards or whatever.

One question we come back to often is, "When in the last little while (six weeks, six months, couple of years) has Galileo felt most like Galileo at its best?" We're asking for specific experiences, actual memories. And over five years, one thing that never fails to make an appearance in multiple small groups is the prayer wall.

I had wondered how to solve the problem of intercessory prayer at Galileo. Like, how will the church, when there is a church, pray for each other? I dislike the practice of asking aloud in worship for people's "joys and concerns." Some people *always* raise their hand; some people *never* do. Some people deflect intimacy by asking the church's blessing for their neighbor's cousin's husband's coworker; some people cannot stop reporting exhaustively on the state of their uterus, to the embarrassment of people who aren't ready to discuss reproductive body parts in public. Almost never does anyone say, "I'm depressed" or "Our credit card debt is out of control" or "My spouse is showing signs of dementia and I'm scared." Plus, we really didn't want to begin small-church practices that would not be scalable. Opening up a time for free-form prayer requests would work best when we were thirty people but not so well when we got to 150.

So the über-pallets became the prayer wall (see chap. 3).

When people are given the chance to ponder and pray and write their prayers anonymously for the church's intercession, it is astonishing what they will share. The deep longings of the heart—for physical health and healing, yes, but also for spiritual restoration, for human companionship, for reconciliation with family, for liberation from addiction, for emotional stability, for strength to forgive, for their own forgiveness, for financial help, for vocational clarity, for diligence in school, all these things for themselves and for the people they love— are added to that wall every single Sunday. We've had self-harm and suicidal ideation on the prayer wall. We've had deep secrets exposed as an early step toward integration and transparency. We've had miscarriages and IVF and parenting fails and parenting brags. And, yes, reproductive organs and all their attendant problems. We've prayed against the raging violence in our world and for the everlasting peace that God promises. Children and others who can't write words scribble their notes to God. It's all there, every Sunday, on the expanding set of pallets that are now mounted, semipermanently, on two walls around an entire corner of our worship space.

Once in a while someone sends me a text on Sunday afternoon: "Please put this prayer on the wall tonight." And then they confess the deep joy or longing of their heart and trust me to transfer it to the pallets and thereby to the people and thereby to God's ear. You could send me one right now, and the praying people of Galileo Church would lift you up. It's what we do when we are at our best, the most Galileo we can possibly be, doing exactly what God has given us to do.

The Holiest Week (Spring 2014)

He was coming up on the one-year anniversary of his dad's death, and it was hurting like hell. He had been laid off from work; his new role as stay-at-home hipster dad was not as hipster as it sounds; his mind was not his friend, neurochemically speaking. And we were coming up on Holy Week, a series of worship experiences that his fundagelical background didn't prepare him for.

Lance built us a tall, somewhat fragile cross out of dry, brittle, used-up fence wood—a cross in 3-D outline held together with metal braces and screws, laced with a grid of fishing line strung on tiny nails to hold anything we might want it to. It lived in my garage till we needed it. We strapped it to the roof of the Subaru with bungee cords and I drove it slowly to G-House to begin our first Holy Week.

On Palm Sunday we gave the kids palm branches and let them dance around while we sang something cheerful. Then the palms went on the floor around the steampunk cross, and we switched gears to read the entire Passion narrative, singing and praying our way through to the burial of our beloved. The cross went back on my car roof and back to my garage.

On Maundy Thursday we arranged tables at G-House in the tightest possible loop to share dinner and communion with crusty bread and red wine. Our youngster czar Erin put her sand table in the middle and told the story of the exodus, sweeping her fingers hypnotically through the sand to show the movement of God's liberated people in the hours after the Passover. It was meant for kids, but every adult in the room was stunned by the power of the story in her telling. We sang together a catalog of songs Jesus might have sung at the Passover meal he shared with his friends. "Great Is Thy Faithfulness." "Be Thou My Vision." "Maybe All Is Not Lost."

On Good Friday we gathered at my house, in the big living room, sofas and chairs pushed to the edges, the cross lying on the floor in the middle of the room, candlelight casting shadows. We opened with that haunting video of an elderly Johnny Cash singing "Hurt." We read the Seven Last Words, snuffing out candles within the cross one at a time, Tenebrae style, till it was darker than dark. We sang and prayed, old hymns, new songs, mostly in minor keys. For "It is finished," Nathan played Metallica's "Creeping Death" on the cello, the strings screeching and howling the indignity of it, and oh! the pain. Most people left in silence; a few stayed around to drink wine and sing along to the bitter, disco-licious end with Judas in *Jesus Christ Superstar*, a tradition we've kept up every year since.

On Saturday we stayed home, quiet and still, and waited.

On Sunday morning the cross traveled roofside again. We met in the dark, in the cold damp of the yard behind G-House. Candles, again, and blankets against the shivering. We remembered Mary, in the garden early, mistaking the risen Lord for a day laborer. We sang the sun all the way up. We disbanded, some back to bed and some to Waffle House. We gathered in the evening for our regular worship to ask each other again the one question that matters: "Is it true?" We filled the empty middle of the steampunk cross with bright flowers—but no lilies; they make me sneeze.

At the end of it all, our grieving friend was emotionally exhausted. "We do this every year?" he asked. "Well, once so far," I said. "But every year from now on. That's the plan."

He sighed. "Is it okay if I was thinking more about Dad than Jesus?"

"Oh, my friend," I said. "Even Jesus was thinking more about your dad than himself. That's how this works. What happened to Jesus happens to everybody, yeah? We die. And we need to believe that God is mindful of that. We need to know that God is paying attention, and God doesn't let death have the last word. That's what Holy Week is all about."

He pondered. "Huh. I think for me it was not Holy Week. Holy is not enough. It was . . . the very Holiest Week."

And thus we have called it every year since. The very Holiest Week.

Maybe All Is Not Lost (Fall-Winter 2015-2016)

Then there's the time we decided to make an album. We had developed a worship aesthetic that we thought was not too traditional, not too baby-out-with-the-bathwater hip, but *just* right, and goldang beautiful. Our worship architect, Paul, had written songs to fill in gaps in our hymnody, songs for what it feels like to barely hold on to faith against the rising tide of hard news and self-doubt, and what it means to come to Christianity hoping to let God break your heart, keep you vulnerable, so you can receive whatever God's got to give you next. He had been paying close attention to Bryan Sirchio's book *The 6 Marks of Progressive Christian Worship Music*, writing songs where God is never "He" and where the singer is never an autonomous, stand-alone Christian. He incorporated language that we used repeatedly in our prayers, like this simple stay against idolatry: "We are yours, only yours, no one else's, yours alone."

We sing at Galileo with full hearts and full throats, as loud as we want, the best we can, so there's a premium on "singable" songs. Yes, I too love that Jon Foreman lyric that turns convention on its head and expresses a brand-new thought about God, but if we can't sing it together, it can't be part of our common worship. The songs Paul wrote for and with us were meant to be sung in worship, among the hymns and Taizé chants and pop songs and other stuff we sing, and pretty soon we knew other people would want to sing them too.

We decided to arrange the album much like the order of worship for a typical Galileo service, including opening with a Quaker-esque query for the worshiper's contemplation: "How goeth it with thy soul?" We got readers from the church for the words of institution when the time for communion came. There are songs for the reading of Scripture, the offering of a sermon, the prayers on the wall, and the closing benediction.

Making an album is hard and expensive. Paul did the hardest part, of course, by writing and recording an album's worth of songs. The church put together an Indiegogo campaign to raise enough money to pay for some technical work on the actual recordings and to cut the CD itself. We contracted with Paul Soupiset (look him up! you'll be glad you did!) to illustrate and hand-letter the CD jacket and make some T-shirt designs. We mailed CDs as gifts to all the Disciples congregations in DFW and to lots of other people we thought would love it. We gave the album as a gift on Christmas Eve to everyone who showed up for our service. We thanked our donors with CDs and T-shirts. It was a whole big thing. We didn't make any money, but we didn't lose any, and we put something beautiful into this world for the sake of our God Who Is Beautiful.

My favorite thing about this project remains the title song, "Maybe All Is Not Lost." It has several melancholy verses about the inevitable decline of human existence—akin to "Change and decay in all around I see" from "Abide with Me"—followed by a gently lilting chorus that charges God with "turning this world around" and "giving us eyes to see / so we can find you / yeah." It's not a loud declaration of utmost confidence that "God is in God's heaven and all is right with the world." It's a quiet, tentative suggestion that maybe, just maybe, if we hold on tight to each other and to our scraps of tattered faith, God might still have something up God's sleeve that will bring this whole thing home. Maybe, just maybe, all is not lost.

I propose that this is the appropriate tenor for our worshipful witness these days: the humble submission of testimony that perhaps God is still reliable, still attentive, still at work on our behalf, even when it's near impossible to see it. Christians have been far too certain in our assertions of God's triumphant reign for far too long, and it's starting to sound hollow in the ears of generations who are facing the truth of humanity's ongoing inhumanity and who will reap the consequences of previous generations' exploitation of our planetary home until it can bear no more. "Maybe All Is Not Lost" feels to me like an extreme word of hope requiring an extraordinary leap of faith these days. That's why we sing it together—we have to help each other make the leap again and again.

It's funny—people who don't hang around Galileo much usually get the title wrong. They call it "All Is Not Lost." I would love to believe that they know that for sure, but until I'm convinced, we'll keep the "Maybe."

CHAPTER 4

This Is Church

Infrastructure Follows Ethos

The Realest Thing in the World

After the flurry of meaning-making that was the first year, give or take, all those #firsttimes and rookie mistakes, all the warmth of filling our lives with lots of new friends to walk this road with, we started to realize that we were actually *doing* it, actually being a church, with consistent people and consistent habits and consistent ways of talking about what we were doing. It was lovely to know that the blank pages were getting filled in with stories and memories we would have forever, even if some of the consistency we now cherished came about mostly by accident.

Accidents like the giant wooden blocks I stenciled for an early worship series called "The Basics." I wanted to articulate what I thought might be the new basic building blocks of Christian faith for spiritual refugees, but it was not a simple task. What would I say is at the core of the gospel? What is at the root of it, this story that I have pledged everything to? About a year before, *Christian Century* had asked various theologians to contribute to their "Gospel in Seven Words" project (August 23, 2012, to be exact). If Brueggemann and Bolz-Weber could do it, I could do it, right?

I knew that for many of us coming from fundagelical backgrounds, the real and present danger to our well-being was the promise of God's judgment. In that scheme, with eternal damnation the default for everybody who doesn't figure out how to get on God's good side, God's judgment fuels all of human existence. From its earliest days,

Galileo was trying to say something else, in direct opposition to that: that God's *love* is the stuff that powers the universe. And furthermore, that God's love is especially *for* the very people who have been told that God's judgment is especially trained on them. And, beyond that, that the receipt of God's love is so delicious, so warm and safe and fortifying, that it's *worth* any effort one has to make to open one's heart to it.

That went on to the blocks, one word per block, with blank blocks between sentences. "God's love is real. God's love is for you. God's love is worth it." (In seven words, if I were competing with the *Christian Century* theologians, which I'm definitely not because I don't have a competitive bone in my body, it would be, "God's love: real, for you, worth it." *Boom*.) In that worship series called "The Basics," I told whoever would listen, "It's the opposite of what they told you, that God's judgment is the realest thing in the world and that God's judgment is especially aimed at you. And it's the opposite of your very reasonable reaction to what they told you, your decision that God's judgment was just not worth it. We understand why you walked away. But we're asking you to come back long enough to consider that maybe what they told you wasn't true. Maybe, just maybe, God would go to incredible lengths to have you home. Maybe, just maybe, God's arms and God's heart are open to you. Maybe, just maybe, you're not too broken to take what God's offering. Maybe, just maybe, all is not lost."

Those blocks, stenciled with markers and meant for one six-week series of worship, have not left our worship space since. They get rearranged and restacked, but never put away. Sometimes they get covered with communion dishes and candlesticks, or moved to the prayer wall area or stacked inside the steampunk cross, which now has a permanent home at the front of the Big Red Barn. But they're never completely absent; their message is the gospel we have made our own and that we have built an entire church to share.

Transitioning from our chaotic, protochurch start-up year into the comparably more stable second and third years and beyond required above everything else that we stay true to the essence of the message on the blocks. We weren't yet all that we were going to be, but we were so much more than a little collection of chili-eating, Bible-reading friends sitting on the floor in Malcolm's living room. Our communal efforts had excavated a gem, a positive statement of what we actually believed was the truest thing in the world and something we believed actually *mattered* in the world. Now all we had to do was build the infrastructure that would support that gospel for some years to come. How hard could it be?

Shh! It's a Conspiracy (Pentecost 2014)

Over Tex-Mex one night after worship we held a meeting. I mean, we were eating dinner, and a conversation that seemed decision-like came up, so we called it a meeting. The question was, How did we know who was "in" with Galileo? How did we know if one of the fabulous people we were meeting at our parties and drinking beer and reading the Bible with on Tuesdays and worshiping with on Sundays was really onboard and thus eligible to be asked for help? Because we always needed help. There was always more to do. And we wanted to dissolve the distinctions between the Redwood Originals and those who came along later. ("Redwood Originals" is from the TV show *Sons of Anarchy*. You know, the one about the old dudes in an outlaw motorcycle club in constant conflict with the younger generation that still wants to ride motorcycles and traffic guns, but they want to do it differently than their old man did—like church but with motorcycles. And guns. And porn. Ah, I feel like I'm getting off topic.)

We *didn't* want to replicate the sense of clubbishness that we had sometimes felt at churches that had "members." Joining a club is a low bar for achieving community, and you end up with people on the congregational rolls that moved to another state or joined another church (or Crossfit) or died. Literally. I had cleaned up the swollen rolls of several congregations in jobs past, and we saw no need to inflict that pain on Galileo Church Future.

"If Galileo's not a club, what is it?" I asked. We talked about how delicious it felt to think new thoughts about God, to be reassured that God's love is the governing force in the universe, to understand how radical submission to that reality could get Jesus killed, then and now. We talked about Galileo Galilei getting excommunicated and how some of us had been too. We talked about how dangerous it felt to declare the treasonous reign of God in the age of American empire. We talked about all the #firsttimes that were coming to life for us and, we hoped, for many more after us. We talked about being small, like a tiny seed, and our hopes that we would grow into a mighty shrub, like Jesus's own parables said. Not too ambitious, just a shrub. But a mighty shrub.

And we talked about how lovely it was to be doing this *together*. Most of us around that table had given SBNR—spiritual but not religious— a try, which mainly just means you're trying to answer life's hardest questions by yourself. ABNT was more like it—"alone but not together."

"The gospel is a conspiracy," I said. "This reeducation that we're doing, this rehabilitative theology we're working on, this subversive practice of letting God welcome all of us the same, of turning trash into beauty, of insisting that you could be queer *and* Christian, that indeed being Christian makes you a little queer, if you know what I mean . . .

"It's a conspiracy. And if we're in it together, we're co-conspirators. Not members. Co-conspirators."

And so it was. To the clink of margarita glasses and Dr Pepper bottles, we declared ourselves co-conspirators with Galileo Church and started to imagine what that might look like as a way of life together.

We stole a page from the playbook of The Church of the Savior in Washington, DC, which I had read about many years before and that my family got to attend a few summers ago. The COTS asks everyone to renew their pledge to support the church's life and mission every single year. You're not in it for life; you're in it for each year that you deliberately say that you will prioritize that community of belonging. We said the same: a covenant of co-conspiracy, to last one year, Pentecost to Pentecost, the same for everyone, even the pastor. We would always have fewer co-conspirators than attenders, and ain't that a kick in the head if you've been part of churches that boast hundreds of "members" but have a sliver of that number in actual active participation. Like, the people that actually *show up*.

I wrote a covenant that our leaders worked on, finishing in time for Pentecost 2014, when twenty-eight souls stood up and said, "With God's help, we will." I was elated. We added five more during Advent. We have continued to invite newcomers to say yes at those same times each year, on our birthday at Pentecost and our half-birthday in December.

Almost every person who says yes to the Co-Conspiracy Covenant each year is serious. Occasionally somebody stumbles in for the first time on Pentecost and stands up when other people do, and they don't know what they're getting into. We don't count the accidental ones in our annual tally. Almost every person who says yes is also highly mobile because of college or grad school or work or going home. Of those twenty-eight early adopters, eleven are still co-conspiring as of this writing (and four of those are my spouse, my kids, and me). None of the Redwood Originals remains; they have gone on to do beautiful things in places far away. In some ways Galileo is on its fourth or fifth complete turnover of people, and I hear the same from other church planters: for a while you're sort of perpetually planting a new church on top of the last one. Some of the ones who don't stick make me sad; they really wanted it to work, and it didn't. But mostly people get what they need from us and give what they can to us and move on. We practice a discipline of holding lightly that which God has lent us. It ain't easy.

Our Covenant of Co-Conspiracy restates our reason for existing and our missional priorities and includes seven habits of life that demonstrate one's prioritization of the church's mission. We're not saying we all do them all of the time; we're saying these are the habits we're trying to grow in our lives. We spend some time in worship each year preaching and singing and praying through those seven practices. We try to imagine what it would mean for our whole church to do these things rather than each individual in the church having responsibility for each of those things on their own.

My favorite of the seven is "Contemplate your baptism, past or future." It means that some people who are co-conspirators are not baptized . . . yet. It means that those of us who are baptized cannot simply check the sacrament off our list and forget about it. It means that every day we're all meant to consider what it means that God has offered to consolidate our lives with the life of Jesus. It means that every day we're allowed to appreciate that starting completely over is built in to our practice of faith. It means that every day we're invited to rejoice in God's generous yes to us.

Once in a while, in worship, we invite people to let someone pour water over their hands into a bucket. The pourer says, stealing shamelessly from Jesus's own baptism, "You, [your name here], are God's child. You are so loved. God is so pleased with you!" Fluffy white towels await to dry the baptisand's hands and sometimes the cheeks. Contemplating your baptism and your place in God's conspiracy of love brings happy tears if you do it right.

Excursus: Covenant of Co-Conspiracy
May 2014 (Updated May 2016), Mansfield, Texas

Galileo Church's Mission: Why Do We Exist?
Galileo Church seeks and shelters spiritual refugees, rallies spiritual health for all who come, and fortifies every tender soul with strength to follow Jesus into a life of world-changing service.

"Spiritual refugees" are any for whom church has become boring, irrelevant, exclusive, or even painful. We especially welcome LGBTQ+ neighbors and those who love them. Millennials (born 1980–2000) are Galileo's particular focus, and all are welcome.

"A bruised reed [we] will not break,
and a dimly burning wick [we] will not quench;
[we] will faithfully bring forth justice." (Isaiah 42:3, modified)

Galileo Church has identified four missional priorities for which God has especially gifted and called us.
- We do justice for LGBTQ+ people.
- We do kindness for people with mental illness or suffering emotional distress; and we celebrate neurodiversity.
- We do beauty for our God-Who-Is-Beautiful.
- We do real relationship, no bullshit, ever.

What Are Co-Conspirators?
Each year at Pentecost (late May or early June), Galileo Church invites every person in our faith community to consider or re-consider a commitment to prioritize the church's mission for one year, from Pentecost to Pentecost.

Since 2014, those who enter this covenant have been called "co-conspirators," as we are experiencing together a delicious sense of being in on the ground floor of God's secret, swelling, inclusive, beautiful reign. Entering the co-conspiracy means that we are actively seeking and sharing God's subversive welcome for all people against the grain of our culture. It feels a little dangerous. Maybe it is.

Co-Conspirators demonstrate their commitment to the church's mission through these seven habits of life:

- contemplation of their baptism, past or future
- presence—physical and emotional—at gatherings of the church
- cultivation of spiritual gifts for the life of our church and community
- sharing of material resources to further the church's goals (money, house, stuff, etc.)
- extension of the church's welcome to friends, neighbors, strangers, and enemies
- gracious receipt of care from the church family
- participation in the church's discernment for our next steps together

It is not assumed that every member of a nuclear family will make this commitment together. Co-Conspiracy is an individual decision of each person in our church family.

Most Co-Conspirators are eligible to serve as Church Leaders in any year during which they commit to prioritize the church's mission. See our document "Servant-Leadership in the Conspiracy."

Co-Conspirators may be dually affiliated with another faith community. We encourage transparency with both (or all) congregations in which one is taking part.

Not Ready to Be a Co-Conspirator? Be a Friend.

Friends are essential to our life together as a church. Friends, in this context, are those who want to explore, study, eat, drink, share, and serve alongside Galileo Church but do not feel ready to commit to a one-year prioritization of the church's mission. We hope to include many Friends in our number for many years to come. We intend that there will be no distinction between Co-Conspirators and Friends in our daily ways of being together.

Individuals who are Co-Conspirators for a time may decide to become Friends in especially busy or difficult seasons of their lives. People can move fluidly between "Friend" and "Co-Conspirator" from year to year.

Children who are not ready to commit themselves to the church's mission may also be counted as Friends at the discretion of their parents or guardians.

Ongoing Conversation

Galileo Church, its Servant-Leaders, and its Lead Evangelist are committed to an ongoing conversation about what it means to be part of this church family. Annual teaching and discussion about the church's mission, as well as the commitments of its Co-Conspirators, should be expected.

Covenant-Making

We ask God's blessing as we form commitments to relationships in the name of the one who embodied God's love for humankind, and for each of us. Our collective commitment is a covenant—a set of promises we make with God's help.

That Time the Church Leaders Fired Me

Galileo Church began with one team of undifferentiated leaders, the "leadership team." They were the Redwood Originals, the planting team, the friends from the old Galileo Thursday night group. From among them, we chose a president (Kayla!), a vice president (Malcolm!), a secretary (Joel!), a treasurer (Kaytee B!). One of our first official acts was hiring Erin as our youngster czar, which I didn't have on our five-year plan until Year Two or Three, but we suddenly had a bunch of kids and needed her help. Which Kayla pointed out because she was the president and really enjoyed being right. Which she usually was. It was far from the last time this group of very young people with very little institutional experience would set me aright.

Those official roles got switched around a lot, and we happily added more people to the leadership team, holding open meetings, publishing the agendas on Facebook in advance, publishing the minutes as soon as we could get them out. It was seriously fun. Those meetings were raucous and intense and substantive and hard. It remains true to this day that when Galileo Church leadership meets, we spend barely any time at all talking through details that are not directly related to our *raison d'être*. We're disciplined like that. Also we laugh a lot and drink a little. It all helps.

Near the end of Year Two, I confessed to the leadership team that I found myself retreating into the role of a *pastor*, meaning that I was taking good care of all the folks who had gathered under the umbrella of Galileo Church. That's what pastors do, right? Take care of the people who are right here, right in front of us, with the presenting needs that we know how to meet, mostly.

But for Galileo Church to remain true to its mission, seeking and sheltering spiritual refugees, I needed to stop pastoring so much and get back to the evangelistic, invitational stance of the church that is constantly aware of the people who are *not here yet*. It's the start-up stance, and the further we got from start-up, the more settled it all felt. And if we settled for a comfortable fifty or so people, I could stay busy every day forever, tending to those fifty. But it wouldn't last; there wouldn't be enough infrastructure or money or relational glue to hold us together much longer.

Based on my confession, "I have become your pastor," the leadership team fired me. I hung out in vocational limbo for a minute while they said, "There are people at Galileo who are doing the kind of work that you are describing, the caretaking of the people who are already here. They're really good at it. Let's ask them to do it officially." We would call that team the care and feeding team (CFT) (which the CFT in short order changed to spiritual care team because they were afraid people would think they actually made food. *It was a metaphor, people!* But at Galileo we call you by the name you want. So, spiritual care team).

Now the leadership team became the missional logistics team (MLT), focusing on nothing but how, concretely, to continue our mission of seeking and sheltering spiritual refugees through the specific avenues of our missional priorities. Very often, members of the MLT leave a meeting with specific tasks they've agreed to accomplish or organize or delegate on behalf of the whole church. How cool izzat?

And what to do with me, the poor, fired pastor? Happy day, reader! They rehired me before meeting's end as their lead evangelist. It signaled their wish, and mine, that my work would be focused more on the people who are not here yet—the spiritual refugees who have yet to hear or be convinced that God's love is the realest thing in the universe. It was an outward turn by the MLT and a release of its members' privilege of having a private pastor at their disposal. It was also a bold reclamation of the title "evangelist," territory that the liberating church had ceded to the conserving fundagelicals decades before. I am glad to have it back.

There was also the pesky matter of fund-raising to deal with. I needed more hours in every week to keep up with everything I had to do to ensure Galileo's survival through another season. The newly formed MLT said, "What can we do in your stead so you have more time to chase the funding?" I said, "I don't know." They said, "At our next meeting, and every meeting after that, there will be an item on the agenda: 'What Katie is giving away this month.' And you must come prepared to hand over a task to us. Do a little work up front to take the work off your plate going forward." And I said, "*Whut?*" Because no church leaders in the history of the world *ever* asked their paid-pastor-planter-person to systematically pass along work to themselves.

If they were sorry they had asked, they never told me. And with that practice we inculcated an ethos of decentering the planter from her own church plant. I added a new sentence to my repertoire: "I am not the boss of that," which I would repeat with a shrug anytime someone asked me something that was genuinely outside my purview, like, "Where are the paper cups?" or "What time do we have to be here to start making margaritas?"

But I'll tell you a secret. Just today I had to confess to a mentor that I really *like* knowing where the paper cups are or what time we're making margaritas. I like solving someone's problem, answering someone's question, being indispensable. I like being in the middle of *all the things*. I don't think anybody who starts a church *doesn't* like that. But as Galileo continues to grow deeper and wider, I keep having to re-let go of my own centrality in this community. I keep having to relearn the astronomer's admonition "I am not the center of the universe." It's true and right; it's gracious and powerful. I'll keep at it. Hang in there with me.

Naming Gifts, Eyes to See (February 2014)

I invited Kyle M. to stay after everyone else had gone home. He's the one, remember, who had watched and waited online, trying to figure out if a church like Galileo could be a real thing in the world. He had been with us for a couple of months now, and his capabilities were apparent to all. He was smart, diligent, and happy to help with whatever would make Galileo stronger. Now, in my dining room, I was bringing him a message from the leadership team: come on board as a member of the leadership team. Be part of the core group that makes this whole thing work. We need gifts like yours, and you've got lots to give.

I told him it wasn't necessary to give an answer right away; we always hope people will take some time to think and pray about it. ("Always" is making me laugh. Kyle M. was literally the first person we had ever asked, after the originals.) So he drove away that night with a promise to get back to me real soon.

I turned out all the lights and did my nightly survey of the socials to check in on everybody, and there was a brand-new tweet from Kyle M. He must have been thumb-typing while driving before he got out of my cul-de-sac. Tweets don't keep after a few years, so I'm paraphrasing here, but he wrote something lovely in the vein of "I never thought anyone would see me this way. But now someone does, and I feel like my life begins again tonight." I gave it a heart and went to bed. Kyle joined the leadership team, of course, and we did a lot of good ministry together over the next few years.

(For what it's worth, searching back through Kyle's Twitter feed brings up this gem from January 2016: "Conversations with my pastor are the greatest. Her: now what do we do? Me: bar? Her: yes, let's.")

What I especially love about this memory of inviting Kyle to serve/lead our church is that I've had that exact same conversation with many, many people over the G-years. I say, "Don't you want to help us figure out what we're supposed to be doing, and do that?" And they say, "You can't possibly mean me; I'm a church reject. I barely believe this stuff. I don't know anything about leading a church. I'm not even really a good person."

And I say, "Yeah, it's you we want, you exactly as you are. We're not inviting you in hopes that you'll become a better person or come to church more or give us money, although if you have some to share we'll gladly take it. We're really inviting you to keep doing what you're doing, but do it officially, with the other folks who are also doing it officially, so we can coordinate our efforts. We see what God is already doing with you and through you. We want more of that if you're willing."

And they say something like what Kyle tweeted: "No one has ever seen me this way before." Or they don't say it, not directly, but I know how they feel. I remember the first time someone said to me, "It would be such an honor if you would come minister alongside us" (instead of the usual, "I guess we can make it work even though you're a woman"). It felt so, so much like love.

It has become something of a specialty at Galileo, recognizing the giftedness of people who probably wouldn't get a second glance in a traditional church. Very very young people, newly baptized people, people who just showed up a minute ago, all manner of queer people, neurodiverse people, poor people, seriously and even pathologically introverted people, cranky people—these have made for some of the best and boldest church leaders I've ever worked with. It makes my stomach hurt to imagine that all these gifted people would *not* have been invited to set a course for the church they love. It makes my head ache to remember all the impediments Now Churches place between certain kinds of people (very young people, newly baptized people, queer people, see the entire list above) and the core decision-making bodies of the church. Where would Galileo be without them, these beloved of God? I just can't. We just couldn't.

Excursus: Servant-Leadership in the Conspiracy (May 2016)

Galileo Church depends on the service and guidance of generous, wise people who are gifted and called to lead us on our journey toward God's good future. Together these are our church servant-leaders, but they function in two distinct teams according to their gifts and tasks.

The following paragraphs are guidelines for our servant-leaders—not rigid rules, but our best discernment of our highest aspirations for these teams.

Missional Logistics Team

The Missional Logistics Team's primary task is to keep Galileo Church true to its mission and missional priorities (see our document "Covenant of Co-Conspiracy").

To do this work, the MLT oversees:

- **the church's staff,** including writing job descriptions, interviewing, hiring, supervising, evaluating, redirecting, setting compensation for, and supporting staff members; and negotiating termination of employment when necessary for the church's good.
- **the church's money,** including preparing an annual budget, making financial recommendations to the church, tracking gifts, expressing thanks to givers, keeping accurate records of income and expenses, compensating staff in accordance with IRS requirements, paying bills and rent, fundraising for long-term health, stewardship education, and operating transparently.
- **the church's calendar,** including the planning, "bossing," and execution of events that support our missional priorities; follow-up about how they've gone, with a special emphasis on the evangelistic (open, outward, inviting) nature of our present life together; and the recruitment of individuals to collaborate in our ongoing work.
- **the church's next steps,** including honest assessments of how well we are living out the work that God has given to us and hope-filled future planning for our long-term life together.
- **the church's resources for the wider church,** including cooperation with the wider church, publicizing what we are doing and learning, and the recruitment and oversight of ministerial candidates.

MLT members make a two-year commitment to this work, with about half of the MLT rotating off each year at Pentecost. The MLT can consist of as many members as the current MLT believes necessary to accomplish its work.

We recommend that MLT members take off at least a year after two terms (four years) before being reconsidered for a new two-year term. We don't recommend that people serve on the MLT and the Spiritual Care Team at the same time. New MLT members are recommended to the whole church by the currently serving MLT and confirmed by the consensus of the Co-Conspirators. In June the MLT decides who will serve as Co-Presidents, Treasurer, and Secretary for a year at a time.

Candidates for the MLT are those who:

- have met the commitments of Co-Conspirators for at least half a year prior to Pentecost, including financial contributions to the church's mission
- are not committed to another church family (i.e. do not have dual membership with another church)
- are consistently present for Galileo Worship and a weekly small group
- can participate in the leadership of Galileo Worship
- have demonstrated loving concern for the life of Galileo Church by extraordinary gifts of consistent service
- can commit to attending MLT meetings about once a month (about 10 per year), as well as to significant roles in the week-to-week functioning of the church.

Spiritual Care Team

The Spiritual Care Team's primary task is to oversee the health of the church's people. In June of each year, people who have become consistent participants in our life together are assigned to specific SCT members, while the Lead Evangelist retains primary pastoral care of newcomers. As newcomers become more regularly involved in the church's life, they are integrated in the SCT members' caregiving work.

The SCT's work is divided into three primary areas:

1. Pastoral Care

- acknowledge and celebrate or grieve life events and transitions
- listen to people in personal crises with a focus on promoting emotional health
- refrain from giving unsolicited advice or problem-solving
- walk alongside people in their ongoing developmental work
- encourage integration with church family
- attend to individuals' attendance (worship, G-group, etc.)
- pray for assigned individuals and families

2. Discipleship Care

- consult and check in with assigned G-Group conveners and facilitators regarding the group's biblical-theological exploration
- be available to assigned G-Group's conveners and facilitators for pastoral consultation; check in regularly

- be available for pastoral conversation and prayer to an assigned group of Galileo people; communicate pastoral availability to them explicitly
- support individuals' vocational exploration
- help with discernment for individual decision-making
- pray for assigned G-groups and individuals
- use SCT meeting time to send cards to individuals who need encouragement

3. Flourishing of the Flock

- nurture community togetherness
- protect the vulnerable
- advise the Lead Evangelist regarding what we should study/think about/ pray about next, and what we should drop
- communicate decision-making process about the church's mission and missional priorities between servant-leaders, lead evangelist, and congregation
- participate in teamwork with other SCT members, and share resources
- pray for the church, for other SCT members, for MLT, for staff

SCT members make a two-year commitment to this work, with those whose terms are complete rotating off or being reconsidered each year at Pentecost. SCT members can serve as many consecutive terms as the church deems sensible. We don't recommend that people serve on the MLT and the SCT at the same time. There can be as many SCT members as the team thinks necessary to accomplish its work.

New members are recommended to the whole church by the currently serving SCT (with the first team being selected by the MLT), and confirmed by the consensus of the Co-Conspirators.

Candidates for the SCT are those who:

- have met the commitments of Co-Conspirators for at least half a year prior to Pentecost, including financial contributions to the church's mission
- are not committed to another church family (i.e. do not have dual membership with another church)
- are consistently present for Galileo Worship and a weekly small group
- can participate in the leadership of Galileo Worship
- have demonstrated wise, compassionate concern for the spiritual nour-

ishment of the various demographics in our church—young adults, kids, parents, LGBTQ+, etc.

• have demonstrated personal spiritual maturity and ongoing development in their discipleship of Jesus

• can commit to attending SCT meetings about once a quarter (about 4 per year), as well as to significant roles in the week-to-week functioning of the church

Ministry Incubator

Galileo Church extends its mission by mentoring and sponsoring Candidates for ordained Christian ministry. Candidates will be considered, received, and supervised by the Missional Logistics Team. To be considered, a Candidate must:

• participate in the life of the church as a dedicated Co-Conspirator for the duration of their ministerial training

• serve a year of internship with Galileo Church in accordance with academic requirements

• fill additional needs of the church in consultation with the Missional Logistics Team

• consistently meet the requirements of the ordination process of the Christian Church (Disciples of Christ). (If the candidate is from another denominational tradition, we will consider the differing requirements of that denomination.)

Covenant-Making

We ask God's blessing as we form commitments to this good work in the name of Jesus, the one who exemplified servant-leadership, emptying himself to take the form of a servant and being exalted for his obedience. Our collective commitment is a covenant—a set of promises we make with God's help.

Frequently Asked Questions about Galileo's Governance and Structure

1. What kind of constitution and bylaws do you have?

We don't have any, for now. We have it on the advice of an attorney that, legally speaking, those kinds of documents are mainly about how to distribute assets if a church breaks apart. Galileo doesn't really have any assets. We own a few thousand dollars' worth of sound equipment, everybody's old iPads, and a whole lot of secondhand furniture. If we get more stuff, eventually, like land and building, we'll have to figure that out. But for now, we're governed more by a set of policies to which we add new policies whenever something new comes up, just so everybody is clear.

2. But what about when you disagree? Who gets to vote?

We have never taken a vote on anything. If we can't reach a general consensus to do a thing (which doesn't mean unanimity, exactly), we usually don't do the thing. We figure God will let most of us know when it's time to do the thing. If the thing is something so small God doesn't really care about that, we don't argue about it in the first place.

Plus, I've been part of churches that voted on stuff. And when the votes weren't close, that felt like consensus. When the votes *were* close, nobody really won, did they? We just knew we were muscling through an idea that almost half the congregation didn't think was a good one. Blech.

Plus, we know that if we try something and it doesn't work or has unintended consequences we can't live with, we can always back up and try something else. We're fans of "a swing and a miss." It just doesn't have to be that big a deal, usually.

3. But doesn't that mean decisions are getting sort of premade by very few people, maybe even just one—the pastor?

Well, that could be true if any of us wanted that. It's definitely true that as the pastor (or lead evangelist or head honcho or whatever) I have a lot of leeway to make things happen without asking too many people's permission. But I choose not to do that very often. I'm a consultative person. I like to process with people; I often don't know what I think until I talk about it a lot. By the time I've done that, most of us have forgotten whose idea it was in the first place, and we start to use plural pronouns about whatever new idea *we* are going to try next. (Indeed, there is a good chance that in this very book I have claimed ideas that were someone else's originally. If it was yours, I'm sorry, and please let me know.)

4. *So what is the hierarchy of authority at Galileo? After God,*
   of course. Just in terms of people.

Well, the Missional Logistics Team oversees personnel and arranges the hiring of new people, so they could also fire me or any of our staff. We report to them. But they take a lot of guidance from me; as the founder, my vision and my ideas hold a lot of sway. On the other hand, I don't always get what I want at Galileo. I too am subject to the consensus of the whole.

And the Spiritual Care Team, while not making programming decisions for the church, has an important advisory role to the MLT. Ideally there's a lot of coordination happening between those two groups.

5. *What do you think makes all that work, insofar as it does?*

I give a lot of credit to the radical transparency and extreme communication we have practiced from the beginning. Because the MLT holds open meetings and publishes their agenda beforehand and their minutes afterward, the whole congregation knows what they're talking about and making decisions about. You don't have to be around Galileo long to know how to suggest an idea, offer your critique, or proffer your help. The whole decision-making process is available to everyone. And because we move quickly, going from a brand-new idea to a yes to the execution of the yes really fast, we find out what works and what doesn't, and we laugh our way out of the mistakes and into better ideas, mostly. I got a fortune cookie once that said, "The way to have a lot of good ideas is to have a lot of ideas." Not a preacher story; actual cookie. Words to live by.

6. *How does execution of ideas happen so fast?*

We try to keep the lightest possible structure for making things go. Like, if the MLT determines that it's time to do something [you can fill in the blank] soon, we get someone to say they'll be the boss of that. The boss assembles a team of people to work on that thing, and the team makes a list of tasks and divides it up. Sometimes that work happens IRL; more often it happens in a Facebook group where people can chime in on their own time. When the thing happens, the team works it together from setup to cleanup and everything in between. Then that team disbands and never gets together again. It's the opposite of "committees."

7. *Don't you worry that you're losing valuable wisdom that accumulates from all those tries when every team has to start from scratch?*

Yep, I'm glad you asked. It's true; we reinvent the wheel sometimes when we don't have to and waste resources relearning how to do what we already know how to do. We have in mind to start building a Galileo Wiki, a crowd-sourced collection of online instructions for how to do things, all the things, at Galileo—how to plan a kickass party, how to clean the Big Red Barn when it's your turn, how to cook a meal for twelve people for under $40, how to fill and drain the baptistery, and the like. We'll get around to that eventually, most likely when somebody sufficiently nerdy shows up at Galileo and thinks a Galileo Wiki is the coolest idea in the cosmos and they know exactly how to make it happen. We're content to wait for that day. So far we've gotten every single thing we need this way. Every single thing.

Gluttons, Drunkards, and That Vegetarian Curry I'm Famous For

One of the most important features of Galileo's infrastructure is our network of G-groups—like small groups or life groups or discipleship groups or whatever. We started out as one complete G-group and divided into two to make room for the people who were not here yet, and we've been adding and subtracting G-groups ever since.

Some G-groups are open—meaning, they run on a schedule with a designated convener no matter who does or doesn't show up. Like Chris and me holding space for Bible & Beer for all those months, someone is always committed to keep open G-groups open. Bible & Beer on Tuesdays, G-Study (where you can come in and out depending on the book they're reading and your interest in it), G-Kids and G-Youth (on Sunday afternoons before worship, with a paid youngster czar to oversee the whole thing), and more—open G-groups are often the first things people come to when they start coming around Galileo. Mainly because open groups are organized around special interests, like G-String, which is a fiber arts group that got together to spin and knit and crochet and drink wine, and if you're interested in those things, you have friends who are too, and it feels normal and nice to invite them to come. Yes, G-String chose their own name, which was a joke for like fifteen seconds until we realized it was the best name for a G-group ever.

Covenantal G-groups are different because, well, *covenant*. These small groups meet once a week, almost always in somebody's house on a weeknight, for eating and drinking and sharing life and doing some kind of work together that helps everybody keep following Jesus. There's a roster of people for each of those groups, worked out mutually between individuals' schedules, geography, and the Spiritual Care Team's oversight. Members of each group covenant together to actually show up and share in the cooking and cleanup and do the work of whatever kind they decide to do together. I'm not the boss of each group's curriculum, but I can help the facilitators figure out what might work. The Bible study I write each week in anticipation of next Sunday's worship is gosh-dang good because the Bible is cool like that, and I'm always pressing for more people to do it, but they do as they discern. They are imbued with the Holy Spirit of the living Christ, yeah? They can figure it out.

Covenantal G-groups meet for ten weeks at a time, with a three-week break in between sessions so there's some built-in sabbath. We've experimented with taking the summer off to do all-church G-group stuff, like pickle ball tournaments in the Big Red Barn. So far, so good. We're a fan of the fourth commandment of the Big Ten, and don't usually do anything in perpetuity without some prearranged downtime.

One happy outcome of nudging everybody to do a covenantal G-group (not required but definitely encouraged, and most seasons we actually have more people in attendance at all our weekly G-groups than in Sunday worship) is that lots of us have learned how to do hospitality for big groups. A "small" group is only small until you're trying to feed everybody and make sure everyone has a fork. We have shared lots of recipes for meals for about twelve that work when (1) you only have $40 to spend, (2) you need to cook ahead #becauseWERK, (3) someone in your group is lactose intolerant, someone else is gluten free, and someone else is experimenting with veganism.

There have been moments we've considered saying "All are welcome except vegans because vegans are so hard to cook for." But we haven't considered it for very long because that's dumb and because we love our vegans. Although there was that one time that a vegan woman in my G-group announced sadly and sheepishly that soy was upsetting her stomach and so she was returning to vegetarian status, and we spontaneously broke into ecstatic applause. It was not our best moment. She did say how grateful she was that we had tried so hard; her own family, she said, had never taken her dietary restrictions as seriously as we had.

It's kind of a joke among early Galileo-ans that the whole thing started with me as the principal dinner cook. I mean, it's true. It did. But it's funny because I'm not that great of a cook, and I learned everything I know from my Texan FOO, so most everything I make starts with ground beef and onions. One time our denomination invited me to tell the story of Galileo in a beautiful video they were paying for, and we jumped on the chance. I wrote a script about how it all started with feeding people who were hungry—physical hunger being a metaphor, of course, for the spiritual hunger only the good news of God's reign could satisfy. In the little movie, I narrate how for that early Galileo group I made chili, tacos, burgers on the grill, and so forth. But the moviemaker thought it would sound more inclusive if I expanded the range of that menu in my memory. At her insistence I ended up saying, immortalized on YouTube, "I made chili, and tacos, and chicken pot pie; butternut squash soup, vegetarian curry, and homemade bread." Let's just say, it was iffy at "chicken pot pie," and by the time I got to "vegetarian curry" the Galileo people who knew better were laughing Dr Pepper out their noses. There are still a few of us around who will crack up at the mere mention of vegetarian curry in proximity to my kitchen or my skills.

But the grace that was extended to me for all those ground-beef dishes and my failure of culinary imagination is the grace we now extend to each other over food and drink in each other's living rooms and kitchens and backyard patios all the time. We've all got to eat, and none of us has time to go gourmet, and some of Galileo's people don't know how to scramble an egg. So we share with each other the best we can. Some people, when it's their turn, know how to order enough pizza to feed everyone for forty bucks and which Domino's carries the gluten-free crust. Breakfast for dinner, including mimosas if anyone is so inclined, has become almost as sacred as the bread and wine for communion. There are recipes named for the people who introduced them to us—Francine's Famous Pasta Salad having been shared far and wide among our beloveds, and D.J.'s queso (which he can't eat, being lactose intolerant) becoming *de rigueur* for weekend parties. When we have an all-church meal, the watchword is, "Find out what Missy or Susan or Wes made, and get that if you can."

There's no way to exaggerate the importance that these communal meals have served for Galileo Church. Remember, a lot of our folks have been turned away from or squeezed out of their FOOs and extended family. Some of them have internalized horrible bigotry and lifelong bullying. Reintegrating into the practice of family dinner means sitting at table with people you can trust, clinking glasses with people who love you, remembering again the common humanity of all those God has made in God's image—all in the footsteps of Jesus, the Messiah who ate and drank with friends and strangers and enemies so often and so enthusiastically that they called him a glutton and a drunkard.

What if they said that about Galileo behind our back? What if they said we spend too many church dollars on weekly dinners and can't go a week without sharing a bottle of wine with #churchfriends? What if they kvetched that sometimes the Bible study gets preempted because over dinner somebody shares something heart-stopping, something so dear that rerouting the evening's plans is the only right thing to do? *"Galileo Church: gluttons and drunkards, just like Jesus."* We're gonna get that on a T-shirt one of these days.

3.14159, Secant, Tangent, Cosine, Sine! (Fall 2014)

Remember how one of my rules for myself was to get dressed every damn day and get out there, in the world, to talk to people about Galileo Church? It's harder than it sounds, especially if you're committed to *never* harassing the waitstaff or the cashiers or the retail workers. There's a power imbalance between worker and client-customer, and they shouldn't have to listen to my Jesus-spiel if I'm there on the premise of commerce. So.

A couple of people in the church were students at Tarrant County College (TCC), a huge, multicampus community college system enrolling tens of thousands of students each year. One of those campuses is in Mansfield's backyard and a perfect place to seek spiritual refuges in need of shelter, right? Except it's supercreepy for a forty-something-year-old woman to just go hang out in a community college lounge or cafeteria trying to meet strangers. Trust me on this one. I tried it.

It seemed to me that the best way to get to know students at TCC was to become one. And as a student, I'd have access to student clubs—I could join one or even start one or get together with students who were also at Galileo and we could call ourselves a club. All I needed was a class to take. And all I needed for that was to be admitted.

At first, I applied online as a "continuing education" student. That's what I would be since I wasn't seeking a degree. But when I tried to register, the only classes available to me were nonacademic stuff, like ballroom dancing and yoga. I wanted to take math—because I wanted to see if my brain could grasp it any better now than twenty-five years before and because my kids were getting into upper-level math and I wasn't ready to let them pass me by. So I reapplied as a regular student and got rejected.

Yep, that's right. I couldn't get into community college, though I have a BA, two master's degrees, and a doctorate (okay, doctor of ministry, not the kind of doctor that helps people, as the joke goes, but still). They wanted transcripts from all my degrees, which eventually (and so much money and time later) I was able to supply.

Then I tried to register for college algebra, the lowest level of post-high school math you can do, and got rejected. My degree transcripts didn't show that I had ever taken any college math, so TCC wanted me to take a "leveling test" to show I was ready for college algebra. I was terrified to do that—what if I flunked?—so I asked for another way. The very young admissions counselor I finally got an appointment to see told me to get a transcript from MIT, my first undergraduate school where I had taken a shitload of math. I must have groaned. "It's not that hard," he said. "You can just go online under your old student username and get it."

He did not quite believe me when I said that three *decades* previous, there was no "online," even at MIT, and I didn't have a student username, never did. In the end I used the actual telephone to call up my engineering alma mater and ask for a transcript to be mailed to my house.

Then, when I couldn't quite work the online course registration system, Jennie grabbed my phone and did it for me. And then she said, "I need to take this course too, and I've been dreading it, so I'm signing up with you." D.J. said, "Count me in," and the three of us were suddenly registered to suffer through college algebra together.

As an evangelistic entrée into the world of millennials, the semester was a bust. (Still kinda creepy to hope to make friends with kids for the sake of getting them to church. Swing and a miss. Not a big deal.) As a pastoral assist in getting Jennie and D.J. through their math requirement, it was a win. (Either of them could have done it on their own, but the added layer of accountability was a good nudge.) The unexpected bonus was the email I got from the TCC math department at the end of the semester inviting me to join the campus Mathletes team.

Well, that and the dawning sense among Galileo folks that there wasn't much I wouldn't do to share the best news in the world with people who hadn't heard it yet. I earned more than an A that semester; I earned credibility. And a spot on the Mathletes team. Don't you forget it.

DIY Church: Chaotic Good

One apt descriptor for Galileo (and most Next Church experiences, I imagine) is "DIY." Like, if someone has an idea for something that we might try, and if we achieve some consensus about trying it, we're very likely to say back to the person who had the idea in the first place, "Here's a little money, and a little help! We'll announce it as soon as you're ready!"

That's how we got G-String. Some knitters and crocheters (I can't tell them apart, but please don't tell them, as they seem to be rather particular about which one they're doing) wanted to knit and crochet together, and some people who didn't do either one wanted to learn how, so they picked a time and started doing it. Galileo happily paid for some refreshments and said we would buy the yarn if they wanted to make hats and scarves for school kids who need such.

That's how G-Study got restarted after a long sabbatical when all the originals were kind of worn out from endless discussion of how our new, progressive faith is different from/better than the fundagelical faith we grew up with. Eventually that conversation wears out, but there are always new people in need of having that same conversation all over again. So when Juliet wrote me an email and said, "I don't really go to your church, because I have another church and I'm not altogether sure how I feel about your church, but I sure wish G-Study would start back up, because I used to come to that back in the day," I wrote back to say, "Let's get together and see if we can make that happen." A few days later Juliet was announcing in Galileo's FB group that G-Study would begin soon with herself as the facilitator. Galileo would buy the books. I don't want to presume too much about Juliet's family, but we see most all of them at worship on Sundays these days, and they're working out what it means that their other church didn't make room for the faithful conversations they really needed to keep going on this path of faith.

That's how GPS (God-Parenting-Support) got started, a twice-monthly group for parents of LGBTQ+ kids of all ages. Jeana was in the middle of her own faith meltdown and came to me saying, "I'm not feeling very Christian these days, and I don't pray anymore at all, and coming to church hurts me. And also I want to start a support group at Galileo for parents of queer kids, parents like me." I said, "Yep." And now she and Melina lead that group twice a month while Thrive, a group for LGBTQ+ teens and young adults, is meeting in the next room.

Same for Welcome 2 My Brain (twice-monthly mental health group), G-Movie (what it sounds like), G-Coffee (same). In each case, somebody wants to see something happen, and we do our best to make it so, asking the idea-haver to make a significant investment of self. It's the difference between consumers/clients and citizens, in that terrific book *Community* by Peter Block. (What?! You haven't read that? Put this book down right now and get after it.) DIY church means lots of citizens because there's just very little draw for consumers.

About a year ago I got an email from a grown-up email address, but the writer was ten-year-old Cash writing from his dad's account. The email said, and I'm going to paraphrase because Cash uses a lot of words, "I think Galileo Church needs a G-Dungeons-and-Dragons group. I would like to be the DM [dungeon master] someday, but for now we should probably have a more experienced DM. I can supply all the minifigs and dice. By the way, can you ask Jack [my teenaged son] if I can borrow his dice? So in closing, all we need is a DM. And Jack's dice. Thank you for considering."

"All we need is a DM" is a rather tall order. But it turns out, upon inquiring, that more than a couple of people at Galileo know how to DM DnD games, and a couple of them were really happy to say yes to Cash's idea. Indeed, a couple of them were actually wondering if the church would ever need the weird set of gifts they bring to us. And Cash, true to his word, was ready to put in the work to make it happen. G-DnD, a monthly, intergenerational role-playing game with experienced players and some who have never played before has slain countless dragons and rescued hundreds of prisoners and redistributed the wealth of despots and vanquished warlords all across their fantastical landscape. They have a couple dozen regulars, some of whom haven't been to our church ever or any church in a long time. I was asked at the outset whether there were any particular story lines a church DnD group should avoid. I suggested that distressed damsels in metal bikinis were probably not a good idea. I suppose they've been true to that restriction; I don't go to G-DnD and I'm not the boss of that.

These next few paragraphs are *for nerds only.*

In DnD, when you roll up a character, you have to declare your character's alignment. You choose "lawful," "chaotic," or "neutral," depending on how your character feels about societal norms and rules; you choose "good," "evil," or "neutral" to describe your personal moral disposition. An alignment combines your two choices: your character can be "lawful good" or "chaotic evil" or lots of things in between.

I have long held that most mainline Now Churches are "lawful neutral." They're concerned with maintaining a kind of social order and conforming to societal expectations—that's "lawful." And, usually in the name of maintaining congregational peace or least absence of conflict, they don't take a stand on many of the moral-ethical issues we are all facing, like immigration and gun violence and women's bodily autonomy—that's "neutral." "Lawful neutral" is, as it turns out, far from my favorite way for churches to be.

Galileo Church, in its messy, DIY, swing-and-miss-and-try-again way, is (obviously!) "chaotic good." We're happy to ignore the trappings of appropriateness and orderliness (chaotic!) but deeply committed to figuring out how to get more of what God wants in the here and now (good!). It's the exhausting and deeply pleasurable way we've learned to be church together. Even our ten-year-olds.

Excursus: "The World's Most Interesting (Hu)Man, or Blessed Are the Interesting" (Blog Post November 2014)

Galileo Church aims to "shelter spiritual refugees" and defines said refugees as "any for whom church has become boring, irrelevant, exclusive, or painful." In all truth, it's "boring" that bugs me most about churches I've known.

While Jesus was certainly not irrelevant, exclusive, or painful in his announcement and embodiment of God's reign, I sort of get the feeling from reading the Gospels that one of his most valuable qualities was *not boring*. Remember all those times Matthew, Mark, Luke, and John report that "the people were astounded-amazed-astonished at his teaching, for he taught as one with authority, not like the super-boring teachers they'd been listening to and yawning at for countless Sabbaths, world without end, amen"? Or something close to that. Jesus was *not* like that, *not* like them. He was *not* boring.

Yes, the demon expulsions were probably part of the draw; the formerly sick people going home healthy were pretty good advertisements too. But even on an idyllic mountainside, with nobody to heal and nothing supernatural to give him a boost, the guy could draw a crowd because he was just . . . so . . . *interesting*.

Which is why I think it's a high good for followers of Jesus to be interesting too. Interesting in some of the same ways Jesus was interesting. Interesting because we love all the wrong people and it causes people to whisper behind our backs. (Like Jesus.) Interesting because we don't have very much stuff to take care of, and we don't seem to want any more. (Ditto.) Interesting because we say and do mildly transgressive things all the time—potty mouths we have, like Jesus. (Don't believe me? Try Mark 7:14–19. Just try to envision what he's saying, especially since there's no word in his language for "sewer.")

Interesting because we're funny, or are trying to be, in the tradition of the one whose sense of absurdist humor was unmatched. Interesting because, if you saw us party and weren't looking closely enough, you might call us gluttons and drunkards. We're not, and neither was he; but if it's good enough for Jesus, it's good enough for us. Interesting because we can get really pissed off about people taking advantage of other people, and we do our best to fix it when we can, knowing that ultimately Jesus fixes everything so God gets everything God wants. He's *interesting* like that.

And Jesus was also interesting because for as long as they followed him around, they could never quite guess what he was going to do next, what he was going to say, where he was going with this story or that. His punchlines were puzzlers. It apparently wasn't his goal to make everything as *clear as possible*. Because that would be *boring*. That wouldn't make anybody hungry for more, wouldn't keep anybody on the hook till tomorrow, wouldn't win anybody's heart, wouldn't prompt anybody's reckless decision to drop everything else to pursue his way of life. Who leaves boats and nets and family for something they already completely understand? So Galileo Church does not aim for clarity or completion in this faith project we're engaged in together. We'd rather be interesting than sure.

Aiming for "not boring" can be risky. We mess it up sometimes, overshooting the target and ending up somewhere beyond "interesting," on our way to an embarrassing "uh-oh—that got a little out of control." But the only way to keep from doing that once in a while is to play it safe. Which is boring. And the gospel just *isn't*. It's just *not*, and neither was he. And with God's help, we won't be boring, either. Now let's go kick some puppies.

No, see, I didn't mean that at all. We would never, ever kick a puppy. But it woke you up, didn't it? Maybe that was a bridge too far. But it was *not* boring. Thanks be to God.

Life Is a Sacrament (December 2014)

Michala and Caroline needed to get married. *Obergefell v. Hodges* hadn't yet made it to the Supreme Court; same-sex marriage was still illegal in Texas while we waited for the Fifth Circuit Court to rule. But Oklahoma, under the Tenth Circuit Court's order, had been issuing marriage licenses to same-sex couples since October 2014. Some county court clerks were stubbornly refusing, but Caroline and Michala had done their homework and knew that the Love County courthouse, just across the Texas border directly north of DFW, was cooperative. And while these women had been together for several years and celebrated a wedding on the beach in their beloved Florida, they weren't legally hitched, and now Michala had a job at Costco that provided health benefits to same-sex spouses. Caroline needed health care. She, like all human beings, *deserved* health care. So I agreed to drive with them to Love County on the first day they both had off from work. I took my pastoral credentials and a white stole and got in the back seat of Michala's SUV with Chris, who was coming along to serve as a witness in case we couldn't find anybody else.

Let me pause here to say, Galileo had taken up marriage equality as a justice issue early in our life together. For me, it was about coming to terms with the very real disadvantages—social, economic, emotional, and spiritual—of the partnerships people formed going unrecognized by the law and therefore eligible for dishonor by their neighbors. I hadn't understood before, and now I did; so Galileo was joining marches and rallies for marriage equality, hoping the Supreme Court would take it up and do the right thing. We waited through June 2015, ready at any moment to be called to a loud protest if the ruling was wrong or a loud celebration if the ruling was right. We celebrated with a rainbow-frosted wedding cake in worship on the one-year anniversary of *Obergefell* in 2016. Also, I love saying "Obergefell."

At the Love County courthouse back in 2014, I presented myself for certification as a sure-nuff pastor. Then Caroline and Michala started the laborious paperwork for a marriage license. The rule was, you could have a wedding on the courthouse grounds, but not in the courthouse itself. It was sleeting outside, and I sat in the hallway wondering if I should cut the homily I'd written.

After a while, Caroline came out to find me. "You saw that couple in there?" she asked. Two women from Dallas were here for the same reason we were, with some of their family, all of them speaking Spanish to each other, one of them translating to English for the county clerk. Caroline spoke a little Spanish, and she figured out that they were going to get their license, but not be able to get married. They had come early that same morning, but one of the brides forgot her wallet at home and the whole wedding party drove *back* to Dallas to get her driver's license. By the time they returned to Love County, the Oklahoma preacher they had employed via the Internet had left, taking off with their money but without doing the deed. They were frantic; they weren't going to be able to take another day off work for a long time.

So Caroline says to me, "Can't you do it?" And with my brain I'm thinking, "No, because I don't know them, and marriage is a sacrament, not to be flung around like so much congratulatory rice, and anyway I don't speak Spanish," but with my mouth I'm saying, "Of course!" and Caroline is running back into the office to share the good news, like a woman running back from an empty tomb.

Did I mention the sleet? One of the Spanish-speaking brides is in a sleeveless, strapless, white gown. She could freeze to death before she says, *"Sí, acepto."* (That's "I do" *en Español*, or did you already figure that out?) I give her my overcoat. We all go outside, Michala and Chris standing by as witnesses, Caroline working hard to translate—how do you say *covenant* in Spanish? *Honor? Cherish? Faithfulness? Till death do us part?* We get it done. We rush back inside to warm up before our second wedding.

And as soon as we're able to talk without teeth chattering, we head back outside to do it again, this time for dear friends whose marriage I know for sure is good for the world. The promises they have already been keeping, the love they have already been generating, the compassionate caretaking of one another—these benefits accrue to all of us when the Carolines and Michalas of the world get hitched. They make the world better by being together.

I would say the same about Dayanara and Mildre, the Spanish-speaking couple who stayed to witness the marriage of my friends, teeth chattering anew. It turns out, the vows are the same in Spanish and in English, the same for two women or two men as they are for my spouse and me. They, and we, in whatever language, promise to pour ourselves into the priority of love.

Before we left Love County that day, a relative of the Dallas brides came up to me and clasped my hand. "*Muchas gracias,*" she said, which I could understand without a translator. She pressed a wad of cash into my palm; I tried to resist, but she was tearfully insistent. This was not the slim packet of clean bills neatly folded that I have sometimes received as a preplanned honorarium; this was an impromptu collection from the pockets and purses of the brides' relatives and maybe the brides themselves. Wrinkled ones and fives, and a twenty: thirty-eight bucks, as I recall. Don't tell the IRS. I did not declare it.

Instead, our happy little band stopped at Babe's for celebratory chicken fried steak on the drive back to Fort Worth. I picked up the check with the cash I had on hand. And Caroline had health care, just like that. Chicken fried steak and health care! The gifts of God for the people of God! Thanks be to God!

Francine's Cancer (Fall 2016)

"Oh, my God . . . Fuck cancer."

There was little else to say. Francine, a near-original at Galileo (who I knew from BG, Before Galileo, as a child-whisperer; we met under a table in a Now Church fellowship hall where we were both trying to persuade a distressed kid on the spectrum to keep his clothes on, literally, and Francine figured it out way before I did), had breast cancer. She was thirty-something. She was ours. She was starting nasty chemo right after a nasty round of hormones so they could harvest her eggs so she might still be able to have a baby someday. Fuck cancer.

The story of her illness (and good health! Thanks be to God! A whole year cancer-free!) is hers to tell, obviously. But it was a milestone for Galileo too because we had never dealt with that level of suffering before. We had not dealt with death.

I said as much to Francine. "We don't really know how to do this," I confessed. "In traditional church there are lots of old women who know how to take care of someone when they're seriously sick. We can barely manage to throw together crude games involving toilet plungers and toilet paper rolls and chugging beer from baby bottles for a new-born shower. How will we know how to help you? How will we tell the church?" Which, I realize, is a shitty thing to ask someone with cancer. But Francine is different. You can ask her anything.

She said, "Let me think about it." And a couple of weeks later, she got back to me with a plan. *She* would tell the church, in worship, as an introduction to a body prayer. (We do a body prayer at the beginning of worship each week, carefully written words arranged around simple physical postures and motions, to involve our whole selves in praying.) She would pray. And then we would, all together, pray our way through a litany that she would help me write.

So we did. And it was awful—and so beautiful. We have used that litany a couple of more times, more times than we would have liked. It helps us remember how to be good companions when we're healthy, and that it's good to ask for help when we're not.

A few weeks into the chemo, Francine and I got together for coffee. She was exhausted and anxious and sick. She said, "It's so ridiculous, but I need to shave my head before all this hair starts falling out. I can't deal with depressing clumps in the shower drain. But I don't want to go to my salon. That's where I go to feel beautiful. And this is the opposite of that." I had not seen tears in her eyes before that moment, ever. I said, "My G-group meets in a couple days. And Andrea B. (a hair artist at a boutique salon) will be there, and I could ask her to bring her clippers and stuff. You could be with friends. Do you want me to do that?"

Two nights later, our G-group was finishing dinner when Francine bounded through the front door. She always bounds, but she was not as buoyant as usual. Andrea B. got her bag, and I carried a chair to the bathroom. And they got to work.

I tell you, there were saints in the bathroom that night. Andrea B. was one of them, carefully and confidently shearing Francine to the scalp, miles of beautiful, black hair tumbling to the floor. Francine was the other, waiting patiently, letting it happen, the embodiment of quiet surrender. I hung back, watching silently from the doorway, not wanting to get in the way of the real ministry, the hovering Holy Spirit covering them both. Total transformation. Holy ground, right there in my bathroom. #Churchfriends, right outside in the living room, waiting to receive their loved ones, Francine, Andrea B., and me, all of us changed. And I thought, "I guess we do know how to do this. God help us, I guess we do."

Excursus: Litany of Companionship in Sickness

Galileo Church • November 2016 •
on the occasion of Francine's breast cancer diagnosis

leader: God of our lives, today we confront the reality of our physicality, our frailty, our mortality.

people: **You have made us from dust,**
            and to dust we all return.

leader: We always know that this is true, but it becomes especially real when someone we love, someone close to our own hearts, is sick.

people: **The reality of one person's suffering**
            becomes suffering for all of us.

leader: Please help us during this time to be more like family than ever before, to be drawn together in strength rather than isolated in worry.

        Specifically, please help us to be present, according to Francine's needs, for appointments and treatments, errands and down time.

people: Help us to be present.

leader: Please help us to be prayerful, less for specific outcomes than for healing peace and healing mercy and healing strength.

people: Help us to be prayerful.

leader: Please help us to be helpful, providing basic necessities like food and toilet paper and laundry and dog-walking and even financial assistance, because being sick is exhausting and expensive.

people: Help us to be helpful.

leader: Please help us to avoid saying things that are well meaning but not well thought out.

Not that "God has a plan," because if this is your plan, your planning sucks.

Not that Francine is "strong," because dealing with cancer is not a matter of her strong character.

Not the stories of relatives' and friends' illnesses and their outcomes, positive or negative. Help us to keep the focus on the beloved who is right in front of us.

people: **Help us to say, with our words and actions,**
that we love Francine unconditionally,
in sickness and in health,
and that we are committed
to being present, prayerful, and helpful
in ways that are good for her.

leader: May we may be people of compassionate action, and may your healing mercies be abundant for our sister and friend. We pray in the name of our brother Jesus, whose own body endured the consequences of mortality, and who knows how we suffer; and in the power of his resurrection, which is our hope.

people: **Amen.**

Barn Raising for Human Beings

You remember how, back in the olden days, pioneer families would come together to build a barn for one family, doing the necessary labor as a community that no one could have done on their own? Of course you don't. Neither do I. We're not that old.

But what if I told you that out here on this spiritual-but-not-religious frontier, barn raising is a necessary Christian practice? We've done lots of it, not because we planned to but because at certain points it became undeniably essential to our life together. This is what barn raising looks like where I'm from.

It looks like that time Kaytee (bartender) and Kyle B (chef) took a huge chance on a new suburban restaurant on the growing side of Dallas, moving in to an expensive apartment, both of them working for the same entrepreneur. As the restaurant slowly petered out (because new restaurants fail at about the rate that new churches do), they found themselves without either of their paychecks some weeks and with dwindling hours on the work schedule, getting in deeper and deeper. And Kaytee was way pregnant. And they were so far away from us, their family of choice, Galileo Originals who had flown the coop. Their FOOs were in Washington but wouldn't have been much more help if they'd been next door. Watching them suffer from far away was miserable. The leadership team told me, "You have to go get them back."

So I drove out to Frisco (please, Texans, appreciate that) and met them for lunch in the near-empty restaurant. "We want you to come home," I said. "We can't afford to," they said. "We'll lose the deposit on the apartment. We don't have money for another one. We can't rent a truck for all our stuff. We don't have jobs down there. We really have to stay."

"What if Galileo pays the lost deposit?" I said. "And we rent a truck? And help pack your stuff? And find you jobs?" I was way out on a limb here. We could muster the money, but jobs weren't so easy to come by. They agreed to think about it and pray about it. I got an email from Kaytee pretty soon after I got home. "We have to do something," she said. "We might as well give this a try."

The spouse of an acquaintance I had met a few months before sells insurance in Mansfield, and he was looking to hire an office manager. I put in a call to say I knew this wicked smart woman who used to be my very own secretary and if I could hire her myself I would, and oh, by the way, she's seven months pregnant and will need maternity leave almost as soon as you get her. That Christian man hired Kaytee without blinking. And in the next town over, an established chain restaurant where Kayla and Ryan waited tables was looking for an assistant manager. Kayla put in a word for Kyle B, and pretty soon he had a job too. They came home to us for a couple more years so we could dedicate their (first two) babies and support their career advancement as a good family should. We raised their barn, as they had done for others before and would do for others to come.

Barn raising looks like that time a family in our church was told they had thirty days to vacate their rental home. They found a new place without too much trouble, but the move itself was excruciating. Neither spouse could muster the executive function to get the packing done, and as the deadline approached we feared they would be evicted. On the last possible Saturday a caravan of folks showed up, knowing one spouse was working a twelve-hour shift that day. The other spouse wouldn't let us in the door. I asked everyone to stay in their cars while I talked to her.

From behind the closed front door she said, "I can't let you see it like this. It's horrible in here. It's like letting you see me naked." I said, "Well, if that's what it feels like, we could make it fair. I'll start taking my clothes off here on the front porch, then I'll be naked too, and we'll be embarrassed together. I'm starting with my shoes. Here I go." She laughed in spite of herself, through her very serious tears. She let us in and we got to work. My big kids took her medium and small kids to get some breakfast and to the mall. "Hang out for as long as you can," I told my daughter. "Here's my credit card." We by God got that family moved that day, got their barn raised. Because that's what Jesus would do, yeah?

I think he would because Jesus said that thing about how, if you come with him, you can lose all the people who are supposed to care about you (Mark 10:29-30). You can lose parents, siblings, and even your kids to be his disciple. And then he said we shouldn't worry too much about it, because he's promising to give all that back to us, *in this age*. Like, now. You lose family to be the person God made you to be, the best version of yourself, brave and dedicated to Jesus and his reign-of-God project, and as a help in that effort you get a family. And I think he meant the church would be your family when you don't have any other family left who will help you.

That promise of Jesus takes my breath away. I mean, what if he's writing checks his church can't cash? What if all we really wanted was to get together in our Sunday best and politely check off items in the order of worship till we're done for another week? But he seems to think we will be family for the family-poor. He seems to think we will raise each other's barns.

Galileo Church has done more of that than any church I've served before because so many of our folks are family-poor. My spouse and I were seriously broke when we were much younger, but we always had our FOOs to back us up. When you're queer or love someone who's queer, the rest of your family may decide they're done with your ass. Or maybe you're a spiritual refugee in part because your family was never all that stable and helpful in the first place. So when you need new tires to keep driving Uber, and you don't have the cash up front, who do you call? When your Obamacare plan changes the formulary and suddenly your anti-anxiety med costs triple, what do you do? When you don't know the first thing about how to buy a house, how to change a car battery, how to write a résumé, how to find a dentist, or how to bake a Thanksgiving pie—or don't have anywhere to go for Thanksgiving—who do you ask?

You ask your barn-raising church, your God-given family, the people you trust who love you as you are. You ask in the Facebook group if you've been around a little while and know that confessions of ignorance and need are par for the course in there. Or you reach out to a spiritual care team member or your G-group or the lead evangelist and ask if there's any way you can get some help. If you start a GoFundMe campaign, we're very likely to kick in there too. Barn raising is the way the church says to each one in it, "We want you to succeed and flourish. Show us your project. Let us help." Or, as we're more prone to actually write on Facebook, "We're glad you asked. You are so loved. Mwah."

Excursus: "How Is This Church Different?" (Blog Post, June 2016)

Spiritual refugees can't always see why Galileo Church is any different from the boring, irrelevant, exclusive, and painful experiences of church they've come from. They're right to insist that stylistic differences—a guitar instead of an organ, jeans instead of Sunday dress-up are not sufficient to earn their trust. They challenge me to articulate something more than our snarky resistance to vocabulary like "committee" and "fellowship" and our now passé commitment to the inclusion of beer for church events. Here's what I say when they ask:

1. About God: we trust that the Deity is ahead of us, not behind us. God is the God of the future, not the past. God didn't just *used to* do stuff, a long time ago in a Bibleland far, far away; God is *still* doing stuff, always a little further out from our comfort zone than we would like. And thus getting a handle on exactly Who God Is is not something we imagine we can do. We just try to keep up and stay amazed.

Someday, we trust, God will get everything God wants. ("The arc of the moral universe is long, and it bends toward justice," somebody said. Somebody with the initials M. L. K.) If we want that too, God's future will feel like heaven to us! If we don't, if we're invested in the status quo, well, God's future will hurt like hell. We find images of that future in the Bible—mountains demolished, valleys raised up, the last made first, the first made last, the despised and forgotten sitting happily with Jesus. We want to want what God wants, because in the future of God's imagining, it will all be true.

2. About Jesus: we trust that his life of ministry was as significant as his death, and that you can't appreciate one without the other. His life was the fullest expression of God-Among-Us, God's Logic, God's Own Self ever. We are much more likely to share stories of his shocking, inclusive, earthly life spent among friends and enemies than we are to dwell on the bloody details of his atoning death.

We're not even sure what "atonement" means, except that God routinely takes the crap we've got (crucifixion, anybody?) and makes beautiful stuff out of it. We insist: If Jesus had not lived the kind of life he did, they wouldn't have killed him. Thus his resurrection becomes a vindication of his choice in life to love beyond the borders of religious propriety; and thus we are saved, because he loved *us* beyond the borders of religious propriety. Boom.

3. About the Holy Spirit: we trust that it's the Spirit of Living Jesus inhabiting us, so that we are kinder, bolder, and more imaginative than we would be on our own because Jesus was the kindest, boldest, most imaginative person ever. And we're pretty sure his Spirit is at work in people who don't even know it's happening, which is delicious. We feel strong and smart and gutsy with this Spirit weaving us together.

4. About people: we trust that people are beautiful and beloved. *All* people. Even us. So we try to act like beautiful and beloved people, even when we don't feel like it, interacting with the beautiful and beloved people in our lives and in our world. This makes us happy, because people are fantastic. We are fantastic. You are fantastic.

This requires constant attention to the flattening of hierarchies, so that race and money and religion and gender and sexuality don't prescribe how we relate to each other. This is the morality we lean into—the corporate morality of Christ's (metaphorical) body (that's us) living into the promise of the dissolution of human distinctions. Whew. That's a mouthful.

So you can see that we're aware that the beautiful and beloved people of God are also broken. We're much more concerned about the deeply systemic brokenness in our world—the way power is used and abused, sometimes to our benefit without our even knowing it happened—than we are in each other's individual little sins. Most of us are pretty good most of the time, and God is merciful; but all of us are caught in sticky webs of systemic sin from which the whole world, even the dirt we walk on, will one day be redeemed, because God is just. Thanks be to God. (*Redeemed* = set free. The churchy language sticks with us sometimes.)

5. About the Bible: we attend to the Bible as one, continuous story about God and how the beautiful, beloved, broken people of God relate to God. Sometimes they get it right. Lots of times they don't. Everything in the Bible points to the God Who Is Ahead of us, calling us forward, never back. Nothing in the Bible is a stopping place. We take the Bible quite seriously, letting it show us how patiently God waits for us to figure stuff out and take the next step toward God.

Oh, and: the Bible is never boring. If it seems that way, you're doing it wrong.

So that's how I explain it, for now. I'm aware that these things could change over time—I couldn't have written this essay at twenty-seven or thirty-seven, so what makes me think it'll still be true at fifty-seven?

I don't know if these words resonate with you, friend refugee. Do they feel true enough (and distinct enough) to make a difference in your experience of our church? Is there balm here to heal your wounds, nourishment here to strengthen your bones?

I guess the last difference in our church from your last one is this: we believe that *the church is for you.* You, the skeptic; you, the cynic; you, the wounded; you, the strong one working to keep your head above water for another day. God is for you, so we are for you. You are why we exist. Come and see.

Excursus: "Galileo Distinctives" (Blog Post, November 2017)

I spend a lot of time explaining our church to people. Not the aesthetics (urban industrial barn? Americana nerd? ironic trash-to-treasure? unironic supergay?); they can see that for themselves. People have legit questions about stuff they've sensed about Galileo that's different from other churches they've known. They can't quite put their finger on it, but . . .

So here's my attempt to say (write) out loud some of the stuff I find myself explaining a lot. I'm calling these "Galileo Distinctives"—the stuff that's purposely *different from* (not necessarily "better than," if churches are in competition, which we shouldn't be) churches you might've known.

1. We're on a slow-growth curve, on purpose. We cultivate relationships like locally grown tomatoes: with care, and time, and food, and prayer. We don't program stuff to attract jillions of people. We would freak out if jillions of people showed up; how could we possibly clink glasses with all of them? We just keep trying to get to know people, and love what we know about each other, and thereby actually love each other. Our idea is, if we can get to a stable number that sustains our missional priorities, probably about 150, we'll send some people out to make another Galileo somewhere else. Like, the other side of the DFW metroplex. Denton, anybody?

2. We plan a lot for the people who aren't here yet. We are deliberately evangelistic. We think what we've learned about God is the best news in the world: that God's love is real; God's love is for you; and God's love is worth it. (Contrast that with what a lot of us learned in church the first time around: that God's judgment is real; God's judgment is for you; and God's judgment is mos def *not* worth it.) So when we plan stuff for our church to do together, it's always with an eye toward whether people who are not here yet might be able to join in, and we adjust to make church stuff as permeable, as *joinable*, as possible.

3. **We're clear about what we're saying "yes" to, and what we're saying "no" to.** We have missional priorities, which you can learn more about on our home page. Here's the truth: there are way more good things in the world than we can possibly join; there are way more awful things in the world than we can possibly protest. So we've narrowed it down. When people in our church want to do or join or fund or protest other stuff, we encourage them to do it—not with the church's endorsement, but as grown-ass people endowed with the Holy Spirit who can make love and fight crime without the institutional say-so.

4. **We've pretty much said "no" to owning property.** Like any of these distinctives, this could change. But for now, most of Galileo's people don't own a home and don't care to shift our ministry to property caretaking (or mortgage support). We suspect that owning a building changes a lot of things churches do, and we like having church in public much of the time. We like the amount of time we spend discussing property usage and upkeep, which is almost none. We even like the idea that our church sort of disappears, or at least dissipates, when we leave the barn we rent . . . and then reconvenes at the taco bar, or the coffee shop, or the next living room. . .

5. **We're kind of a DIY church.** Not very slick; more on the homemade end of the scale. Our furniture is hand-me-down, or made from recycled junk, and we like it because it reminds us of ourselves in a way. Moreover, our programming (the stuff we plan to do together) is kind of *ad hoc*. It changes depending on what we need next. So we have Little-G for preschoolers during the sermon until there's not a critical mass of toddlers, then we stop; we put together teams to plan events and disband them when the event is over. When someone says, "Why don't we have . . . ?" we listen, and if it's a good idea, we ask that very same someone to make it so, with plenty of support from the whole church if now is the right time. The church usually knows what it needs.

6. **Our Lead Evangelist isn't necessarily nice.** Maybe she's not someone you want to emulate, or even be friends with. She's busy and bossy and brash, although she also deflects a lot of decision making by saying, "I'm not the boss of that." One of the dynamics we're interested in at Galileo is, what does the official-pastor-person *mean* in a system like this? What if you didn't like some-

thing she did or said? What if she really pissed you off, and y'all couldn't get reconciled? Could you still be a valued part of the Galileo Church fam? What if you pointed out something about Galileo you think she should fix, and she didn't fix it? Could you still trust her theological teaching? And what if your kids heard her drop the f-bomb in a sermon, knowing that's seriously against the rules in your house? Could you say, "She's a bang-up preacher and has some really good thoughts about God, but we don't talk like that around here, mister"? *Would that be okay?* We're thinking the answers to these questions might be yes. We really hope so.

7. **We're banking on inter-generational friendship** rather than demographic-specific programming to keep our kids interested in Jesus for the rest of their lives. It's not so much a question of whether our kids *like* coming to church—it's not our job to entertain them to death. Rather, we want our kids to think of Galileo Church in all its iterations (Sunday nights, G-groups, parties, etc.) as safe and brave space for working out what it means to be disciples of Jesus. Do they have people, including kids younger and older than themselves, who are happy to see them? Do they have grown-ups besides their parents who know their names, and ask about their lives, and share their own? Are they able to enter into meaningful conversation about the biblical-theological stuff the church is exploring together?

Toward these ends, we don't do a lot of kids-only stuff at Galileo. If the kids want to do an all-night video-gaming lock-in, *everybody's* invited, and expected to come. Same with roller-skating, mini-golfing, karaoke-ing. Also, kids mostly stay with grown-ups for worship, even the littlest ones. Bring in da funk, bring in da noise; we're in this thing together, *with* our kids, not because we can't afford to hire a caretaker but because we don't want to disappear them out of our life together.

8. **We do a lot of life together on social media,** mostly Facebook for now. We have an active Facebook page where we make announcements and curate resources, much as we do on Twitter and Instagram. But we also have a jillion Facebook groups where different configurations of G-people interact in mostly meaningful ways, with the occasional random cat GIF thrown in.

- We have a big FB group that's like a dorm commons area, with people wandering through to see who else is there. That's where people share real life, from "Woohoo! I got a new crappy job!" to "This day sucks balls and I can't do it anymore; please pray for me."

- We have small FB groups for G-groups to coordinate dinner plans, or share more personal prayer requests.
- We use temporary FB groups to plan events, like the most recent "Halloween for Grown-Ups Planning Group" where we invented a signature cocktail and argued over decorations.

And our Lead Evangelist wants to be in all of them, and be "friends" with everybody, so she can keep up with everything all the time. It's cute.

9. We'd rather eat and drink together than anything else. We figure Jesus did that a lot with his friends, an idea we got from reading the gospels. So a lot of our church budget is dedicated to food and beverages. If the Lead Evangelist invites you out for coffee or beer, and offers to pay for it, she's likely using Galileo $$ to do that. (Remember, she's not that nice.) If you make dinner for your G-group, don't *not* get reimbursed because you worry about using up the church's money. Just give as generously as you can to our work together, and it's like we're all buying each other dinner all the time. Thanks be to God!

10. We're really into transparency. In the same way that we're hoping to "do real relationship, no bullshit, ever," we're trying to model truth telling in our institutional life. Meaning, there shouldn't be any decision making or procedural details you don't have access to. Missional Logistics Team meetings are open. Our budget and other admin docs are online. We ask for volunteers to help "boss" stuff all the time. We run a G-101 class every quarter or so, to make explicit what we might otherwise tend to assume "everybody" knows about Galileo. We consider lots of input for decision making and strive for consensus; it's quite possible we've never actually taken a vote on anything.

(We do keep private stuff private, though, meaning that you can count on your Lead Evangelist and Spiritual Care Team members to keep strict confidentiality, and you can count on your G-group friends to honor privacy. Be careful on social media, however; even in "private" spaces online, there's no truly secret space.)

Look at that—I got to a nice, round Decalogue for this list of Galileo Distinctives. You could push us into prime numbers, though, if you suggest 1 (or 3 or 7) more.

CHAPTER 5

Missional Priorities

Get You Some

But What Can I Do?

For a while we carried on with that reason for being that I wrote when I first started imagining Galileo Church, shortened to "We seek and shelter spiritual refugees." Those words carry a lot of weight for us—"seeking," "sheltering," "spiritual," and "refugees" each doing part of the work of forming our life together.

But once we got a critical mass of said refugees, I discovered that they didn't want to *be* the mission. They wanted to *have* a mission. Like, they wanted to know what God had planned for them to *do* in the world God loves. Like, what is our church *for*?

I'll tell you a secret. I practice a kind of discrimination in welcoming newcomers to Galileo Church. If you come in the door sick to death (but not kicked out) of your old church, burned out on the exclusion and meanness even though it wasn't aimed at you, ready for the Spirit to blow some fresh air through your musty faith life, voluntarily slumming with us in the Big Red Barn—*and* you are cisgender, straight—*and* you shake my hand eagerly while asking, "How can I get involved? How can I help? What do you need me to do?" I'm very likely to say, "We don't really need you to do anything. Just keep showing up, because showing up is important. Consistent presence alongside those who have been kicked to the curb is important." And if you do that, keep showing up, eventually there will be more stuff for you to do. Trust me.

If you come in all beat up, scars of rejection crisscrossing your spirit, some of the wounds too fresh to have scars yet, barely able to muster the energy and courage to take *one more chance* on God, barely able to believe that any of God's people calling themselves a "church" could ever receive anyone like you—because of your LGBTQ+ identity or neurodiverse way of being, or because you're the parent of a queer kid who's been kicked out of their church youth group or because you're the kid of parents who couldn't/wouldn't/didn't love you without attaching a great big "but" to their love—*and* you ask, tentatively, terrified, "Is there anything I can do to help?" well, then, I've got a long list of ways to say yes to that audacious question. I will make things up for you to do so you will know how valuable and loved you are. Often the time between first showing up at Galileo and being assigned some gigantic, mission-critical task is ridiculously short. Ryan tells how after his third Sunday visiting, I asked him to decorate G-House for Easter Sunday, spending no more than a couple hundred bucks. But the random (or not-so-random) assignment of tasks as we invent them was not really what Galileo's people were hungry for way back when. We were hungry to know how God would use us, all together, to make this world more like the world God wants. All we had at our disposal to satiate that hunger was about a year's worth of life together and a whole bunch of Post-it Notes. It was enough.

Discerning Missional Priorities:
It All Came Out Okay (Fall 2014)

The task was simple but not easy: figure out what God is equipping and calling Galileo Church to do in the world God loves. How is it that we embody Jesus in the place where we are?

There's some dispute about whether this happened around my dining room table in a marathon meeting or whether church leaders went on one of our famous twenty-four-hour working retreats to the nearby Disciples campground. Either way, the Post-it Notes are not in question.

We asked one question in several ways: "When, in this first year of our life together, have we felt happiest? most like ourselves? at ease with the task at hand? useful in the world God loves? What have we done together that has brought us joy, joy that we've been able to share with people outside this room? On what occasions have we looked around and thought, 'This is where we are supposed to be'?"

We had a year's worth of experiences. We took our time. Each of us wrote short descriptions of our memories on Post-it Notes, one memory per square. There were scores of squares on the table.

- Marching at the marriage equality rallies
- When we sing at the top of our lungs
- Katie seriously apologized for something stupid she did
- Candles all lit for worship
- I told my life story, no one left or laughed
- We talk like real people talk
- Praying at the prayer wall
- Rainbow flag hanging up
- Communion (too much to say)
- Bringing cookies to Labor Day workers
- Tips for Jesus (an experiment in which we went to dinner after worship on Sunday nights, each person buying their own supper but Galileo leaving a $100 tip for the restaurant's workers—super-fun but expensive and ultimately unsustainable)

Everybody worked in silence on their own growing cluster of satisfying moments. As that work wound down, we grouped together in trios, comparing our notes, finding commonalities, sticking together similar memories. Each group of three chose their top three to share with the whole group.

As the trios shared, we stuck the proffered Post-its on the walls of the room. (My dining room, I'm sure, but someone will argue with me. Hey, it's my book!) We grouped together similar-sounding experiences, searching for themes. Degrouping, regrouping, till it felt just right.

Then we tried to name each group. Advocacy for LGBTQ people was certainly clear.

Being generous to people who worked for tips, or for low wages, was something we loved.

Gratitude for our worship style and space, the whole Galileo aesthetic, came into focus.

Permission to be our whole, integrated selves—indeed, an expectation of such—*at church* was something most of us had never experienced before and now found that we could not live without.

We named these as our missional priorities and began saying them every time we gathered:

1. We do justice for LGBTQ+ persons.
2. We do kindness for low-wage workers.
3. We do beauty for our God Who Is Beautiful.
4. We do real relationship, no bullshit, ever.

In seasons to come we would find that priority two needed to change. Not that we were going to be *un*kind to low-wage workers! But when it came to kindness, there were people who needed it even more at church: people with mental illness or in emotional distress or who were nonneurotypical. In other words, people whose brains worked differently than most folks' brains do. We think the spike at Galileo in numbers of people with mental health diagnoses and neurodiverse persons came about because of priorities one and four on our list. In declaring ourselves advocates for LGBTQ+ justice, we telegraphed our intention to celebrate the fullness of anyone's humanity. And in practicing "no bullshit, ever," we made safe and brave space for people to be whoever God made them to be, including people who tended toward depression or anxiety or landed on the autism spectrum, or had Down syndrome or Tourette's or OCD, or any other thing that would make it hard to participate in churches where everyone pretends to be "normal," whatever that is. No pretending at Galileo.

So after another year or so, we developed a new priority two, not as succinct as the first one but more attentive to who we were becoming:

2. We do kindness for people with mental illness or in emotional distress, and we celebrate neurodiversity.

Our missional priorities help us decide what to do as a church and what not to do. There are a million possibilities for joining God's work in the world; we're so glad that other churches are working on other missional priorities. And while ours serve us well for now, giving us clarity about next steps, we hold them lightly, knowing that God may have other plans for us at some point.

Here's something I didn't expect: we don't usually get the luxury of working on just one missional priority at a time. They get all tangled up and ask us to pay close attention to the complicated little miracle that is about to be born. Like the time Wanda posted in our FB group, "Anybody got an enema bottle I can borrow?" And she described her efforts to find one large enough, the smaller ones being too hard to work with. It was a *lot*. Unusually, nobody chimed in on the FB post right away. I waited and watched, and finally commented: "I can honestly say that this is the strangest request we've had in this group! And also, that you and your small intestine are so loved, Wanda. I truly hope it all comes out okay. (See what I did there?) Love, for real."

It turns out that our Wanda had, before we knew her, experienced a painful and dangerous small-bowel obstruction that left her truly afraid of it happening again. Her request was not just for medical equipment; it was for comfort, even at the risk of embarrassing herself. (*We do kindness for people in emotional distress . . .*) Wanda is trans and happily part of a church that advocates for her right to exist and have health care and feel well. (*We do justice for LGBTQ+ people . . .*) She needed an enema and said so. (*We do real relationship, no bullshit, ever . . .*) And the slow tide of sympathetic comments that rose on that FB post was a lovely outpouring for a woman who is precious to us, created as she is in the image of God. (*We do beauty for our God Who Is Beautiful . . .*)

I'm saying, it's not exactly how we thought our missional priorities would play out in church life. It's not what we *planned*. But having given ourselves over to those priorities, we find that God makes up stuff for us to do. God knows how hungry we are to be useful and how good it feels to be needed.

And in case you were wondering, Wanda is fine. Everything came out A-OK.

About That Queer Thing

Here's what I knew when we started: when millennials are asked why they aren't at church, one of the things they say is, "I don't want to go any place that all my friends can't come." They are unwilling to make anybody else a refugee, even if it means becoming a refugee themselves. Ain't that a kick in the pants? (To check my research, look for Robert Wuthnow's *After the Baby Boomers* and the Barna Group's data in David Kinnaman's *unChristian* and *You Lost Me*.)

Therefore, to reach the spiritual refugees among a generation that was already important to me, Galileo Church would need to be clear from the outset about LGBTQ+ inclusion. I had served churches that were explicitly exclusive, and I had served churches that were of the more subtly bigoted "don't ask, don't tell" variety. I had tried moving the needle on that at one church that said, basically, "We'll be nice to them, but we never want to talk about it, ever." Being firmly convinced in my own mind and spirit that LGBTQ+ people are created in God's image and beloved by God's heart, I did not want to get stuck in the hush-hush indecision that would make LGBTQ+ people and the people who loved them *guess* how welcome they truly were at our church. I asked the start-up team, a bunch of het-cis folks, all of them married except for Malcolm, if it was okay to proceed with LGBTQ+ inclusion as a fundamental commitment. They were genuinely surprised I asked. Eyebrows went up. "Of course," they said, as if to a small child who has asked if it's okay to breathe the air.

In our worship exploration during those first several months, we had shared an experience that doubtless emboldened our willingness to be explicit about that welcome. We heard of a little start-up church in Denton, a university town north of Fort Worth, that met in a gay bar. Not the fancy-schmancy kind like you find in Dallas, but a hard-core, gritty place with buzzing neon and dark corners and a cloud of cigarette smoke hovering around the front door. The bar was called Mable Peabody's Beauty Parlor and Chain Saw Repair, and the church meeting there on Sunday mornings was called—wait for it—The Church at Mable Peabody's Beauty Parlor and Chain Saw Repair, the Rev. (now Dr.) Jeff Hood presiding.

I called up Jeff and asked if we could come over, a bunch of clean-cut, white, straight students and suburbanites. Probably subconsciously I was asking if we would be safe there? And he said, "Sure, you can come, but it's best if you come to the bar on Friday night to get to know some people." His church was doing some karaoke or something on Friday, and we'd be welcome to come have a beer, and then when we came on Sunday we'd be less like lookie-loo tourists and more like worshipers. I understand that even more now—Galileo gets tourists all the time, and while I used to be excited about each and every newcomer, I now understand that some folks come to observe us, not to engage the Deity who meets us there. Which is fine. We've been tourists before too.

So we piled in my car on Friday night and drove to Denton. (Traffic, ugh. I-35.) And y'all, that bar was rough. People passed out in the booths. People of indeterminate gender dancing alone, feeling no pain. Couples (more than couples?) making out against the wall. No bouncer, but a bartender who looked like she could bounce anybody she damn well pleased and who took very good care of our silly selves that night. We drank politely, getting no attention from Jeff (appropriately) while he tended to church folks who were also bar patrons and vice versa. When we decided to leave, he was still going strong, listening and commiserating and laughing with anyone who needed his ear. We were like scribes and Pharisees, the VRPs (very religious persons), getting no love from Jesus if there were sex workers or tax collectors anywhere in proximity.

We came back on Sunday morning expecting to be surprised by how the bar would transform into a sacred space. But the cloud of cigarette smoke had not dissipated, and the lights were not any brighter, and some of the folks who were there on Friday night had not gone home in the meantime, I swear. Everything smelled, um, exactly the same. When we walked into the room where worship would be held, the only visible change was a six-foot-by-eight-foot plywood sign, painted in broad strokes as if with house paint, announcing, "JESUS IS QUEER." Jeff would later do a doctoral project in queer theology, exploring the queerness of God as one who finds Godself othered, rejected, and persecuted by mainstream society because God will not conform to mainstream expectations. Sounds pretty queer to me.

I said before that we experienced some pretty crappy worship during our explorations, but this was not one of those times. Jeff is a weird dude, and everything about that worship service was weird, but it was the most gorgeous weird I had ever seen. He gave a sermon during which he lay in a fetal position on the (filthy) floor at one point, in his alb, to embody the story he was telling about Jesus and Nicodemus, each of them trying to figure out what it's like to be born again, anew. While he preached, his wife painted on a large canvas from buckets of house paint, with wide brushes, his words giving shape to her strokes, until a fascinating, enigmatic portrait of pregnancy and birth and light emerged.

We sang with a shy black woman whose guitar sounded cheap and thin, but oh! when she sang! During communion she quietly warbled endless verses of "We Shall Overcome," the rest of us joining in when we could. Each worshiper came forward to meet Jeff before getting to the bread and wine. He held each one's head in his hands, made significant eye contact, and said, "This God, this gift, this grace, is *for you*." I think he might have kissed my head. I would not have minded. We ate and drank. Sang some more. "Deep in my heart, I do believe / We shall overcome some day." It was a day more sacred than any we had experienced in a long time.

And I think that's when we knew. We knew that it would not be enough to be *nice* to gay people. We knew that people who have been pushed to the fringes of society, kicked out of church, left out of their families, stepped on, turned out, talked about, put down, and in every other way shit on did not need a nice church to be nice to them. Galileo Church didn't have to be Mable Peabody's, and I didn't have to be Jeff Hood, but we felt ourselves sli-i-i-iding significantly in that direction, out to the margins, beyond the bounds of propriety, that day in Denton.

Right around the same time that summer, my spouse and I traveled with Erin and Joel to the Wild Goose Festival in North Carolina. That year there was a talk listed in the program: "How Queers Are Saving the Church." And of course I went because I didn't get that at all. Until I heard this gay Episcopal priest talk about how seriously insulting and outright vacuous it was for straight churches to offer "welcome" to queer people. "Oh, no, honey," he said. "What you need to understand is, queers have what the dying North American church needs. We're closer to Jesus than you can imagine because Jesus has always been out here with us losers, all the rejects from your respectable churches. Queers know more about getting real with God than straight people can fathom. And we have a killer sense of style, and frankly your churches are looking stale." I mean, that was his talk in a nutshell. I could have listened to him all day.

Are you sensing that the summer of 2013 was a big one for me, spiritually and ecclesially? Because, yeah. World turned upside down.

So, practically speaking, it was pretty simple to get Galileo registered with gaychurch.org. I had heard from a seeker who found us online that Roger Wolsey's book *Kissing Fish* advises young adults who are looking for a progressive, science-friendly church to check out gaychurch.org because any church who's bothered to register there is not advocating six-day creation or a six-thousand-year-old earth. We were vetted somewhat by that website—I seem to remember a phone call, but that couldn't be right—and then there we were, right there on gaychurch.org, declaring ourselves open for business and open to all people, just waiting for someone to Google "gay church 76063."

It was less easy to get our denominational *bona fides*. The "open and affirming" ministry of the Disciples of Christ has a process for achieving O&A status, which involves congregational studies and guided conversations and (shudder) *voting*, with minutes produced to show that you've done all these things over a sufficient period of time. But we were in more of a hurry than that and couldn't ever imagine studying and deliberating for months about the basic dignity and inclusion afforded all people by God's own Self. So I called up the director of that ministry and said, "A church like Galileo is never gonna make it if we have to go that route. Couldn't you just believe these youngsters? This is what's in their heart. Plus, we've already bought a rainbow flag." He sighed and said okay. I think the sigh was the same sigh I get from a lot of Now Church loyalists who can tell we're onto something but can't quite make it fit their time-tested processes. I feel them. And I'm so grateful when they're willing to let us do it the Next Church way.

From there it wasn't long before we were welcoming queer people of all kinds—including many for whom the rainbow letters in L-G-B-T don't apply. We became bolder about using *queer* as a catch all for all the ways people don't quite fit. We stopped short of a house-paint sign declaring Jesus's own queerness—the landlord church might have imploded if they'd seen such—but we got clear about the welcome we were sharing.

That is to say, we got clear about the welcome that all of us had received, the same, from God Who is the Welcomer. We became suspicious of declaring that "we" welcome "them," no matter who "they" may be, influenced by Jacques Derrida's brilliant little riff on the similarities between *hospitality* and *hostility*, hospitality being that "virtue" that preserves power for the host and keeps the guest on their toes. Sometimes we say, in our opening for worship, that "All are welcome here—not because we are so nice, because we're not actually all that nice, but because God is good, and God welcomes all of us to God's heart just the same."

So, listen. This book about Galileo Church is not really very much about the queerness of it all, at least in terms of sexual orientation and gender identity/expression. Yes, we have hung multicolored flags for trans people and genderqueer people and bi people and whatever else—I lose track—around our worship space, signaling that this space is safe for you to be your whole, beautiful self. We are attentive to queer interpretations of familiar Bible stories, and we substitute gender-neutral language in our hymns. We each say our pronouns when we get to the microphone, for the first or fiftieth time. We've married gay couples and blessed babies born to same-sex parents. We've baptized trans folks in the same trough we use for cisgender people. That's all true.

But it makes me a little cranky when people of a certain age ask me, as they sometimes do, *sotto voce*, wanting a private convo, straight person to straight person, "So, uh, how many of your folks are, uh, you know . . . ?" If I'm feeling my oats I'll play dumb and make them ask more explicitly. But usually I just tell the truth with a shrug: "I dunno. I haven't really counted." It's not the same as "I don't see LGBTQ+"; it's just a recognition that here, in this space, we are doing so much more than that. We're living into that Ephesians 2 thing, where buff Jesus uses his cross like a sledgehammer to demolish the dividing wall between us.

I like to think we'd be "doing justice for LGBTQ+ people" even if there were no actual LGBTQ+ people in attendance, but I don't know if that's true. I really hope they stick around; this church is no church without them, and I am no Christian without them.

Excursus: "Samaritans in the Gayborhood" (Sermon Preached at the Wild Goose Festival, Summer 2015)

Just then a lawyer stood up to test Jesus. "Teacher," he said, "what must I do to inherit eternal life?"

He said to him, "What is written in the law? What do you read there?"

He answered, "You shall love the Lord your God with all your heart, and with all your soul, and with all your strength, and with all your mind; and your neighbor as yourself."

And he said to him, "You have given the right answer; do this, and you will live."

But wanting to justify himself, he asked Jesus, "And who is my neighbor?"

Jesus replied, "A man was going down from Jerusalem to Jericho, and fell into the hands of robbers, who stripped him, beat him, and went away, leaving him half dead.

"Now by chance a priest was going down that road; and when he saw him, he passed by on the other side.

"So likewise a Levite, when he came to the place and saw him, passed by on the other side.

"But a Samaritan while traveling came near him; and when he saw him, he was moved with pity. He went to him and bandaged his wounds, having poured oil and wine on them. Then he put him on his own animal, brought him to an inn, and took care of him.

"The next day he took out two denarii, gave them to the innkeeper, and said, 'Take care of him; and when I come back, I will repay you whatever more you spend.'

"Which of these three, do you think, was a neighbor to the man who fell into the hands of the robbers?" He said, "The one who showed him mercy." Jesus said to him, "Go and do likewise." (Luke 10:25–37)

The lawyer is good with all that talk about love. The lawyer just wants to know, "How far do I have to take this thing? Because I was born to help people,

Jesus. When they have a problem, they come to me. I've got answers; I've got solutions; I've got resources to share. But if I get spread too thin, I'm no help to anyone. Give me a measure. Give me a rule. Because I was born to help people, within the reasonable limits of my proximate neighborly obligation. How far does this thing go?" Or, in the ever more succinct rendering from Luke, "And who is my neighbor?"

The curtain opens on a motionless body, mostly obscured by the Joshua tree scrub that grows by the side of the road. We hear a low moan; we see a twitch of the exposed feet; the pain is unmistakable. There has been violence here. We have missed the main action and have arrived to witness the aftermath.

Enter stage right, a well-dressed somebody on her way to something big, something of which she is, no doubt, in charge. Noticing our casualty, she checks the time on her phone, shakes her head. People are waiting for her, people whose problems are her problems and her responsibility. She hurries on.

Not far behind her, another well-appointed traveler, another somebody with a destination, a schedule, and no time for the friction this complication will introduce. Entering stage right, crossing stage center, exiting stage left, and . . . scene!

Our victim languishes for lack of help.

I can see Luke's lawyer, in the front row of Jesus's audience, practically jumping out of his pew—"Pick me! Pick me!" Because he was born to help people. It's a sign, finding a wounded man by the side of the road. Our lawyer would stop, sure he would. Wouldn't you?

But the third act introduces a new character, a Samaritan, and surely you know that this is the one least likely to have a good reason to help, the best reason to walk on. Samaritans have to be careful. Traveling Samaritans have to be especially careful. Samaritans on the road in the vicinity of Jerusalem have to be doubly, triply on their guard. You can get pulled over just for "walking while Samaritan" in these parts. "You're not from around here, are you, boy?" the temple guard will ask with a sneer. And what happens after that is anybody's guess.

But the Samaritan, not the lawyer, is the one Jesus has chosen for the starring role, the neighborly exemplar whose own plans drive into the ditch he'll be pulling this guy out of. It'll be his resources shared—who even knew Samaritans had that kind of money?—and his instructions followed—who even knew Samaritans could manage a situation like that?

And it's clear to everyone, including our lawyer, that the Samaritan has rightly understood the boundaries of neighborliness—that is to say, there are none. Even when the neighbor-in-need is one who very likely despises you and everybody like you. Even when it feels dangerous to your person and your personhood. Mercy isn't measured; it's simply given wherever and whenever it is most necessary.

Which is all well and good, thinks the lawyer, but not the answer he was looking for. "Excuse me, sir, Jesus," he says. "I wanted to know, Where am I in your story? My honorable colleagues, the priest and the Levite, clearly don't understand you as well as I do. I'd've stopped to help; I know I would have. But I'm not even in your story, so I'm not sure you've answered my question. Who is *my* neighbor? Where beginneth and endeth my responsibility to the people who need something from me?"

"Oh, my friend," laughs Jesus, "don't tell me you didn't see yourself in that scene. You were on stage the entire time, till the Samaritan's ass carried you away. You, sir, were on the ground. You, sir, were the injured man."

Not so long ago my church was working hard to press the issue of marriage equality. In 2015 Texas had a marriage equality case before the Fifth Circuit Court, but there was a good chance the Supremes would rule before the Fifth got around to it. It was exciting, and to keep the pressure on and our spirits up, we were rallying in Dallas, holding signs that said, "God is love," in all the colors of the rainbow.

To one of those rallies, I drove. There were four gay men in my car, all in their twenties, who wanted to fortify themselves for the long-term struggle in the bars of the Gayborhood, and I was to be the designated driver. We marched and yelled and prayed and sang, and then it was time to party.

Or so I thought. As it turns out, my young friends weren't that interested in a party. What they really wanted to do was show me around a part of the city that had never been mine to explore. A dance hall where cowboys in hats and boots glide across the floor cheek to cheek, the finest Texas two-stepping I have ever seen. A loud place with a thumping bass beat that made the floor quiver and my head ache. A giant club with glow-in-the-dark drinks and body-to-body room only on the dance floor. We found a table at the last club, scooting in to watch the dancers, barely able to talk over the music. I was, um, not nervous, but not exactly in my comfort zone, you know what I mean? "I'm glad you're here," Kyle M. shouted directly into my ear.

You know, I had said those exact words to him probably one hundred times on my home territory, every Sunday at least, for two years, in the worship space our church rented in the back of a small-town, decidedly non-Gayborhood bar. I had stood at the table of our Lord and insisted loudly that all were welcome there. I had played the gracious host to these young men, feeling justified, I must confess, that I was doing my part to create space where they were welcome, where they would feel safe and beloved. I was born to help people, see, to use whatever privilege I've got to make things better for whomever needs my help.

But on this night, in the Gayborhood of Dallas, I was utterly out of my element. A het-cis woman in her (let's say mid-) forties, wearing sensible shoes and a sensible jacket for the rally, of course. Married a quarter-century, two teenaged kids to prove it, a hetero-ordinary life, and from the suburbs no less. An ally, sure, but also a fish out of water, not at home, not at all.

But here we were, my friends and I, gathered around this Dallas gay club table, laughing and yelling, clinking glasses. I slipped off my shoes under the table. I lay my hat on the table. I rested my elbow on the table. We made room for another couple of friends at the table. We ordered some appetizers for the table. We ate and drank from the table. We crammed in more chairs for more foot-weary dancers at the table. We moved another table to make a bigger table. The table, the table, the table, the table, the table, the *table*! It was a *table*, not mine but theirs, a table I had been welcomed to, though a stranger, though I was clearly passing through, out of my element, no longer the pastor or the welcomer-in-chief or even the designated driver, but a guest, one in need of help and welcome, one in need of love. "I'm so glad you're here!" Kyle shouted directly in my ear. "All are welcome at the table of our Lord!"

Well. He didn't actually say that last part. But he could have. It would have been true. We were on sacred ground in that pulsating light and throbbing music. *Their* sacred ground, not mine, but I swear all I could taste in those appetizers was unleavened bread and the fruit of the vine.

Jesus said, "Which of these three, do you think, was a neighbor to the man who fell into the hands of the robbers?" The lawyer said, "The one who showed him mercy." And maybe what the lawyer is supposed to see—

Oh, who gives a fuck what the lawyer is supposed to see? What matters is what you and I are supposed to see. And what if we are meant to see our woundedness, we who are the church? What if we are meant to see how utterly incapable of saving ourselves we are, much less offering help to anybody else? What if we're meant to see the ditch of our own institutional upkeep we've fallen into, how we've been robbed of purpose, beaten, and left for dead by the politicians who have used us for their money-making, war-making, self-making agenda?

What if we're meant to see how very dependent we are now on the kindness of the people we have scorned, or ignored, for the sake of our traditions and our doctrines and our institutional survival? What if we are meant to hope that some of them are still willing to take a chance on us, to offer us a hand up from this morass of self-preservation we've fallen into?

To be more specific, what if our neighbors in #blacklivesmatter protests this summer are the Samaritans who will save our lives just by uncovering and airing out the racist wound we have let fester, very often in the name of our Lord, for so long? What if our LGBTQ friends, especially in this moment our T-is-for-Trans friends, who insist simply on the basic human dignity of all people—an ethic Jesus insisted upon first—what if they are the ones who will notice us down here, kicked and robbed and bleeding out our tiny reserve of kindness, and extend a hand to us?

What if Jesus just isn't interested in my self-assessment as a helper who needs his guidance to set limits before I just give it all away? What if he knows better than that? About the lawyer, about me, about the church we love. In which case, we'd better be on the lookout for Samaritans, y'all. We need their help.

Nathan's Cello, Nathan's Self

About a month into our worship life, an old friend showed up. Actually, Ken and I had mutual friends and not much friendship of our own back then, but over the decades (!) he kept stepping into spaces where I was. He was always gentle, curious, and kind. When he stepped into Galileo's space, he said, "I have a son in college, Nathan, who plays the cello, who might like to come play here." I, knowing nothing about the cello and even less about Nathan, said, "I'd love to meet Nathan, anytime." I was noncommittal about the cello.

Pretty soon I was corresponding by email with Nathan, who did indeed want to play the cello for Galileo. I said, "What if you just *come* to Galileo for a bit without the cello, and we'll see what happens?" He did, and within a matter of weeks he was collaborating with the worship architect to add beautiful, low tones to Paul's guitar. We called him Paul's Consigliere-on-Cello, and scheduled monthly Cello Sundays.

A few months after that, Nathan asked to be baptized at our church. It hadn't really occurred to us that Nathan wasn't already baptized; he had grown up in church and was very committed to his faith. But he told me that he had never known a church that he wanted to be joined with in the sacrament. Darn good reason, right? So after he and I studied for a few weeks, Ken baptized him in the Adventists' sanctuary, as the tub in the G-House bathroom was seriously too small and we didn't have our trough yet. After his baptism we promptly added him to the church's leadership team.

A few months after that, in a leadership meeting, Nathan proposed an idea that pushed one of my buttons. I don't have many buttons, but this one was/is a big one, and I lashed out. I think my lashouts are pretty mild compared to some I've been on the receiving end of, but it was enough of a rebuke to set off Nathan's anxiety and shut him down for the rest of the meeting. I felt like shit and couldn't fix it on the spot without drawing more attention to Nathan, who had retreated into his hoodie like a turtle in its shell. So I wrote him an email late that night with the subject line "soft underbelly." I apologized for fucking up, for displacing my crap onto him, for not taking his idea more seriously and less personally. I revealed why I felt so vulnerable around his perfectly reasonable and generous proposal. I offered a way to fix what I had broken between us. He wrote back to say, more or less, "You're right; it hurt; and you are forgiven. Everybody has a soft underbelly, but not everybody admits it. And yeah, let's do your idea and fix it." I re-read both those emails every once in a while for my own good.

A few months after that, in a worship service celebrating our missional priorities, Nathan read our email exchange out loud to the whole church to exemplify our fourth missional priority: "We do real relationships, no bullshit, ever." He said, "This is what it means in our church: even our pastor will fuck up, and when she figures it out, she will apologize, and she will mean it. No bullshit means we all have to be ready to offer grace to each other." I swallowed hard. We were in uncharted waters. Not unlike baptism. We were dying to self. I was dying to self.

A few months after that, I hosted a house concert in my living room for a singer-songwriter whose music I love. He came down from Oklahoma with his little family, and his own consigliere-on-cello, and we had a grand weekend. Those musicians drink whiskey rather than beer and stay up rather later than my usual bedtime, so Saturday night stretched on and the whiskey settled in. Nathan stayed late too, and several hours after sundown asked if we could talk in a serious way, privately. I said, "Sure, let's walk around the block. But I'm going to have to hold your arm, and if you feel me leaning a little bit, it's the whiskey." I leaned more than a little bit, I'm sure.

We walked around the block about a zillion times while Nathan told me that his gender identity was in flux. He liked dressing in femme clothes. He liked to think of himself as *her*self. He didn't know where it would go or how it would resolve, but he wanted me to know. He was showing me his soft underbelly, trusting me not to hurt him. I think the whiskey and the Holy Spirit worked in concert to help me talk less and listen more. Let's call it a love-mixed-with-curiosity cocktail, shall we?

A couple of months after that, Nathan came to worship with a duffel bag. He disappeared into the bathroom and changed from his regular collegiate musician clothes into a short skirt and boots with impossibly high heels. We told him he looked terrific. He changed back before he left that night to go back to his dorm.

A few months after that, Nathan shaved off his long Rasputin beard and asked us to use she/her/hers pronouns. She was becoming the genderqueer person she felt herself to be. She would still be Nathan and still be our consigliere-on-cello (now, consigliera!) and still be our sibling through baptism into Christ our Lord—and she would be more of herself than she had ever been before. I can testify: there is *more* of Nathan now than there was before. And the world is better for having more of her in it.

It's only fair that Nathan gets to be Nathan's whole, entire self in the exact same space that I get to be my whole, entire self. Neither of us has to pretend anymore. Nathan doesn't pretend to be cisgender; I don't pretend to be invulnerable. What has become increasingly clear to me is that neither of us was keeping those secrets from God; God was only waiting for us to show each other what God already knew. So, yeah, to Nathan and everybody else who brings their soft underbelly to Galileo Church: I'll show you mine if you'll show me yours. We've got missional priorities that practically say we *have* to. To the glory of God. Amen.

Excursus: "Generation to Generation: Gender Role & Identity in the Church"

"Generation to Generation: Gender Role & Identity in the Church" was originally published in *Just Women*, Spring 2018.

Rev. Dr. Katie Hays, Lead Evangelist of Galileo Christian Church (Disciples of Christ) in the suburbs of Fort Worth, Texas, is 48 years old. She is a cisgender woman who grew up in the Church of Christ, where a strict patriarchy threatened her call to ministry. Nathan Berry, former co-president of the Missional Logistics Team of Galileo Church, is 24 years old. She is a genderqueer person who also grew up in the Church of Christ, where binary gender definitions threatened her full expression of self.

Nathan is in St. Louis on an XPLOR internship through the National Benevolent Association. Katie and Nathan had a conversation by email about gender role and identity in the church.

Katie: Nathan, one thing you and I have in common is how much of our identity development has to do with our self-understandings of our gendered selves; and how much those gendered identities were formed by the churches we grew up in.

Being a girl in a conservative church in the 1970s meant my voice was encouraged until adolescence, when I was expected to hush myself and learn how to serve quietly alongside the women of the church, including my strong and smart mother whose voice I respected deeply. I remember when my little brother was about 5 years old and he was invited to start helping in worship.

I was itching to be acknowledged as capable in our little congregation, but it simply could not be. It would be years before I could articulate a clear "call to ministry" because it simply was not allowed for girls and women to think that way. You can't hear God when you have never been invited to imagine God could be speaking to someone like you.

Nathan: From as early as I can remember I have wanted to express myself in a way that I now understand to authentically reflect who I am. However, because my birth certificate says "male," the church ingrained in me that any behavior that was outside the norms for "male" was sinful. As a result, for the first 20 years of my life I considered my desire to wear femme clothing, and to otherwise identify more closely with women than men, to be a weird sexual fetish.

Given how invested the conserving church is in the culture of sexual purity, it's no wonder that I developed a hard-wired sense of shame about who I knew myself to be. I buried my identity so deeply that before I could dig through the shame I had piled on top of myself, I had to first tear down the barriers in my mind between church and God's own desire for justice for all people, even people like me.

Katie: Shame is such a powerful weapon that churches usually don't even know they're wielding. The church communicates the mind of God to us, whether it intends to or not. Whatever the church thinks of us is what we assume God thinks of us; whatever the church wants for/from us is what we assume God wants for/from us.

In my case, there were these binary assumptions about gendered *roles*: men and boys do these things, behave this way, want and deserve a future of this kind. And that set is different and in most ways opposite for women and girls. My own abilities and interests and deep-down desires didn't fit the given role for women, so there was this inner conflict all the time.

For me, the conflict manifested as anger in my young adulthood. I was angry at the church, at the men who ran it, at the women who accepted it, at the historical power structure that ensured the status quo, and ultimately at God. I began to accuse God: "Why did you make me this way if I'm not supposed to be this way?" And Nathan, you know, because you've experienced me lashing out from the depths of it, that the anger of my youth can still be triggered today around these questions of role and power related to gender.

It's a heaviness that I pray to be released from, but it's also a fuel for the hard work of institutional reform.

Nathan: Those binary assumptions of gendered roles were pervasive in my own church experience as well, and my reaction to that went in a couple of directions: towards myself in the form of depression, and towards the church in the form of anger.

When I was very young I became passionate about justice for women, particularly within the church, and for LGBTQ+ equality; even though it was not safe for people in our church to openly advocate for such justice issues, let alone identify as a feminist or as a queer person. I did not yet have the vocabulary to articulate my identity, but something in me knew that I did not conform to the church's expectations of gender.

Toward my advocacy and toward my private development, the message I received from the church was the same: "You are a problem. Your existence is a burden, not a blessing. Leave who you are and what you care about at the door; they don't have a place in God's house."

I took these messages to heart. I became a perfectionist to a destructive extreme, and eventually every mistake I made (whether it was in school, social interaction, or anything else) drove my self-worth lower and lower. Negative feedback impacted me deeply, and positive feedback had little effect. That's an emotional imbalance that continues to be a part of my life.

However, I have always had a strong sense of fairness, and I knew that my church was harmful to many. So I also grew angry. I was angry that church leaders did not seem to care about how their theology was harming people. It wasn't fair that dissenting opinions were shut down. It was so easy for me to see that all of this was so *wrong*. How blind did they have to be to not see how wrong things were; or how selfish did they have to be to see it and just not care? By the time I went to college, moving away from the congregation I grew up in, I had become cynical and resentful towards church.

But here's what's funny to me, Katie: despite our similarly rocky histories with the church, and all the anger we confess, we are now quite "churchy" people. We have worked together happily in ministry at Galileo and can't imagine not being part of it! What did the journey between those two disparate points look like for you?

Katie: Honestly, I was just stubborn enough to keep beating my head against the church's wall. Church is in my bones; church is where I'm *from*, you know? They couldn't get rid of me. And it felt normal, I guess, that my church was a source of struggle and sorrow, because I didn't know any better.

But at a certain point, much later in my adulthood than you, I recognized that it's *not* normal. And it's unnecessary, if you can find a church that thinks you are *not* a "problem" to be dealt with.

So it required a transition to the Disciples of Christ, where justice for women was already happening, and where I thought I had no argument left to make. For a while, the acceptance itself was disorienting—like, how do I be part of a church with which I don't have to fight regarding my own personhood? How do I serve and lead and teach and learn in a system that has already made ample room for me?

It would be a little while before I understood that my acceptance in the Disciples of Christ was setting me on a platform from which I could advocate for the acceptance of . . . well, you, Nate. It felt like such a relief to have my own gender-based constraints dissolved; I didn't understand right away that gender-based constraints were still tightly wound around the Nathans of the world.

And when I think how close I came to missing you—I mean, a couple of years later on my own evolutionary timeline and you would've passed right by!—it makes my heart pound. And I feel the same way about all the LGBTQ+ people who are passing by our churches right this minute. They aren't going to wait for us to figure this out. At some point, people who have been told repeatedly that they don't belong start to believe it. And they disappear.

Why didn't you disappear? What made you keep seeking church, when church was the source of so much heartache?

Nathan: That's another reason I still deal with anger towards the church of my youth: while you wait for your congregants to get on board with progress, how many more marginalized people have to disappear? And how many more have to die? Because it's not just that they disappear from the church's pews. They disappear from this life.

As far as why I kept seeking out church, it comes down to two things: I am also exceptionally stubborn, and I had examples of people of faith who embraced God's justice that I found lacking in the churches I knew. My parents always pushed me toward basic fairness for all people. The theology of U2; Christian feminist writers; and a small circle of Christian friends who shared my convictions kept hope alive that faith and justice could co-exist.

There is a bitter irony that much of my understanding of God came from seeing church do things that I knew were not of God. I thought that if a church comprised of people like those who kept my faith alive existed, church could be worthwhile.

That's why I was willing to try out Galileo, but there are two reasons I stuck around. First, in an LGBTQ-affirming atmosphere free of patriarchal structures I could let my guard down enough to actually feel Jesus in the room.

Second, Galileo invited me to become a part of the group leading the church. In a church that wanted *all* of me, and wanted my thoughts and opinions, I was finally empowered to explore my authentic identity and deconstruct the shame that had accumulated around it.

At Galileo I became the person God made me to be. And now that I can confidently share my authentic self with the world, not only am I part of the church but I am doing ministry in and for and with the church. That would have been unthinkable to me six years ago.

Katie: That pretty much sums up our common experience: that the church can be the place where we are invited and empowered to be the people—not the roles, not the binary identities—but the *people* God made us to be. Or the church can be the place that diminishes and shames us for who God made us to be. There's so much power in the church. May God help us to be wise and kind with that power. I'm grateful to be in ministry alongside you, Nathan Berry. Peace to you.

Nathan: Peace to you.

Excursus: "It's Not Binary" (Blog Post, February 2016)

You already know that sexuality is on a spectrum, from super-gay to super-straight, with lots of people falling somewhere along the spectrum on one side or the other, and a couple of oddballs in the exact middle. (Just kidding, my bi friends. Chill.)

And you are learning that gender itself is on a spectrum, from all-the-way-male to all-the-way-female, with so many degrees of biological and emotional and social expression in between that it makes sense when some people identify as a gender other than the one they were assigned at birth.

Now here's a third spectrum that you probably want to know about: the range of responses to LGBTQ+ inclusion among people of faith. It turns out that there are *not* two kinds of people in the world, the homophobic, non-affirming nitwits and the purely good, #allmeansall advocates. Imagine that.

William Stacy Johnson points out in his book *A Time to Embrace: Same-Gender Relationships in Religion, Law, and Politics* (Eerdmans, 2006) that individual Christians and churches locate themselves all along a spectrum of acceptance to which he assigns seven numbers and descriptions. Here they are.

1. *Prohibition* does not approve of and seeks to ban same-gender relationships (and trans identity, etc.) in church and culture.

2. *Toleration* does not approve of but would not prosecute or reject LGBTQ+ people. A "don't ask, don't tell" attitude prevails here.

3. *Accommodation* does not approve of LGBTQ+ identity generally, but allows for exceptions, especially if someone they love comes out. "Hate the sin, love the sinner."

4. *Legitimation* wants to include LGBTQ+ persons in the community and church, and wants to protect individuals from being singled out or condemned. "They're people, too." "We're all sinners, you know."

5. *Celebration* believes that same-gender relationships and marriages should not be scorned but affirmed as good for individuals and for society.

6. *Liberation* views LGBTQ+ acceptance in the context of wider injustices in society, and seeks remedy for injustice generally.

7. *Consecration* argues for the full religious blessing of LGBTQ+ identity, including the sacrament of marriage.

I identify as a 7 on this scale, but that was not always the case. I remember being a 1, and a 2; and I remember the person I met who converted me to a 3. The ascent through 4, 5, and 6 was rapid and smooth, thanks be to God and the brave LGBTQ+ people who helped me figure it out.

So, when we're thinking about people we love who have not figured out how to love all people exactly as they are, can we imagine them as something other than hopelessly homophobic and hate-filled? Of course we can. With practice, and patience, and prayer, we can.

And maybe you find yourself somewhere on this spectrum, somewhere short of #7. And you're wondering whether <7 persons have a place at Galileo Church. Well, sure you do. Because you have a place in the heart of God. That's always been true, and it always will be.

God, as it turns out, is pretty good at this spectrum thing. And we're getting better at it all the time.

Yvonne, the Atheist Evangelist

She sent an email to our info@ address. "I don't believe in God, so perhaps you will not want to speak with me. But I have many questions about God." I wrote back: "When/where can we talk?"

She didn't have a car, so I drove up to her university and we met at the McDonald's across the street. It's a weird Mickey D's with lumpy concrete forms that serve as furniture on a little outdoor patio. We swiped the condensation off the seats and settled in.

It would be impossible for me to reconstruct that long conversation, because Yvonne is way smarter than I. She's from Hong Kong, and while earning a degree in physics at UTA she decided to do a second bachelor's degree in *philosophy*. In her *second language*. In her *second culture*. Both physics and philosophy were causing her to question the nature of existence, so she needed to talk with someone about God. She chose Galileo because she loved the name Galileo—thinking we would not shame her for being a scientist—and because she's queer. Nonbinary. Something. Doesn't matter. (I mean, of course Yvonne's identity matters, but she never made a big deal about picking a label, so I don't want to give it more attention than she did.)

I'm telling you, it changes everything when you start preaching and planning worship and writing Bible studies for Yvonne. No ontological claim can be assumed. She was never, ever rude (Yvonne is one of the kindest people I've ever known), but she was rigorous in her questioning of Christian faith claims. She made me a better Christian, y'all. We're hoping we made her a better agnostic, a better seeker of the truth she is ever after.

But what's really worth reporting here is that Yvonne told all her friends about Galileo Church. Queer friends, science-y friends, one and all. She told them that we were smart and unafraid and funny and queer and kind, just the kind of people she really liked hanging out with. When she graduated from UTA, we threw her a party, to which she invited #schoolfriends to meet #churchfriends. One of those #schoolfriends was Ros.

Ros grew up locally, in a family that loved her gay self, in a church that didn't. She was earning a PhD in social work at UTA, researching the intersection of queer identity and religious identity. She partied down with us for Yvonne's graduation and just never left. In short order Ros was a leader at Galileo, helping us organize our first peer-to-peer support group for LGBTQ young-uns. It was kinda perfect: we had Ros, a black, queer woman, paired with Travis, a white, straight man (and a PhD candidate in pastoral theology) for the facilitation of It Gets Better (a previous iteration of what is now called Thrive).

And Ros introduced us to Jenny, a Vietnamese American convert to Islam, and Jenny introduced us to Munira, her Muslim sister friend. There have been seasons in which Jenny attended a covenantal G-group faithfully because being a queer Muslim woman in Texas cuts down your options for mosque membership. Progressive Muslims in our neck of the woods have more in common with progressive Christians than either of us do with the fundamentalist folks on our respective religious spectrums. (Spectra? Whatever.)

And Jenny and Munira have brought lots of friends to Galileo worship both times we've invited them to present their everyday faith to us. "The Coolest Muslims We Know" Q&A forum is one of our favorite explorations of how young adults work through faith, religious tradition, queerness, and prejudice in this very conserving cultural milieu. Like with Yvonne, we learn better how to articulate what is essential and particular about Christian faith when we are in conversation with people who are equally serious about their commitments and genuinely curious about ours.

Last we heard, Yvonne the atheist evangelist was in France working on the Large Hadron Collider for CERN. She sends us postcards once in a while. I hope she's still telling people about Galileo Church and asking hard questions of all the Christians she meets.

Excursus: "I Saw the Kin-Dom of God Last Night" (Blog Post, August 2016)

I saw the kin-dom of God last night. I've been busy today, no time to write, but I thought you'd be mad if I saw it and didn't tell you about it.

(Sometimes these days I experiment with saying "kin-dom" instead of "king-dom" because while I believe God's sovereignty is a Big Deal, I'm almost sure God is always using God's power to draw people together, like family, like love, like kin.)

Last night there was an "It Gets Better" meeting. You know, people a lot younger than I getting together to talk about their lives. Specifically, about their lives as LGBTQ+ people—the queer and beautiful people of God—though they are sometimes not so sure about the "beautiful" or the "of God" part of that. So they talk about it.

I guess they talk about it. I never actually go in there; that meeting isn't for me. I have to be there because I'm the one with a Mansfield address so I can rent that room in that place. Galileo pays for the room. Galileo pays me to go sit in the lobby and work a little and pray a little for the group that is meeting behind a closed door a few yards away.

And somebody else from Galileo sent homemade cookies last night, cookies of a kind I cannot get out of my head. Yes, they shared one with me. Sweet baby Jesus, those cookies were good, and the milk that came with them. The cookies were not the point, but they could have been. They were that good.

But the people. The people were the point. They met for the 90 minutes that we were on the books for that room, and then they shambled into the public space where I was, only they weren't ready to leave. By accident they formed themselves back into a circle, standing now, and talked some more. Laughing. Bending at the waist from laughing. Heads thrown back, laughing.

And oh, I wish you could have seen it. They were dark brown and light brown and peachy-pinky-yellow. They were all the colors, a rainbow of God's beloveds. They were Christian, Muslim, decidedly non-religious. Students, workers, wishing for work. In relationships. Alone. Lonely. Content. Depressed and joyful, anxious and brave. Women and men, all along a spectrum, just themselves.

Laughing.

Their departure from the building and the parking lot took another 45 minutes, I'm guessing. Forty-five of those kin-dom of God minutes, precious minutes during which every single person knows for absolute certain that they are God's children, beloved by God, with whom God is well pleased. Transfigured, bright shining as the sun.

I know, because I saw it. With that vision in my recent memory, I am the luckiest person on God's green earth today. So I thought I would share it with you, so you could feel lucky, too.

I Can't Always Get What I Want

And then there was that time I argued for a change in our missional priorities, and I lost.

After the Supreme Court's *Obergefell* decision for marriage equality in June 2015, I suggested at a leadership team meeting that we should shift our justice focus (missional priority 1, "We do justice for LGBTQ+ people") to focus on #blacklivesmatter, joining a growing wave of progressives protesting police violence against black bodies. I figured that after the Supreme Court ruling, injustices against LGBTQ+ people would fall like so many judicial dominoes.

Others in leadership said I was an idiot, not to put too fine a point on it. "This work is far from finished," they said. Kind of loudly, but still respectfully, over wine at Palio's Pizza, with our neighbors listening in. Never underestimate the power of having church leadership meetings in public places; your conversations will always, always be about things that *matter*, and you will really have to think about what your neighbors will assume your church actually cares about, depending on the meeting's agenda and how you treat each other when you disagree.

There was no vote that night about missional priority 1. I'll say it again: we've never actually voted on anything at Galileo, because if a bunch of Spirit-filled people who love each other can't reach consensus about something, maybe that means they don't know what to do yet. We sometimes don't know what to do yet. So we wait.

And that night, nobody was saying, "We'll never relinquish missional priority 1." But people whom I love and trust were saying, "It's not time yet." So I backed off.

The next year, in mid-2016, we addressed it again. It seemed true that LGBTQ rights were being worked out in the courts, and there was still so much work to do around racism, white privilege, and the whole system of white supremacy upon which our country is built. We had to confess, though, that lots more of us Galileo-ans were white than not. We didn't even know how to get into that racial justice conversation with integrity. We decided to ask the church to spend a year in discernment with us, listening and learning about intersectionality—the reality that we are all complex entanglements of identities, including race, including sexuality, including gender identity, including class. We put together a curriculum for that year's study, and here are the highlights:

We bought forty copies of Ta-Nehisi Coates's *Between the World and Me*, asked the church to read it, and set up five conversation groups about it. We invited Sandhya Jha, one of our denomination's go-to voices for antiracism education, to do a long-form intersectionality seminar. We hosted Allyson Robinson, trans activist Baptist preacher, for preaching and conversation around her, and our, various ways of belonging. We asked Nancy Ramsay, professor of pastoral theology at Brite Divinity School, to lead us in a privilege walk, highlighting the various ways that Galileo Church itself houses an immensely diverse collection of intersectional identities. We read. We processed. We prayed. We spent over a year learning intersectionality, right on through 2017, right on up to The Election.

The Election blew a gigantic hole in our confidence that the world (or at least our American corner of the world) was getting safer for LGBTQ+ persons. The dog-whistling, the gaslighting, the emboldening of bigotry of all kinds—we were afraid like we had not been afraid before. Every day after the inauguration there was new cause for alarm. Would marriages between gay people be honored? Would name and gender-marker changes for trans people still hold? Would basic civil rights for LGBTQ+ people be protected? Would hate crimes be named and prosecuted?

After The Election the Texas legislature found new energy for inflicting meanness. A "bathroom bill" was introduced, but not passed, during the regular legislative session. The lieutenant governor called the legislators back in the summer of 2017, saying he would not let them adjourn until they passed the bill restricting public bathroom use for transgender people. The church tweeted, "[The Texas lieutenant governor] is a terrorist, holding #txlege hostage, demanding #trans lives as ransom." All spring and summer long, we sent beloveds to Austin, paying for gas and meals and whatever else it took for them to testify and protest and lobby at the state capitol. We sent homemade cookies to our representatives, in the mode of cookie evangelism, with notes that said we wanted to complicate their votes so they would stop imagining that all of their deeply religious constituents believe the same thing about the humanity of LGBTQ+ persons. Also, the note said the cookies were made by LGBTQ+ people, so, you know, eat at your own risk.

We spent a ton of money in 2017 fighting that ridiculous legislation, about 300 percent more than we had budgeted. We asked our generous friends to help us make up for it, and they did. Thanks be to God.

With respect to our first missional priority: at the time of this writing, it remains specific to LGBTQ+ persons. But Galileo Church has recently experienced several months' worth of fierce womanist preaching from Rev. Dr. Irie Lynne Session; a bunch of us have participated in a reading group on white fragility; and we remain committed to further conversation around broadening our justice focus to include more identities than only LGBTQ+. It's on the table, I'm saying. We're holding lightly, I'm saying. I don't always get what I want, I'm saying. But eventually, God will. And through the embodiment of our missional priorities, we'll keep trying to want what God wants. That's really it: we want to want what God wants.

Excursus: A Pastoral Letter (February 2017)

Galileo Church
February 3, 2017

Dearly beloved,

Grace and peace to you in the name of God our Parent and the Lord Jesus Christ.

I'm writing this longish letter to communicate some things I've been thinking about the life, health, work, and care of our church. I've consulted with the church's servant-leaders (the Missional Logistics Team and the Care and Feeding Team) for help with these thoughts, and I'm grateful for their discerning wisdom.

1. A pastoral observation

We observe that it's been a grueling social-political season these past few months. Our families, our work places, our schools, and just about every public space are buzzing with conflict, negativity, and alarm. There is an onslaught of news every day, much of it truly frightening. Basic protections and kindnesses we thought we could take for granted, for ourselves and our neighbors, are jeopardized.

Many of us have reported feeling increased anxiety tending toward terror. Many of us convert fear into anger tending toward rage. These feelings can fuel productive action, but they can also lead to spiritual exhaustion, both personal and communal. Spiritual exhaustion often takes the form of overwhelming hopelessness. Negative changes seem sudden; working for positive change seems discouragingly slow.

2. The church's dilemma

The church in every place and every season is called to be engaged with the world God loves, speaking out against injustice and working diligently to pull God's future into this present moment, especially on behalf of neighbors who have less voice and more to lose. Galileo Church is committed to having a public voice in the cultural conversation about who has value (every human being!) and how our government demonstrates human value through public policy decisions. We are an activist church, and our voice has gotten stronger over our few years together, with the Spirit's help.

At the exact same time, the church in every place and every season is called to provide sanctuary from the world's brokenness. God intends that our communal life would produce peace in our hearts, and strengthen us for our individual lives. We are meant to multiply hope and joy for and with each other—not fake optimism or false cheer, but the deep-down hope and joy that come from remembering that God is in charge, despite all appearances to the contrary, even when we are in distress. This is our work for each other, and we're pretty good at that, too, with the Spirit's help.

The dilemma is, sometimes our call to prophecy (justice! engagement! protest!) and our call to pastoral care (kindness, sanctuary, caregiving) are in conflict with each other. Pastoral care can tend toward a kind of slothful escape from reality—not really our tendency. Prophetic engagement can tend toward a kind of alarmist frenzy—oops.

3. Recommendations

Keeping in mind that dilemma, and our collective preference for activism tending toward alarmism, we make the following recommendations.

a. **Be careful with yourself,** for the sake of your mental and spiritual health. Absorb news and social media judiciously. Curate your feeds in Facebook, Twitter, etc., so that you're not assaulted with content that scares or enrages you so often. Listen to or read enough news to stay current, but try not to obsess. Choose a reliable newspaper online and check those headlines, rather than letting social media curate all the news you receive. Try using the "Groups" app for Facebook to stay connected while avoiding the triggery stuff that steals your hope.

b. **Employ your *personal* social media voice with confidence.** Use it to inform each other about things you've learned from good, reliable sources. Recommend good reading to your web of connection. Announce your own actions with clarity and pride: "Here's what I'm reading; here's the next action I'm taking; here's what I'm praying for; here's where I gave money." Reveal yourself as an engaged Christian who actively loves this world God loves—whatever form that love takes for you.

c. **Let Galileo Church remain a haven from the chaotic urgency of every alarm.** We do not mean that we are squelching political conversation at Galileo; we just mean that there are better and worse ways to have that conversation.

Please don't:

• **Please don't post each new Trumpian assault in the Galileo Facebook group.** Not everybody agrees on everything all the time. (For example, in the case of the Uber CEO who was on the president's economic council—some of us wanted to boycott Uber, while some of us make our living driving for Uber. Another example: some people think all our energy should go toward getting one Cabinet appointment disapproved, while others are much more worried about a Supreme Court appointment. Priorities differ; positions differ; even as we find common ground in wanting to make the world a more just and generous place. Respect the difference.)

- **Please don't post language that makes it sound like everyone should show their activism in the same way.** Some people are energized by public protest; others are praying powerfully at home; others have money to share to shore up front-line justice work; others are powerfully engaged in social media activism. It's easy to insist that "everybody" or "we all" should show up or write a letter or make a call or give money or retweet—but it's almost never true or helpful.

- **Please don't commandeer our weekly G-group conversations** with litanies of political/social bad news, to the neglect of other kinds of conversation. People are still seeking work, coming out, grieving loss, celebrating change, loving their kids and dogs and cats; and all these things still need to be shared. Our G-groups are a great place to practice loving the neighbor who is sitting right in front of you. Some of our groups really enjoy political conversation, we know; perhaps they can consider setting aside a designated amount of time for it, then letting it go? We will not run out of bad news to share, it seems. But we can be the boss of how much of it we need on any given day.

Please do:

- **Please do continue diligently in the disciplines of prayer and communal study of the Bible**. Our G-groups are a rare opportunity to consult with each other about God's beautiful vision of the world God wants. Use your time together to do the things churches do—Bible study and prayer, shared over food and drink as a sign of God's generous provision to us. Consider also whether your group might benefit from reading books that help inform the Christian way of life in the worst of times. Your church leaders have suggestions, if you need some.

- **Please do let your discipleship of Jesus call you into deeper engagement with the world God loves.** Follow your passion into activism—protest, boycott, write letters, phone the reps, whatever works for you—and share your experiences through your *personal* social media, so your church friends can rejoice with you and pray for you.

- **Please do trust the missional priorities of Galileo Church to guide our communal action,** developed over several years together, through the Spirit; derived from our strengths and gifts; and flexible enough to shift with our growing life in Christ.
- **Please do trust the theologian-in-residence** (that's me!) to continue to connect Biblical theology to the world as it is, always. The teaching and preaching we share is meant to show us each how to be the light of Christ in and for the world.
- **Please do trust the Missional Logistics Team** to call us to communal action when the time is right. We are keeping alert concerning local, state, and national policy issues that connect with our missional priorities. We are seeking opportunities for Galileo Church to exercise its voice all together. If you have ideas about that, you can contact any of the MLT members: Aisling, Allison, Corina, Kaytee B, Malcolm, Nathan, or Susan.
- **Please do trust the Spiritual Care Team** to care for you in your distress and to strengthen you for good work in the world. You can call on any of our shepherds for help: Aaron, Francine, Harmony, Jenny, Kyle M., Missy, Ros, or Travis.

4. Confession and benediction:

Your church leaders don't know yet exactly what Galileo Church is called to do and be in this new season. Most of us have never lived through anything like this. So we are working on it, faithfully and prayerfully. Will you pray for us, as we pray for you?

Receive this blessing from the ancient church, still our promise and our hope:

May the God of peace, God's own self, sanctify you entirely.
May your spirit and soul and body be kept sound and blameless
at the coming of our Lord Jesus Christ.
The one who calls us is faithful. God will do this.
(1 Thess. 5:23–24)

grace and peace,
Katie,
in consultation with the Missional Logistics Team
and the Spiritual Care Team

Excursus: Letter to Our Legislators (July 2017)

Dear legislator,

We know you're on your way to Austin for a special session of the Texas Legislature. We thought you might like some sweet treats to take with you. As you nibble, we ask you to consider:

- These cookies were made for you by devout Christians who believe that God made, knows, and loves all people, including LGBTQ+ people.
- *Because of our Christian faith*, we are deeply opposed to legislation that discriminates against LGBTQ+ people. We believe that such laws promote fear, distrust, and even violence among neighbors.
- The legislation we're talking about includes *any* form of "bathroom bill" that requires transgender or gender-non-conforming people to use the bathroom that matches their gender assignment at birth. That's a silly and mean-spirited idea that will, for example, "out" kids at school who would otherwise blend in with their friends. Bullying, emotional distress, self-harm, and even death by suicide are outgrowths of systemic discrimination against LGBTQ+ people. You can help prevent this by protecting trans kids and adults with your vote.
- Additional legislation we oppose: any kind of "religious exemption" law that allows individuals and/or businesses to discriminate against LGBTQ+ people (or anybody else) when they imagine their religious beliefs call for it. Medical professionals, civil servants, nonprofit organizations that serve the public, entrepreneurs—these should all be prepared to serve, protect, help, and do business with *all* people. Our opposition to "religious exemption" laws is based on our deep commitment to Christian faith.

We think it's highly unlikely that we will change your mind about these issues. But we want to complicate your vote: don't imagine that by supporting "conservative" social policy you are a standard-bearer for all Christian people.

We're calling these cookies "Stubborn Hope Sweets" because we keep stubbornly hoping that our political system will help curb citizens' anxiety and suspicion; instead producing compassion and generosity through policies that protect the most vulnerable of our neighbors. We stubbornly hope that policymakers such as yourself can actually do that. You and your colleagues are in our prayers as you head back to Austin.

grace and peace to you

—the co-conspirators and friends of Galileo Church

Mansfield • Kennedale • Burleson • Fort Worth • Arlington • DFW

Lead Evangelist Rev. Dr. Katie Hays • katie@galileochurch.org • 817-773-XXXX

Excursus: "Overspend, Overspend! For the Love of God, Overspend!" (Blog Post, September 2017)

We need your help. **We overspent, by a lot.** And we're still spending.

Here's what happened. In our 2017 Ministry Finance Plan, we budgeted $1,800 on "justice for LGBTQ+ people." It should have been enough.

But who knew 2017 would be like this? Who knew the Texas State Legislature, in particular, would devote so much energy to stripping the rights and dignity of LGBTQ+ people (heavy emphasis on "T")? Who knew the national environment of acceptance and fairness would melt so quickly under a new administration? (Okay, maybe you knew, but we didn't.)

So we have spent more money than we planned. Like, a *lot* more. On things like these:

- January: We took **rainbow-frosted donuts** to protest (sweetly) the anti-LGBTQ meanness mailed from a nearby church to every household in that town. We gave away the donuts outside that church.
- January: We sent two learners to the **Gay Christian Network** conference in Pittsburgh.
- January: We sent six learners to the Texas Tribune's **Race & Public Policy conference** in Austin.
- February: We hosted a visit, a seminar, and a sermon from **Rev. Allyson Robinson,** pastor-preacher-trans-activist.
- February: We sent one learner to **ClexaCon** in Las Vegas, a conference advocating equity for queer women characters in TV and movie storylines. (We're pretty sure she was the only one whose church paid her way . . .)
- March: We offered **free *tae kwon do* self-defense training** for vulnerable LGBTQ+ people.
- March: We showed up for **local parade and booth activism** in our suburban home base.
- April: We hosted a big screen **viewing of *Gender Revolution,*** the National

Geographic documentary on gender, in partnership with Transcendence International.

- April: We hosted an **anti-racism / intersectionality workshop** (and preaching!) by **Sandhya Jha,** co-sponsored with the Trinity-Brazos Area.
- May: We sent three learners to the **Contemporary Relationships Conference** in Houston, a weekend with special emphasis on strengthening **LGBTQ+ couples.**
- June: We hosted **Trans Ally Training** with Transcendence International, and provided free dinner for all.
- Spring & Summer: We **paid for numerous trips—so many! —to Austin** to lobby, protest, challenge, and enlighten our **Texas State legislators** concerning discriminatory legislation, including several G-people who **testified before the Senate and House Committees** concerning the **"bathroom bills"** that threatened all summer long.
- June: We delivered **homemade cookies to our local legislators** as they prepared to return to Austin for the special session, asking that our Christian witness to God's inclusion of all people be allowed to **"complicate your vote."**
- September: We set up a booth presence at the UTA at Activities Fair and **Rainbow Reception for LGBTQ+ students.**
- We supply monthly rental and refreshment costs for **It Gets Better,** a peer-to-peer conversation group for young adults around LGBTQ+ identity, going on three years now.
- We incurred a few printing costs for the **"justice table"** in the Big Red Barn, helping people stay aware of current threats to civil liberties for LGBTQ+ persons, with ways to reach out to legislators at every level.

And there's still more on our calendar for the remaining months of 2017. We're christening a brand-new float for the **Tarrant County Pride Parade** in October, laying hands on it to bless its witness during worship the weekend before. (We'll roll it right through the big garage door into the barn.)

Bottom line: our total spending for the year, against that budget of $1,800, is **closer to $5,200 at this point,** the treasurer tells me. Almost three times what we planned. **300%.** With more to come.

So . . . don't these things sound like the kinds of things a church should be overspending on? If we're gonna blow the budget, isn't this the way to do it—by announcing loudly, proudly, everywhere we can think of, that **God's love**

is the only law, the realest thing in the world, the beginning and ending of every conversation about what really matters?

And if you think that's true, can you help replenish our coffers? We're not broke, but it's tight. And frankly, we think there are **people out there who would** *love* **to fund this kind of ministry,** specifically and strategically. We think it's good work, and exactly the work God has called and equipped us to do. You could help with the "equipping" part by **clicking the "donate" button** right down there. Thanks for considering. Peace of Christ to you and yours.

Excursus: "I've Been Away So Long" (Blog Post, February 2018)

Tamara, a newish soul at Galileo Church, posted one night in our Facebook group, where we share prayer requests and knock-knock jokes and outrage and other stuff. We shared her post on our blog as an extraordinary example of what can happen when spiritual refugees are invited back into the spaces they were once excluded from. "This is how the Spirit of the living Christ works in us," I wrote as an introduction to the post.

I hope it isn't too late to post on the page, but I need to share. I just got home from a very fun night with S and J, who are great friends and fellow musicians. Even though J and S are very liberal, they have some friends that come to hear them play who are not particularly my cup of tea.

I've tried so hard for a couple of years to keep my distance from a particular couple among their friends. His FB posts are Anti-Everything-I-Believe and I have personally witnessed him being an absolute dick to his wife. I've just thought it best for him and me to not have that confrontation. It's always been very cordial and polite; you know, the plastic, "Hi, how are ya"; "Good, thank you."

BUT as it happens, I was leaving the event tonight and they happened to be fumbling around trying to figure out how to do the Uber thing. Something came over me and I said, "Get your asses in the truck; I'll take you home." Jesus!!! Must have been the whiskey!

Just so happens, he had a serious health scare in December. I had kept an eye on it via FB just to make sure the ol' SOB made it. Obviously he did.

They got in my truck and off we went. I spent the next hour-and-a-half visiting with them. Keep in mind, I've known these people for a couple of years, but just refused to get too close because he is such an old, white man with conservative leanings. Royal asshole!!!

(It's not that I can't love someone like that. I just don't want to tell him to his face what a jackass he is, and he makes me so mad!)

SO, we talked, laughed, and sang songs; and I told him how lucky he was to be alive, and how he should appreciate his wife more because without her he would be a dead piece of crap. My words exactly! He hugged me and complimented me, told me how much he admired me, blah blah . . . I took a few deep breaths, then hugged him back. And then . . .

I headed home and tears filled my eyes. I began to think: "It's Galileo's fault!!! I want to NOT LIKE them so much!!"

Maybe, just maybe, I've spent the last 25 or so years filled with anger, resentment, suspicion, caution—and now I have to face the fact that for my life to be peaceful, I have to accept the people I just don't like. I guess it is after all, "What Jesus would do?" UGH, I really hate that phrase, but I know it is the ultimate goal and where I will find the ultimate peace.

Sorry if this sounds like the ramblings of a fool. I've been away so long, it's hard to be open and vulnerable again. I really just don't want to. I don't want to. But here I am.

Bathrooms, Coffee, and the Reign of God (Spring 2016)

Then there was that time we drove out to Rockwall to attend the city council meeting. Rockwall is a little town on the far east side of Dallas, a long drive from Galileo territory. But their mayor had introduced a local version of a "bathroom bill" requiring citizens to use public bathrooms that match the gender identity on their birth certificate. Rockwall is a small town, and to be honest some of us social justice sophisticates were pretty sure their citizens wouldn't know how to articulate a good argument against such a law. We decided to make the hike.

I drove with Glenna, a trans grandpa/ma who is known to me only as Glenna, the lovely soul who texts me every several days to simply say, "Katie, I hope you have the best day." Seriously, I have scores of those on my phone. Glenna never asks for anything; she only wants me to "have the best day." I got to hear some of Glenna's life story on the way to Rockwall, and I treasured that time.

What happened when we got there was also lovely. There were a few hundred people there, far more than could fit in the city council's chambers. The mayor announced that only Rockwall residents would be allowed to speak during public comments because there were far too many of us signed up. Those of us who had driven a long way to get there, who feared what would happen if this local law became a precedent for other municipalities, groaned.

And then, one by one, the small-town citizens of Rockwall stood up and told their city council members why they didn't want this kind of law in their town. It was mean-spirited, they said. It was unnecessary, they said. One man said, "Mr. Mayor, we've been friends for a long time. You keep talking about protecting everybody from everybody else's private parts in public restrooms. What I want to know is, brother, what kind of public restrooms are you using?" In the end, after all that public comment, the mayor's motion died for lack of a second. Not a single city council member was willing to assist his bigotry and fear-mongering.

It was like that scene in Stephen King's *The Stand*, where East Texas and the other guys go to Las Vegas thinking they're supposed to stop the destruction, but really it turns out they were only meant to *witness* the salvation brought about in the most unlikely way. Trust me on that one if you haven't read it.

What I mean is, it was incredibly uplifting and humbling all at the same time to remember that we don't have a lock on virtue, that God speaks to and through all kinds of people, not just the ones we like or expect. And because it was so uplifting and humbling, I told everybody that story a *bunch* of times. Including the G-Study group meeting at America's Best Coffee on Wednesday mornings. I told them about it with gusto: about the lovely car ride with Glenna, about the angry mayor, about the humble saints in Rockwall, about our shock and delight at the outcome. The G-Study group was a terrific audience, egging me on, the celebration heightening.

Out of the corner of my eye, I could see a young woman with a little child sitting nearby, having coffee and cocoa, respectively. The woman kept glancing over at us; I knew they could hear everything we were saying. When they finished their drinks, depositing cups and napkins in the trash, they took a couple of steps toward us. The woman cleared her throat. "Excuse me," she said. "I couldn't help but overhear what you were talking about."

"Oh shit," I thought. "I really should've toned down that telling. Mansfield moms don't want their little girls hearing this kind of stuff—private parts, bathrooms, gender identity . . . "

"What I wanted to ask you is," said Mansfield Mom, whose actual name is Hannah, and whose daughter's name is Zoe, "where is this church you're talking about? And can we come? Because my husband and I wish we had one, but we've never heard of a church like yours."

Ah, see? God knew I wouldn't catch it the first time, the lesson about how I do not know who thinks what just by looking at them, about how I am not the judge of people's hearts, about how humans are infinitely varied and infinitely beautiful in their variation. Rockwall, then Hannah, two in a row, and maybe now I've understood. But please, God, keep showing me anyway, because these are the encounters that fuel my spirit.

Neurodiversity, Unpacked

Our second missional priority, "We do kindness for those with mental illness, or in emotional distress; and we celebrate neurodiversity," is a mouthful. Doesn't exactly roll off the tongue. But it says some important things. For one, it doesn't overpromise. "Doing justice," as in our first missional priority, is a tall order requiring an activist mind-set. "Kindness" feels more realistic for what we have resources to do concerning neurodiversity, and combined with our fourth missional priority (the "no bullshit" one), it produces a community that is forthright about and appreciative of the different ways our different brains work.

This is what this particular kindness looks like at Galileo. Worship is never boring, but mostly predictable. There is an order of worship, not written down for every worshiper, but recognizable after you've been there a couple of times. Transitions are marked with "stitching," a way of pulling the pieces together and giving sufficient instruction so that anyone can join in. Movement around the space is encouraged. An invitation is spoken at the opening of the service: "This service is designed to help draw your heart near to the heart of God. But if at any point you find that it's not working for you, that you need something else, please feel free to do that."

There are individual marker boards and dry-erase markers in bags for any worshiper who needs a hand-eye activity to help them listen or stay calm. Reflection stations each week are multisensory, often not requiring reading or writing for participation. There is a quiet room in the back that we point out in the welcome each week: "In the Quiet Room, you can expect quiet, if not solitude." There are disposable ear plugs in there for anyone who needs them, plus grown-up coloring books and lots of colored pencils. We have mostly kept our kids from spending the entire service in there playing games on their phones unless said kids seriously need to check out from the big group, which some of them do sometimes.

No fluorescent lights anywhere. Low lighting in the main worship space. No loud drumming. Unscented candles. Body prayers that call for gross motor movement. Trigger warnings if we're going to pop balloons or make other sudden, loud noises.

Roles for worship leadership for anybody who wants to help. Grace when that worship leadership doesn't go exactly as anyone expected.

A picnic table outside under a shade cloth, with a flowerpot ashtray. We recognize that some people need to disengage from what's happening inside but want to stay proximate to that safe space. It's okay. We trust everyone to know what they need. It's not infantilizing; it's giving options to everyone.

In Bible studies, if there's round-robin reading aloud, we always say, "If anybody doesn't want to read tonight, just say pass." Same for praying or sharing in a circle or whatever. It's never compulsory; nor is it assumed that everybody knows it's not compulsory. The weekly query that begins worship gets two minutes for conversation with a neighbor, but we say, "If you prefer not to talk tonight, just bow your head and close your eyes and nobody will give you a hard time."

Some of our leaders don't process well on the fly, but after a couple of days, they have thoughts that are important. We're learning to respect the delay. (Or maybe I'm the one who's hasty, and their "delay" is actually contemplative and wise. It's worth considering.)

Perhaps most importantly, we don't hug each other without asking. It's not a rule, exactly; it's more of a community practice that people pick up from being asked themselves: "Are you hugging today?" Even kids get to say, "No, but here's a fist bump." We recognize that not everybody likes being touched the same as everybody else and that people feel differently about it on different days. Which is completely fine. There's nothing particularly Christian about hugging, you know? (Jesus wasn't a hugger. Or at least we don't know that he *was*.) And if a body prayer calls for laying a hand on a neighbor's shoulder or grabbing someone's hand, we invite those who don't wanna to "give yourself a hug instead." That way we who are chronically extroverted know whom to let be.

Our kids' group has run for a long time as a one-room schoolhouse, but sometimes it makes sense to separate the kids who want to have a mature theological discussion from the ones who happily join in making crafts, acting out stories, or playing games that are geared to let everyone participate. But we're trying real hard not to say "little kids" and "big kids," or "kids group" and "youth group." We find that some young kids are smart and mature and need to be in the discussion-based group, and some kids who are chronological "youth" may actually flourish in the activity-based group. We let them decide along with their parents.

I've mentioned already our three, facilitated, peer-to-peer groups: Thrive for LGBTQ+ older teens and young adults, GPS (God-Parenting-Support) for parents of LGBTQ+ kids, and Welcome to My Brain for adults with mental health diagnoses. All of these groups honor the neurodiversity of the people who come, provide safe space for disclosure and discussion of all kinds of emotional distress, and serve to destigmatize the very human need for trusted friends who can listen in love. Facilitators of the groups have gone through extensive training with a psychotherapist who is a Galileo co-conspirator. We're not messing around with people's psyches, you know?

Welcome to My Brain actually began as a one time event in 2017, an open-mic night with the subtitle "an evening of art inspired by neurodiversity, mental illness, and emotional distress." For two hours on a Friday night an incredible range of vulnerable and mighty souls sang and spoke their truth to the world in the Big Red Barn. Some of those people had never spoken or sung into a microphone before. Some people brought paintings and papier-mâché and poems that we displayed around the space. I gasped and cried and shouted alleluias all night long. It was all our missional priorities rolled into one. It was so beautiful, the offering up of all that truth telling to our God Who Is Beautiful.

That night ended the way such nights often do: with a sing-along of Bill Withers's "Lean on Me," made gender inclusive, made every-human-being inclusive. It was our pledge to each other to be kind by being present and available and telling the truth about ourselves as best we can. Bill knew the no-bullshit ethic:

> *Please swallow your pride*
> *If I have things you need to borrow*
> *For no one can fill*
> *Those of your needs*
> *That you won't let show.*

What if church could be the place that your needs *can* be filled because here you *can* let them show?

Song, Vera, Finn

For Song's baptism at the theater a few months after Caroline's, we did it all again—propane, hoses, heater, pump, the whole shebang. Song has a slew of siblings plus parents who love her, so it was hard for her to choose just one beloved to join us in the baptistery and help me bury her under water. But ultimately she chose Vera, one of several sibs with Down syndrome.

But let's back up: Song and Vera were the daughters of Jill, who has eight kids altogether, some of them adopted, some of them bio. Jill married Tricia, mom of three. I don't know that I ever saw all of them in one place except at the Jill and Tricia wedding. Jill and her kids used to attend a fundagelical church where at some point her three kids with Down syndrome were disallowed from receiving communion because they couldn't pass some kind of doctrinal test to prove their understanding. (Although, if I know Jill, she never let any of her kids take such a "test" because she fiercely believes God is not *like* that. Anyway, who "understands" communion? Or any sacrament? Come on.)

At Galileo Church, not only could Jill and Tricia be married but *all* their kids could participate in worship in any way they wanted. The main thing sixteen-year-old Vera wanted was to sit on the front row, right next to me, every Sunday of the world. Which made us both very happy.

When Vera started going by the name Finn (after a short dalliance with Michael) and using he/him/his pronouns, his Galileo fam was right there. We made the change. We were happy to be one of Finn's happy places and to celebrate what God was doing in his life.

There came a time when that beautiful blended family didn't come to Galileo Church anymore (see "Dumpster Fire," coming soon to a chapter near you). I missed them all, but the one whose absence I grieved every Sunday was Finn. Suddenly I was all alone on that front row, and it felt like Galileo had lost a huge chunk of God's own merciful presence right out of our core.

About fifteen months after the last time we saw their family at church, Finn became ill, went to the ER, and quickly deteriorated, dying just hours after getting to the hospital. Jill invited me to help lead the memorial service over at her parents' conserving church, and I said, "Of course." The family invited Galileo Church to come if they could, and they said, "Of course."

That's what they said publicly, anyway. Privately there was much anxiety about whether Finn's grandparents' fundagelical church would be a safe space for our queer selves—especially for the gender-diverse among us. After some sharing of that fear, the group who could get time off for the funeral decided that indeed the funeral *would* be safe space because Galileo Church would be there together, making shelter for each other, beautiful bricks built into a mobile temple for God's Spirit. Isn't that the best ecclesiology you've ever heard?

I was still nervous, though, for my own work that day. I had been asked not to use he/him/his pronouns for Finn during the service, and I couldn't figure out how to respect the (extended) family's wishes (not that I respected them for misgendering our beloved Finn, but you know what I mean) while also communicating to my church my steadfast commitment to honor the gender identity of the deceased. I chose to preach on the Beatitudes from Matthew 5, Jesus's Sermon on the Mount, as proof that Jesus has favorites—the pure in heart, the poor in spirit, the meek, the merciful, the ones who won't fight because they'd probably lose. I said that Finn was one of Jesus's favorites, and then, with no pronouns needed:

> At our church we begin worship each week with a query, an old question that people of faith have been asking each other for a long time. "How goeth it with thy soul?" we ask, and we take two minutes to talk about it with whomever we're sitting next to. Some of you know that for just about the entire time this family was in my church, Finn sat next to me on the very front row, with a notebook and pen, ready to draw and take notes throughout the service. But when the query came, Finn would stop writing and wait for me. "How goeth it with thy soul?" I would ask. About half the time Finn would talk for the whole two minutes. I confess I often didn't catch all the details, but the honor of Finn sharing life with me was no less for my lack of understanding.
>
> The other half of the time Finn would give a shake of the head, didn't want to talk. But Finn would listen to me, nodding sympathetically to whatever I poured out about the state of my soul. And knowing as I did that Finn is one of God's favorites, I felt that God too was especially attentive to me in those weeks.
>
> From that front row in our little church, I prayed with Finn and sang with Finn. Finn sang with gusto, my favorite way to sing, too. I served communion with Finn, lots of Sundays, as I often forget to ask someone before the service, and Finn knew the drill and would join me at a moment's notice if I asked, usually with a look of reproach because Finn knew I was scrambling. But Finn never turned me down.

And one beautiful day, Finn and I baptized Song together. We sat on opposite sides of the cattle trough and cooperated wordlessly to get her in and out of that water. It remains one of the holiest moments in history, in my estimation. Because of, you know, what Jesus said about Finn: pure in heart, blessed are those, blessed is Finn.

See, it's not just that Finn was an excellent specimen of a human being. I mean, that's true, no question. But it's more than that: Finn helped so many of us recalibrate our own sense of what makes a human being excellent, what God actually wants from and for us. We receive our Lord's congratulation insofar as we are like Finn. And so to have lived any part of this life alongside Finn, to have been invited into Finn's heart, is valuable beyond measure. I am forever grateful. Thanks be to God.

Thanks be to God.

CHAPTER 6

Things That Were Harder Than We Thought

(And That I'd Rather Not Tell You)

You Can Skip This Part

At Galileo, some of the hardest conversations begin, "In the interest of no bullshit, ever . . ." because what follows is going to be something that's hard to say and to hear, and it would be a whole lot easier if the person saying it would just stuff it down and keep quiet.

I'm aware too that sometimes the "no bullshit" ethic gets abused as an excuse for people to say harsh, judgmental, mean things to each other. We remind each other that the fourth missional priority is "*Real relationship*, no bullshit, ever," which demands that "no bullshit" be measured in proportion to "real relationship." You can only tell as much truth as the prior relationship can bear, see?

So, because you've read this far, I feel like we have some kind of relationship. Is that presuming too much? At least, I'm assuming that you don't want bullshit from me, that you're actually interested in the not-so-inspirational tales of Next Church. I was warned that it was hard before I started, but I couldn't get a grasp on what, exactly, was so hard about it. Now that I know, I feel like it's important to share. But nothing is compulsory here: it's okay with me if you skip this part.

Holding Lightly

We practice this motion sometimes at Galileo: first we clench our fists tightly, as if we are holding on desperately to the stuff we've been given (faith, fear, God, salvation, guilt, shame, money, self, beloveds); then we unclench, opening our fists, splaying our fingers wide, palms up, hands empty. We practice holding lightly and letting go.

One of the things we have to hold most lightly is people, even and especially people we love. Very young adults are very mobile; they move for work, they move for school, they move back home, they move away from home. Sometimes they move across the Dallas–Fort Worth metroplex, and sometimes they promise they'll keep coming around from the other side of the city. We mostly haven't found that it works that way. We have learned to hold lightly the people we've been given.

With Erin and Joel, who were Galileo Originals, we knew in the back of our minds that their time with us would be short. Joel was applying to PhD programs and would definitely get in. It was just a question of where—locally? Across town? Another state? We were in the sanctuary of University Christian Church in Fort Worth for Ministers Week the night he told me, his face flushed red with excitement for his own future and in anticipation of my grief, I'm pretty sure. He said, "I heard from Chicago today. I got in. We're going." My own red face signaled a swirl of feelings too. I couldn't hold back the happy-sad sobs as I told him how crazy-proud I was. And am! A University of Chicago PhD in history! (Joel, if you're reading this, put it down right now and get back to your dissertation.) And Erin swiftly secured a job at an established Next Church in Chicago, in part because she had been with Galileo. We had no doubt they were leaving us for the best possible reasons. We spent a little minute in the "What will we ever do without them?" phase, and then found how efficiently God fills the gaps left by the very best people.

We try to say an intentional goodbye to folks when we know they're going. We tell the whole church what's happening; we gather around them during worship and lay our hands lightly on their shoulders, or someone's shoulders, in a chain of touch that makes its way to the person in the middle. (Or, if the person we're goodbye-ing doesn't want all that touching or all that attention, we modify. We're cool like that.) We pray our thanksgiving for the time we shared; we pray God's help for the days to come, for them and for us, as we grieve and rejoice for how things change. I usually cry. Saying goodbye sucks.

We don't always get to do it this way, though. Some people never get in all that deep, for all that long, and after six weeks or six months they just stop showing up, and no one quite knows why. I've tried asking some people; it's not very satisfying data. I tend to think that people don't always *know* why they stop. I tend to think spiritual hunger can be like an itch—you scratch it for a second, and the itch goes away. It might come back again later. We'd like to think people could come back later if they needed to, and sometimes they do.

Sometimes people just fade out—they're here, in the hot middle of all our stuff for months and seasons and years, and then they get caught up with other stuff and stop coming around as much, and then they're altogether gone. No announcement, no conversation, no laying on of hands with a prayer. Those are the hardest ones, and I have sometimes reached out with a short message—in the vein of "We miss you; we love you; we hope you're okay"—but it's hard to know whether that makes anyone but me feel better.

And then sometimes this miraculous thing happens: somebody launches out of Galileo like a rocket, better when they leave than when they got here, ready for God to do all kinds of amazing things with their life. Take, for example, Serena, a neurodiverse, lesbian undergraduate who had been at the heart of Galileo's life for a while, then faded out, and who sent me this email in the spring of 2018:

Katie!

I hope the book writing is going well. I hope that you're also finding time to rest and recharge (JV says y'all are going to Israel this summer? How fun!).

Apologies in advance for a long email, but I wanted to let you know as Pentecost approaches that I am not planning on being a co-conspirator at Galileo this round, and perhaps not for quite some time. I know it isn't really necessary to inform you beforehand, and I imagine it isn't surprising to you as I have not been around much. The reasons are primarily logistical. But in my last few days as a co-conspirator and partner in ministry, I want to thank you. I have no doubt that you are aware of the life-changing, life-giving nature of your little (not so little anymore?) church, but Galileo changed my life and revived my faith. My first year at TCU was spiritually tumultuous, but you welcomed me in all my quirkiness and patiently walked beside me as you taught me how to untangle the web of untruths ingrained in me from an early age. I had been so hurt by the church that when DoC [Disciples on Campus, a campus ministry group] began their church visits, I cried for an hour before going to Ridglea, my first venture into "big church" after being kicked out of BCoC [Serena's family's fundagelical church].

Paul played a song about a year ago called "Not Scared Here." That should be Galileo's theme song, tbh. I learned how to not be scared at Galileo so I could not be scared everywhere else. Now I'm able to participate fully in the life of UCC [University Christian Church, where Serena is a youth mentor] because of Galileo. The growth and healing that took place on Sunday evenings at Red's and Thursday nights at Travis and Harmony's (modern day Priscilla and Aquila, I swear) cannot be overstated. Galileo is where I learned how to hold a baby, how to cook, how to drive at a four-way stop. Galileo is where I learned how to love and be loved in church, how to accept the gracious care from my church family, and how to embrace the love of a God who created me intently and perfectly, who loves me wholly and completely. I did not think that was possible after the CoC. This church you've started is the Spirit of the living God in this world. The presence of God is so palpable in everything you do, everything Galileo does that it made this doubting dyke into an annoying church girl once again. I'm able to tell others that God's love is real, God's love is for them, and so totally worth it because I finally believe it about myself. I would not be where I am now without this church. I am more grateful than words can express for your influence on my life, Katie Hays. Thank you for loving me so well.

-Serena

I don't know how many goodbyes we've said over five years. But by the summer of 2017 we had released all of the Originals: Kayla and Danny, Erin and Joel, Nicole, Malcolm (and Lacey, who came a little later but was every bit ours), Kaytee and Kyle B. Paul the worship architect moved on that same summer. Other than my nuclear family, Galileo was completely new, and the vision for what we were doing together had been transmitted to new leaders, new worshipers, new staff members, new everything. It's actually happened more than once, that near-total turnover, and it's likely that by the time you're reading this, it will have happened again. There are surely books about what it means, sociologically speaking, but what it has meant to me is this: it's my job to love people the best I can while they're around and to let them go with grace when it's time. And they, not I, get to decide when it's time. It's not what I would choose if I were choosing. But I am not the boss of that.

Excursus: "We Are Not Okay without You" (Blog Post, March 2016)

Dearly beloved human, who used to come around our church a lot but now doesn't, mostly,

We are not okay without you.

I know it looks otherwise. If you're following us on Facebook and Insta and reading our tweets, you probably believe we're fine. God keeps us thinking great thoughts and doing amazing stuff and loving our life together. That's all true. Galileo Church is still Galileo Church; the ethos and the people you fell in love with haven't changed.

Except that we have, because you're not here. And what I want to say, without pressing you to feel one iota of guilt, is that we really wish you were. Here are my three best reasons why:

1. Galileo Church is about helping people know for sure that God loves them, which some folks among us have a hard time believing. The only way we can prove it is by being here ourselves. Every single time we show up, just by putting our bodies in proximity to each other, we are communicating acceptance and community and love. It's the easiest act of kindness we ever do: sharing love by simply being here. When you were here, you were helping us with that, and we appreciated it so much. I'm worried we never told you how important it was.

2. When you were here, you shared significant parts of your life with us, and we feel responsible in no small way for your health and wholeness. It's not that we have a messiah complex—or maybe we do, because we are, after all, the body

of Christ. We say we exist to "shelter spiritual refugees," and insofar as you were (are?) one, we intended to be of actual help. And now you're gone, and we don't really know how you're doing, and that worries us. We still pray for you. We still give thanks for your amazing and beautiful life, and we still worry about how easy it is for you to think otherwise if no one is around to tell you the truth about that. We wish you'd come back so we could tell you to your face.

3. Because the thing is, we love you. I know it's weird; in some important ways we barely knew you. But nobody crosses the threshold of Galileo Church by accident; we have learned to respect the deeply felt reasons each person brings, and we have learned to love people for their vulnerabilities and brokenness. So when we don't see you, it hurts—not because we need your ass in a chair, or because our numbers are falling (they're actually not, there are always new people coming around), or because our ego is suffering (though we would confess that we're not above that, just working to make it less true all the time). It hurts because losing a part of your body hurts. It hurts because letting go of someone you care about hurts. It hurts because we love you. You can stay away, but you can't make us love you less.

This is a letter I want to print and put in the mailbox with your address and a stamp on it. But I won't, because there's just no way to unattach it from the potential for shame. That is the very last thing we want for you (see #3 above). So how do we convey that we're not okay without you, and that we would love to see you and catch up on your life and welcome you the way God has welcomed all of us? How do we communicate how good that would feel to us, how grateful we would be, to you and to God?

Maybe we don't. Maybe we just write it down to keep our hearts soft, so that if our People-Whisperer God whispers you back to us, in such a subtle way that you'll think it was your idea, we'll be ready to receive you with open arms. And then we'll all be okay.

Peace—KH

Excursus: "Find a New Church!" (Blog Post, November 2017)

When Galileo people move on from here, literally to a new city or state, I'm often asked to help them find a church family, "one like Galileo," near their new home.

It's rare that I have a specific suggestion. But here's what I share about what it's like to search for a new band of travelers to share this Christian journey with.

Friends, I'm glad you asked. God's good people are everywhere in the world. I really believe this. Whether they've formed communities that look like Galileo isn't guaranteed, but still: God's good people, everywhere in the world, even Miami (or Roanoke or Plano or wherever).

Here are some things I hope you'll remember after your boxes are unpacked and you find the grocery store and gas station:

1. Churches deserve several chances to show you who they are. More than one visit is important. Not every Sunday at Galileo is our best Sunday, you know? And if a church has gatherings other than Sunday, try those a couple of times, too. Some of our best stuff happens on Tuesday nights at Fuzzy's, or on Wednesday morning at AB Coffee, or in somebody's living room.

2. Sometimes you can find a little "church within a church," like a young adult subgroup that is doing life together, no bullshit, within the larger structure of a traditional church. It might take a little while to find it; they don't show up in your Google search.

3. Don't underestimate your power to form the church you want simply by being present and sharing yourself. The church IS the people, and if you become part of the people, the church starts to look more like you from the very first time you start sharing yourself in that space. Galileo is not Galileo; Y'ALL/WE are Galileo. Same with other churches. You know what I mean?

4. It was always the hope of the Galileo originals that what we learned by doing community together would be exportable to other places, because Millennials are mobile, and y'all are all going to live somewhere else eventually. If this way of Christian community hasn't equipped you to be/make the church you want to go to, we haven't done our work very well.

5. Take care not to idealize the experience of Galileo—it is soooo human, as we've learned recently, and has never been exactly right about anything for everybody. It's important to know where our broken places are so that you can see the advantages of a community that's significantly different than ours— because they have some stuff figured out that we're still stumbling through.

6. Be brave. You are God's address. The Spirit of the risen Christ lives in you. You have the power of discernment, and you can do this. But don't neglect to do it while you're feeling strong—because while God doesn't need

the church, God knows we do, or will eventually. Get some people to travel this path with. That's what a church should be, ideally.

7. Remember how hard it was to find Galileo, and how miraculous it seemed when we discovered each other? Well, if God worked in your life once, what makes it any less likely that God would work in your life again? I'm praying for you. I hope to hear all about your explorations, your earnest and energetic efforts to find the right place. You are so loved. Keep the faith. Peace.

Our House in the Middle of Our Street

One year for Christmas, way back when, I asked for additional dishes to match our wedding set. "I like having people over," I said. "We need more plates." Those came, but a few years later I found myself buying dinner plates from Goodwill, a buck apiece, in mismatched colors and sizes, so I'd have enough for Galileo. A lot of things changed in our house for Galileo: we started keeping beer in the fridge, a baptistery in the backyard, and stacks of G-stuff in the garage. Galileo didn't have a building, but it had our house, and that was just as good, right?

The Galileo Bible study group had been meeting at the Hays-Pape house on Hampton Drive for quite a while before Galileo Church began, and it felt natural for us to keep it up. We have a big dining-room table and plenty of chairs; we have three sofas and lots of small tables. The Hampton Drive house had a big, open floor plan. We could push the furniture to the edges to make room for dancing or add a bunch of chairs around the fireplace hearth for a house concert or make the TV the centerpiece for karaoke. The kitchen opened into the living room, and it was easy to set up a bar from there. The back bedroom was large; we called it "HQ" and sent kids back there to play video games and do crafts.

A covenantal G-group met in our house every week for about a zillion years. We used every plate and cup in the cabinet every week, sometimes having as many as thirty-five people in the house, including kids. When the number of kids got to be more than we could safely release to the back bedroom without supervision, we asked Erin to serve as our first youngster czar, and she ran a one-room schoolhouse biblical-theological education program out of HQ for months. The idea

was to divide G-groups when they got too big, but sometimes we literally didn't have anyone who was ready to invite ten to twelve people
into their home for something churchy. Plus all those kids—we needed
them consolidated under one roof for Erin's sake.

When we rented space for worship, we would negotiate for several hours on Sunday afternoon and evening. We paid a few hundred
dollars a week to have enough time to set up, worship, take everything
down, and put it all away each week. But if we wanted to have a party,
say, or an educational forum, a study group, a leadership meeting, or a
non-Sunday worship service (think Maundy Thursday, Good Friday),
those were scheduled for the Hampton Drive house. We had forty people for a "Who Are the Disciples of Christ?" program on denominational identity, taught by President Newell Williams from nearby Brite
Divinity School. (Newell and a newborn we had dedicated a couple
of weeks earlier were the only cradle Disciples in the room.) We had
forty-plus for a seminar on LGBTQ+ inclusion by a guy from the Gay
Christian Network (from whence came Jennie's famous declaration,
"This is triggery as fuck"). All of this, all these beautiful people in my
living room, squeezed in and leaning forward to figure out what God
will be up to next.

Parties, though—that's what we did best at Hampton Drive. Friends
and strangers came for real occasions like college graduations and
wedding showers and made-up ones like "We Survived the Holidays"
and Dos de Mayo, eating and drinking and playing in bracketed tournaments that we concocted (Pictionary, bocce, game shows, dance
contests), which had no prizes except bragging rights. Those parties
were loud and long; they bore little resemblance to the polite potluck
dinners that pass as "fellowship" in Now Church. One time we were
taking turns belting out karaoke when someone requested Sir Mix-
a-Lot's "Baby Got Back." Suddenly the whole room was karaoke-ing
every obscene word to gales of gleeful laughter—because who would've
thought we all knew all the words, and it was just so *not* church, which
made it all the *more* church. Many, many people found their way to
Galileo Church when they were invited by a friend to a party we were
throwing and figured out that we were real human beings who love
laughing together.

Suffice it to say, our big suburban home was a huge asset I did not even know I needed when we first started. There were long stretches when every single day saw its use for Galileo: couple's counseling in the study, lonely souls invited to family dinner, G-groups with nowhere else to go, several epic back-to-school all-night video-gaming lock-ins, team meetings to plan *more* parties, always *more*! I loved it. My family tolerated it. More on that later.

And then one day after a particularly raucous night, I was spending the hours it always took to put everything back together for our family's regular life. I cleaned candy out of the sofa cushions and mopped margarita splashes off the floor. Furniture got wiped down and scooted back into place. Twinkly lights and paper streamers were unhung. Dishes went into the dishwasher (probably the second or third load, as other people would have loaded and washed dishes the night before; there was a time in Galileo's life where you weren't really "in" if you didn't know where to put away all my family's dishes). In the middle of the cleanup I found myself in the entryway scraping queso off the wall with a putty knife, hoping the tomatoes hadn't stained the paint, and thought, "We probably need a better place to do this."

Well, yeah. But we didn't have one. I kept scraping.

A lovely consequence of the Hays-Pape home's openness to the church is the long chain of sharing that it inaugurated. The expectation that you don't just "go to" church but sometimes the church *comes to your house*—that was something we wanted to bake into Galileo's way of being. From the very beginning, starting with Malcolm's living room, Galileo people opened their front doors and back porches and kitchen tables to their #churchfriends. Eating and drinking, sharing life and praying, Bible study and theological rehabilitation, all of it happening in the homes of beloveds remains a way of life for many people at Galileo. I can't any longer count all the individuals and families who have shared their private spaces with our church. We invite everybody in, including strangers who show up for companionship and dinner, not necessarily in that order.

And so we continue the story of Jesus, who was completely dependent on the hospitality of his friends and plenty of strangers. The Son of Man has no place to lay his head, except when we open our doors to him.

Though I think if Jesus splashed queso on your wall, he'd probably clean it up himself, don't you?

Excursus: "A Theology of Parties" (Blog Post, May 2014)

Today I've trimmed up the hedges, cleaned the bathrooms, made room in the fridge for homemade salsa and Mexican beer, and made a run to the liquor store for tequila and margarita mix. And I've counted it as ministry. Sure 'nuff work that I'm called to do on behalf of, and alongside, the people of God.

Because here's the thing. You cannot swing a dead cat in the Bible without running into one of God's parties. You know how they make that Bible with red letters wherever Jesus speaks? Or the one with green print every time earth and its ecology are mentioned? Or the really hard one with highlighting over all the parts that talk about God's special concern for the poor? I humbly submit that some publisher should add a new one to the collection: I want a Bible with hot pink confetti sprinkled over all the parties in the Bible.

Hot pink confetti for all the times that God's prophets predict a big banquet in God's dining room when God finally gets everything God wants. God's been cooking all day, and there are enough chairs for everybody—me, my friends, my neighbors, and my enemies. Check out Isaiah 25:6–9 for just one example. Rich food. Aged wines. Nom nom.

Hot pink confetti for all the times God's people are instructed to bring their first fruits to the altar, the tithe of their herds and crops; and, when they've sufficiently submitted those gifts to the priest, they're instructed to use that stuff to throw a giant party for everybody who doesn't have stuff of their own, a party to which they themselves are also invited. Don't believe me? Check out Deuteronomy 26:1–11. "Then you, together with the Levites and the aliens who reside among you, shall celebrate with all the bounty that the Lord your God has given to you and your house!" Tithing = par-TAY! Who knew?

Hot pink confetti for all the times Jesus goes beyond base-level sustenance for the people he loves and feeds them till they're full, sending them home with doggie bags; or gives them the best drink they've ever tasted even when the peak of the party has passed. I don't have to give you scripture and verse for those. You know them already.

Pink confetti for all the times Jesus describes the "kingdom of God" like a feast, a banquet, a wedding reception, a party you don't want to miss. Pink confetti for all the times Jesus is accused of eating and drinking too much, celebrating too much with all the wrong people all the dadgum time. "The Son of Man came eating and drinking, and they say, 'Look, a glutton and a drunkard, a friend of tax collectors and sinners!'" (Matthew 11:19). They meant it as an insult. I say, who *wouldn't* want to follow a messiah like that?

So here's something we count as important kingdom work at Galileo Church: we throw parties. If there's no reason to have one, we make one up. After Christmas we threw a "We Survived the Holidays" party, because a lot of our friends suffer through holidays with—or without—their loved ones. When it was my birthday, there were no presents (because that wasn't the point!) but there was lots of cake, and there were lots of people, and we blew off a lot of steam. We all went roller skating one night for no good reason other than it helped us have an intergenerationally hilarious good time. I'm doing chores today to get ready for Dos de Mayo tonight—because, you know, Cinco de Mayo is on a Monday, and that's a lousy party day.

We do this as a form of kingdom work, because we believe that in the future of God's imagining, "the shroud that is cast over all peoples" and "the sheet that is spread over all nations" will be ripped away, and God will swallow Death as an appetizer, and all God's people will be invited to boogie down as tears are wiped away and disgrace is erased from our existence. The table will be laden with deliciousness and no one will be turned away. (This is Isaiah 25 again.)

So we're doing our part to puuuuullllllll God's future into our present, one party at a time. This is good work, church. Y'all come on over.

Finding Space: The Farr Best
(Winter 2014 through Summer 2015)

Look, I'm not kidding when I say I'm glad Galileo doesn't own its own building. I've done that kind of ministry before, where it's my responsibility to unlock and lock up, plunge a toilet between Sunday school and worship, hang out waiting for three different sets of roofers to give us a bid for repairing the hail damage, manage the custodian. I didn't go to school for that and I wasn't called and ordained for that.

But there are days when I would take it all back, and those are the days I have spent looking for new rental space for Galileo Church.

You know about the *terrible worship service* at the community center, and why we decided not to rent there long-term. You know about G-House, and why our time there ended prematurely, counting as eviction 1, if not officially, then *de facto* as we became unwelcome as soon as we announced our collective queerness.

As the G-House era came to a close, we tried a bunch of things. One deal we came close to making was for an old Fina gas station in the industrial section of Mansfield. It had an empty feed store in the back, and we felt like we could raise money to renovate the whole structure if the owner would be reasonable about the rent. That's the time I did shots at the Fuzzy's bar with the owner's son (or was it her nephew?), hoping he would put in a good word for us. I was not convincing. After stringing us along for a long time, she decided our renovations were too much, and she would lose too much time before we paid any rent. That old Fina is still empty; I drive by and check every once in a while. Bitter much?

I went back to Felix, the city manager, and asked if he had any other ideas. "Have you tried the Farr Best?" he asked. I had, in fact. That early twentieth-century theater on Main Street, with red velvet seats and a heavy red velvet curtain that swooped down across the movie screen, loomed large in my imagination. It was almost always empty, save for a few music concerts each year. I knew it would be perfect for a start-up church. But the owners had turned me down the first time around. They were conserving Christians, and they didn't want "that kind of stuff" in there. (Which makes me want to ask, "*What* kind of stuff?" What does anybody imagine we do in church, other than churchy things?)

Anyway, after a death in the family, those owners had recently turned over management of the theater to a committee appointed by the city. That committee was looking for a consistent renter to keep the utilities paid, and we could be it. We were able to move out of G-House ahead of our actual expulsion and into the Farr Best Theater, into the red velvet seats.

The Farr Best Theater was both so right and so wrong for us. We discovered early on that there were secret stairwells leading to the balcony so that African American moviegoers could get up to the balcony without being seen by white patrons during the long extension of Jim Crow in Texas. We did walk-around prayers as soon as we moved in, praying God's blessings into every corner of the building, praying away the stink of segregation.

(No, that's too simple. We can't pray away the stink of segregation. But we wanted to tell the truth, to God and everybody, that we were embarrassed about those stairwells, about the lingering legacy of white supremacy and racism. Telling the truth about it seemed better than pretending it wasn't there. It felt like our church being there just might redeem the space, you know? Spoiler alert: it didn't work like we thought it might.)

We loved the quirkiness of the tiny lobby with a glass ticket sales window, the dim light from the colored glass sconces, and the swoopy velvet curtain. The aesthetic was pleasing. But the cast iron seats were bolted to the floor in long, lateral rows. The aisles were narrow. Our habit of moving around for communion, for prayer at the wall, for reflection stations of multisensory activities meant to stimulate engagement—this did not go well in the Farr Best. Movement was constricted. There were too many seats for too few people. Attendance at worship bottomed out. There were a few Sundays where the only people who showed up, really, were the ones who had a role in leading the service. I wrote a letter to the church saying, "Hey, do we want to keep doing this?" I mean, that's not what it said, but that's what I needed to know.

And then, after we'd been there about eight months, somebody graffitied the Farr Best. It was weird stuff about Mansfield—sprawling, spray-painted gibberish about how it's a terrible city and no one should shop here. Very strange. We helped to clean it up; we pledged our support to the city as they sought to find out who had done it and why. We reported that some of our stuff, stored backstage, had been roughed up, and some of it had disappeared. A microphone, some cables, a couple of pieces of furniture. We thought whoever did it must have had a key.

The second round of graffiti appeared in broad daylight one afternoon soon after. This time the city manager Felix was called out in a racist, spray-painted scrawl. And this time the vandal could be identified: it was the owner himself. Weird much?

When asked, he let it be known that he had discovered that our church was desecrating his precious property. He didn't want us there; he wanted to take back control of the place from the committee that had rented to us. This is not what we were told at first; the committee wanted to spare our feelings (and perhaps avoid a lawsuit, if I'm feeling cynical). A friend who was privy to those meetings spilled the beans sometime later. Anyway, with the city's management committee out of the driver's seat, we were given thirty days to get out. I hit the streets again to find another place to rent.

Just a few days into our thirty, though, I got a phone call from a friend whose optometry office is across the street from the theater. "He's saying you have to leave now," she said. "He's putting your stuff out on the street." Our communion table! Our thrift-store dishes! All those IKEA candles! I was about three hours away, visiting my FOO in College Station. I posted on our Facebook page, "We're being evicted. If you can help us move Galileo's stuff to my house, meet me at the Farr Best at 3 p.m."

I got on the road fast, making phone calls the whole way back to Mansfield. I called the leadership team members. I called the police to let them know we were going to be at the theater soon, in case of confrontation. I called the newspaper editor; she met us there and wrote a story about our sudden homelessness.

The most important call I made was to Jan, the owner with her husband, John, of a local brisket restaurant. The restaurant hadn't been interested in hosting our church, even though it was closed on Sunday nights; it just wasn't a good fit for their business model or for ours. But Jan had always been kind to me in her quiet way. She answered the phone from the beach in Florida where she was vacationing with her family. I told her what was happening downtown. I might have been crying a little. Snuffling, anyway. "It's Thursday, Jan," I said, like she didn't know what day it was. "And my church has no place to go on Sunday."

Jan listened to the whole story without comment, then said, "I'm not due home for another week. But Rusty [or whatever that kid's name was] has a key. I'll tell him to have it unlocked for you on Sunday at 4. Y'all can stay there till you find another place." Very matter-of-fact. Very Texan. Very Christian.

We met at Steven's Garden and Grill (weird name for a brisket restaurant, I know) for the next six Sundays. Steven's is a true Texas smokehouse. Every material in the place, like the chairs and walls and oxygen, is saturated with smoked meat smell. It has a long bar down one side with dozens of glass bottles of warm liquid on display. On Sundays we shoved the liquor down to one end of the bar and set up communion on the other end. We moved tables to the back and put chairs in curvy little rows in the front. We hauled in everything we needed from my garage, where Galileo's accoutrements were now living, and hauled it back at the end of the night. We made it work. Attendance stayed steady and even went up a little; some people were just curious to know what had gotten the Farr Best guy so mad. Everybody went home smelling like brisket at the end of the night; if you went to bed without washing your hair, your pillowcase would smell like brisket of a morning. It was hard on the vegetarians.

Corina is the one co-conspirator we got out of that deal—Corina, a theater student at UTA. Corina, who went on to serve a term as our MLT president and lead co-conspirator. Corina, whose cheerful spirit rarely dims. No amount of smoky-meat smell could keep her away; no number of evictions could keep us from making space for her. God gets what God wants. Thanks be to God.

Excursus: The Farr Best Schlump
(Email Sent to All Galileo's People, December 2014)

Subject: it's urgent [and important]

#Dearly beloved,

#This is a different kind of email from me: not funny, not ironic, mostly serious. And so, a serious greeting: grace and peace to you, from God our Father and the Lord Jesus Christ.

Galileo Church has a problem, and I'm asking you to enter with me into a period of prayerful discernment to figure out what it means and how to address it. Here it is, as plainly as I can state it: Sunday night worship attendance is down for the months of October, November, and, so far, December. We have dropped below 30 worshipers for several weeks, counting every soul including babies and employees. That is a big change from our consistent 40, 45, even 50+ a few months before.

The problem is *not* "there aren't enough people to glorify the Lord in worship." God is pleased to receive our offerings of ourselves, I still believe. Our worship is still beautiful and true. We remember Jesus faithfully at the Lord's Table each week.

But the theater feels empty on Sunday evenings. If I were coming in for the first time (or the 20th time), I would feel discouraged. It feels strange, to be among so few people in a space prepared for so many.

Additionally, we're putting a huge percentage of the church's resources (money and people-hours) into making worship happen. You might recall our pie chart of the church's expenses—about 36% of the money we receive and share goes to Sunday nights. That's a lot of money. It's also a LOT of hours, including the creative team's hours of preparation, and the weekly set-up and clean-up each week to transform the plain space into a beautiful space filled with holy possibility.

So . . . what do we do? Simplify worship? Change locations? Maybe the theater was too much, too fast? Maybe we subconsciously liked the more intimate space of G-House with all its flaws? Maybe something about our worship format is a subtle turn-off and can be fixed? Maybe we're in a normal season of "schlump" and the pastor needs to chill? Maybe Galileo is meant to be a small-ish house church, and that's okay? So many possibilities. So many possible answers.

Please believe me: this is *not* a passive-aggressive email designed to guilt you or anybody else into "coming to church" more often. I believe that Galileo's people are grown-ups in whom God is at work. We have always pledged to hold each other lightly, offering full welcome whenever and wherever God's people show up. Our empty-theater problem won't be solved by a temporary attendance spike fueled by shame. Blech.

Please believe me, also: the sense of urgency I feel about this is *not* financial. We have enough money to keep doing exactly what we're doing for a good, long time. But there is (always) the question, as stated above, as to whether we're being good caretakers of the money and talents and time and energy that so many people are sharing with us.

So I have several specific requests of you to address this problem:

1. Enter with me into a period of prayer and discernment, beginning this Sunday night at 5 p.m. We'll meet at the theater as usual, but we are suspending our regular liturgy to dedicate the worship time to prayer. We'll have prayer stations in the theater with instructions. We'll have a labyrinth set up in the parking lot out back. We will share communion together. I'm asking you to pray during that time specifically about next steps for us regarding Sunday night worship. (I won't say much about this on Sunday when we meet; we're having guests for the Second Sunday Forum and I don't want to generate anxiety for them.)

2. Let's complete the holiday season with joyful worship, beautiful and true, just as we planned. We'll continue with a Christmas Eve service at 11 p.m. and all the regular Sunday plans through January 4. Come when you can.

3. The leadership team will meet in January 2015 to consider how to continue with our discernment process regarding Sunday worship. It will probably involve lots of conversation with each other and with you. Please continue praying about this on your own, asking God to grant our whole church family insight and hope. If you are given any particular insights through your praying, feel free to drop me a note or give me a call. But please wait a while. We're trying to avoid knee-jerk reactions here. We're trying to listen, all together, and wait quietly for clarity to come.

There is a happy word of gospel in all this. Galileo Church, for all its layers of complexity, remains light on its feet. We are still able to make course corrections with relatively few impediments. Our friendships remain strong and are not endangered by changes in infrastructure. We know how to change; our spirits are limber; our hearts are strong. We can figure this out. With God's help, we can be the people of God that we have been called to be.

Thank you for your consideration. It's been a hard week, coming to terms with this reality; I won't lie to you about that. But it remains true for me now as always: it is a privilege and a joy to be in ministry alongside you. Thanks be to God.

peace—Katie

Justifying the Price of This Book

In the category of "things that were harder than we thought," I have to talk about people who have worked for Galileo as part of our itty-bitty pastoral staff. Not that the people themselves are harder than we thought but the work is hard in ways I didn't understand at first and for a long time.

I work full-time-plus-plus and receive a full-time salary, but the other people we pay have to have "real jobs" to also work for Galileo. We try to compensate generously, but we can't pay for very many hours each week. I don't like the reality that we're building our church, in some sense, on the backs of these workers for whom we can't provide a living wage or health care or even a Christmas bonus.

Add to that the reality that we're creating this whole thing from scratch. There's not a template for how to do worship architecture for this kind of church; there's no curriculum for our youngster czar to buy and copy. (No, for real. Don't send me suggestions, unless you've got one that affirms a spectrum of gender identity and sexual orientation in a kid-appropriate way, works for our one-room schoolhouse model, celebrates neurodiversity, and is also deeply grounded in biblical theology, Genesis to Revelation.) People who have formal theological training want full-time ministry jobs, not the little quarter-time-or-less positions we can offer.

So what we're always looking for is people who have a zillion ideas before they get out of bed in the morning, a baseline of progressive theological maturity, and a cocktail of sufficient time, energy, and sheer dedication to pull some of their best ideas into reality, mostly in their spare time—oh, and a high tolerance for failure. Without much of a budget, without any locational stability (doing a youth group without a youth group *room*, for instance), and among a bunch of people who, because they are spiritual refugees, don't feel themselves qualified to help much with the heavy lifting.

Add to *that* the reality that I'm not that great of a personnel supervisor. I have superstrong opinions about just about everything (are you surprised?), and I might tend toward micromanagement, except that I'm hyperaware of that tendency and instead overcompensate by mostly leaving our staff completely alone with their work. Sort of a "Call me if you get into trouble; have fun!" mode of nonmanagement, until I'm sufficiently disappointed that you're not magically intuiting what I wished for and I'm suddenly critical with little warning. At the same time, I'm hoping for every staff member to be my boon companion in this wild endeavor of church planting, sharing the risk and the exhilaration and the vision of all that it can be. I'm always wishing they would love it as much as I do. That's a lot for people who are paid by the hour for a few hours per week.

Thank God, we have had some the most talented and dedicated people on our payroll that any church could ever boast. Erin, Jess, Kelley, Ryan—they have each brought a wide range of talents to their work as our youngster czars. (Nobody strings donuts from a tree for kids to eat without their hands like Erin. Nobody genuinely laughs at kids' dumb jokes like Jess. Nobody loves the hardest kids to love like Kelley. Nobody writes DnD adventures for intergenerational play like Ryan.)

Paul and Steph have helped every worshiper learn to raise their tentative voice to the heavens as our worship architects. (Nobody writes postmodern hymns like Paul. Nobody wears strength-making sorrow and a Canadian tux like Steph.) And Steph has had the doubly difficult task of following the guy who pretty much invented the way we sing in worship. Watching her develop her own voice for our context, and thereby *change* us for the better, is exactly what we say will happen whenever anybody new decides to journey with us. Steph has embodied it better than anybody and against harder odds.

But we have burned through the gifts of some of those folks in significant ways—always asking for more than we can really pay them to give and usually surprised when they come to the end of their time with us and describe how hard it was. I'm learning to be less surprised, which is not really a solution, I know.

Here is a golden nugget about employing people that I wish someone had told me when we first started, a piece of advice that would have saved us a great deal of anguish and money: pay a payroll service to do payroll for the people you pay. Payroll is hard. Payroll sucks. Payroll will get you in trouble with the IRS in ways you do not understand and cannot rectify without writing *big fat checks*. Just budget it in, thirty bucks or so per month, to let someone else work those numbers.

That, and be good to the people who catch your vision, or some percentage of it, and come alongside you for the ride. Buy them presents that show you know who they are. Send them to conferences that will help them do the work they love. Thank God for them, publicly, in the hearing of the whole church. And, did I mention, get a payroll service? I feel that by telling you these things I have justified the price of this book. You're welcome.

Money Is the Worst: Financial Sustainability

Money is the absolute worst. I hate it.

But we always need more of it. Because, as we like to say around here, "Money makes it go." I wish we were saying something more spiritual, something more theologically appropriate. "The Holy Spirit makes it go," would be nice. But making space where the Spirit is welcome and responding to all the things the Spirit suggests takes moola. Look, even Jesus had financial backers: Joanna, Susanna, Mary Magdalene, "and many others," says Luke 8. And that man could make wine out of water, yo. I cannot.

Here's the broad-strokes outline of how Galileo makes ends meet. In the first place, we got a big-ass grant from the Trinity-Brazos Area (TBA) of the Southwest Region of the Christian Church (Disciples of Christ), which is our denomination. We asked for funding for four years, $100,000 in the first year, and then dropping off each year until in the fourth year it would be something like $20,000. We got two years' worth—$100,000 and $85,000—but not years three and four. I don't really know that whole story, but I think most people thought new church plants only take a couple of years to get on their feet, and our denomination doesn't have a lot of money and tends to think that risk-taking is . . . risky. I think it used to be true that church plants only needed a couple of years of support when they were mainstream congregations in fast-growing zip codes recruiting baby boomer churchgoers who were already predisposed to support institutions with their money and presence. But not anymore.

From the first time we met for worship, we asked people to contribute financially to the church's life. And we make our ministry finance plan (aka the budget) completely transparent, including posting it on our website. That goes against some conventional church-growth wisdom. But I (1) don't buy that millennials don't have any money, (2) don't believe people can be truly invested in something if they're not financially invested, and (3) don't think the church's money, or mine, should be a hush-hush topic. I'm a stewardship advocate from way back, and I bring a kind of frankness about money to Galileo that has served us well. And millennials, as it turns out, are hella generous with whatever money they've got if they trust who they're giving it to.

We also began raising money from individuals who don't come to Galileo because they live far away or because they are not spiritual refugees (i.e., have a church of their own) or because they just don't wanna. (I see you, Stacy; you just don't wanna, and it's totally fine. You are a grown-ass woman and God loves you. Thanks for the support, always. Let's get lunch.) Along the way a huge number of folks have sent us checks with prayerful notes, hoping that Galileo "makes it" because they've got something at stake in its future. They have a kid or grandkid who doesn't feel at home in Now Church, or they just want to see the wider church try something new. We have a few dozen consistent backers, from small contributions of a few dollars a month to very large gifts. There are also Disciples congregations nearby and far away that count Galileo as one of *their* missional priorities, sending us gifts from their outreach dollars every so often. *We are so grateful.* We think of as many ways as we can to say so, lots, including handwriting a couple dozen thank you notes at every meeting of the missional logistics team. Mom, did you hear that? All those thank you notes you made me write to my grandparents after birthdays and Christmases, it paid off! My mom seems so much smarter now that I'm so much older.

When the big-ass grant from the TBA dropped out in the middle of 2015, we thought we might shrivel up and die. I realized all of a sudden that I was going to have put on my fund-raising hat—and that was bad because I did not own a fund-raising hat and did not think I would look good in one. I honestly had not done any serious work on finding money in our first two years together, past securing that initial grant.

The church leaders made some adjustments in our infrastructure, discussed elsewhere in this book, in part to free me to add that work to my portfolio. And I got busy. And I got bold—asking everybody, everywhere, all the time to back this project. Taking speaking engagements wherever I could and asking that the honoraria go directly to Galileo. Writing grants, whether we were eligible or not, hoping to strike a chord with some committee somewhere.

And again, we got truthful with the whole church. When that big chunk of funding dropped out, we had enough cash in the bank to keep going, just like we were, without any major scalebacks on staff or other expenses, for about six months. Or we could do some major restructuring (like I could go part-time, and we could quit paying for so much food and drink) and make the money last longer. The leadership team went for the former, like they do, because they actually believed me, like they do, when I said that risk taking is inherent to the practice of the gospel Jesus preached. And we told the church what we had decided, and the church said "Amen." We had written two budgets for the coming year, one of them titled "Full Throttle." That's the one we went with.

Somehow we have always found the money, or the money has found us. Only one time were we in major danger of not making payroll, and we asked a big church that had already awarded us a small grant to accelerate its distribution so we wouldn't bounce checks. (That was surprisingly recent, like early 2018. No lie.) Another time we went to our landlord and said we didn't feel we should have to pay the balloon note at the end of the year, considering all the August Sundays the air conditioning hadn't worked. He agreed. Whew.

Sometimes we're lucky like that, and sometimes we're just dumb. One night the leadership team met at a BYOB pizza place, and by the time the meeting was over we had hired two interns for the coming year, which would eat up a significant chunk of our financial reserves, money we would wish we had back a little later when we got unlucky. The financial catastrophe I lost the most sleep over involved the IRS— aren't they in your nightmares?—because we made some basic payroll errors early on and didn't do the required repairs on that situation in a timely fashion. Suddenly (it seemed to me) the IRS was angry with us, and they did not care that we are a church and we do Jesus stuff and we are nice people. They did not care at all.

Recently (last summer!) we had a treasurer's report that showed we were $94 in the hole. Not overdrawn, actually, but once we paid out payroll and made rent and covered a couple of other expenses, we were going to be dry as a bone. The agenda for that meeting of our missional logistics team, published on Facebook as always, literally said, "How do we feel about that number?" And we talked through it—how we're not that interested in building a fat cushion of cash "just in case." I mean, just in case *what*? Someone said, "How can a church be in the business of accumulating assets? When there's actual ministry to be done, for Christ's sake?" (Like, literally, for the sake of Christ.) So we all raised a glass to being $94 in the hole and trusted God to work it out. God did.

A metric we've been using all along: we're banking (!) on data from the Center for Progressive Renewal that says new church starts aimed at millennials take eight to ten years to be financially self-sustaining. (You can find their research at progressiverenewal.org.) We're aiming at the high end, ten years. Which means that in our third year, we needed for Galileo Actual (the folks who come to church here) to supply 30 percent of our operating budget, 40 percent of our operating budget in the fourth year, and so on to the tenth year, 100 percent of our operating budget from local folks who actually come to our church. So far we're on track, both by increasing our giving and by making sure our budget doesn't grow unnecessarily. The whole operation costs about $180,000 a year for now. I hope that number blows you away. It's so much and so little, all at the same time.

I still don't know how to raise $180,000 a year. I'm telling you, God works it out. For this work God cares about, for these people God loves, God does. Thanks be to God.

Ministry Finance Plan

If I publish Galileo's most recent ministry finance plan here, it will be out of date before Amazon processes your credit card transaction to buy the book. But if I don't, I risk vague-booking about something I wished desperately someone would get clear with me about, way back when. Look, the most recent budget is always on our website. You can look it up. Let me use this space to tell you how we worked that out.

I had worked closely with the accounting and stewardship teams in traditional churches for years, so I knew the basics of church finance. What I wasn't sure about was how to translate that knowledge into a form that would match Galileo's own institutional ethos. Budgets, as you know, are theological documents; they communicate what we do (or don't) believe about what God is asking us to do in this world. Or they communicate that, like the corporations in a capitalistic system, we're mostly worried about property and personnel. But that can't be what God is actually asking us to do, can it? So what, we wondered, was God asking Galileo to do?

The percentage answer to all Christian theological questions is "Jesus," so we went with that. What did Jesus do with his hands and feet and mouth and body and *money* during his ministry? Maybe we should do that and write a budget that reflects it. So we worked through the Gospel stories about him and applied some verbs to his work. We got these:

- *Announcing the Reign of God ("It's at hand!") and Inviting People into It ("Come and see!").* This category holds the stuff we do explicitly for the people who are not here yet: parade entry fees, college fair registrations, website upkeep, T-shirt printing, and parties. "Parties and celebrations" is actually the first subcategory in our budget. Tell me that's not biblical.
- *Preaching and Teaching, Healing and Shepherding.* My salary and benefits go here along with lines for books and conferences for my ongoing education, coffee or beer with whoever needs a pastoral conversation, and the expenses of the missional logistics team and the spiritual care team, who keep making sure that the good news of God's reign is emanating loud and clear.
- *Worship and Spirituality.* Here's where we count the Big Red Barn rent, the worship architect's salary; a monthly appearance by the consigliera-on-cello, and all the froufrou we collect for our beautiful, intergenerational, multisensory worship services. Also bread. Also wine.

- *Friendship and Hospitality.* Because Jesus ate and drank with his friends! And everybody else! All our G-groups have a little budget of their own.
- *Calling, Sending, Bringing Good News to the Poor.* This lumps together our justice and mercy work, stuff we do that's about sending money out (e.g., to our denominational ministries) or funding our efforts to pull the reign of God a little more into the present (e.g., helping build a Habitat for Humanity house or getting folks to Austin to fight those bathroom bills).
- *Welcoming Children and Youth.* Here we pay our youngster czar, a kid wrangler, and 50 percent of camp registration for anybody who goes to our denominational church camp. Plus snacks, markers, glue sticks, Scotch tape.

Okay, some of those are nouns, not verbs. But you get the idea. We wanted to make a document that, as dry as spreadsheets can be, would be a strong basket to hold the juicy, sweet fruit of God's purpose in us. Thus the point of this annual plan is to spend it all, everything we've been given—not always exactly the way we thought we would at the beginning of the fiscal year, but always in service of these things Jesus still needs a body for and still needs money for.

Excursus: "What Had Happened Was" (Blog Post, July 2015)

What had happened was, there was a resolution on the floor on the very last day of the biannual General Assembly of the Christian Church (Disciples of Christ). (In our denomination, we take "sense of the assembly" resolutions that say what the people in attendance think about important things. They're not rules or doctrine; they're a somewhat reliable pulse check on the denominational diehards who still show up for biennial assemblies.)

Resolution 1526, "Resolution to Celebrate and Reaffirm Our Commitment Towards the Vision of Planting 1,000 New Congregations by 2020," followed up on a promise we made some years ago. It was basically a reminder to us all that starting new churches is beautiful and essential work. It would be easy to say, "Yes, yes," to that.

The procedure is thus: whoever wrote the resolution introduces it, and then people get a chance to talk to the whole assembly about it, using some funky parliamentarian protocols that you don't want me to explain here. Suffice it to say, I found myself walking toward the appropriate microphone to get permission to address the assembly. I had no plan, no notes; I'm not a great extemporaneous orator. But I knew I had to speak. "The Moderator recognizes the speaker at microphone number one," said the Moderator.

"Thank you, Mr. Moderator," I said, my gigantic face turning blotchy red on the humongous screens at the front of the plenary hall, my voice reverberating through the arctically air-conditioned air. I shivered. "I am Katie Hays, pastor-planter of Galileo Christian Church in Mansfield, Texas. I rise to express gratitude for the congregations of the Trinity-Brazos Area of the Southwest Region of the Christian Church, which granted us extremely generous start-up funds for our first two years of life. And Galileo Church has made good use of those funds; we are welcoming people to the heart of God in the name of Jesus and in the power of the Spirit." (A couple of people "Amened" at that.)

"However, I need to tell the whole truth about that. Two years is not enough. Galileo Church has legs, but it can't walk on its own yet. Our start-up funds have run out. And the truth we should acknowledge is that new church starts very often fail for lack of money. Not for lack of interest from the community; not for lack of the minister's good work; not for lack of the gospel's power to transform lives. It takes money, real money, to make this ministry possible. And while Galileo is progressing toward sustainability, we have not achieved it yet.

"I will vote 'yes' on Resolution 1526, but I just want to say that it's not enough. We already have the prayers and encouragement of our sister churches. I already have the friendship and commiseration of my colleagues. What we don't have, what we really need, is more money to extend our life to the time when we can fund our life together.

"I'm hoping that established, traditional, aging congregations that are holding tightly with clenched fists to the resources that are slowing their inevitable decline will find the courage to open their hands and release some of those resources in service of the church's future. I'm hoping that we'll find a way to share with new congregations all across the country that are struggling to stay alive because their pastors are working full-time jobs and planting churches in their spare time.

"I will vote yes on this resolution. But it's not enough. Thank you."

And I stumbled back to my seat, panting a little from anxiety. I closed my eyes to concentrate on breathing deeply while the talking continued.

When I open my eyes, she's kneeling beside me. I've never seen this person before, and I didn't hear her come up, but there she is, *kneeling* on the concrete floor beside my chair. She says, "I don't have very much money. But I want to share with Galileo. This is such good work. Can I write a check?"

And while I'm gaping, unable to say anything, she starts to scribble, her checkbook on her bent knees. No, not a huge amount of money, but who cares? The real gift is her presence. The real gift is the power she's sharing with me in that moment. She rips out the check and hands it to me with a smile. "Take heart," she says. "It will come." And we both stand up into an automatic embrace.

By this time I was crying the ugly cry—blotchier face, lots of snot. A friend from Georgia crept up to offer me Kleenex. I let go of the check-writing angel to wipe my face and she was gone. I didn't see her again for the rest of the assembly. It's hard for me to believe she even exists outside of that moment.

Over the next two days, I received notifications from PayPal that donations had arrived from a couple more of my colleagues, and that recurrent donations from one had been set up. Another friend wrote to ask what kind of plan we have for our long-term sustainability, and to offer her considerable administrative talents to help realize it.

But that's not all. When I landed at DFW after a long travel day, I got a call from a pastor saying that her church had voted to include Galileo in their outreach budget; she would be mailing a check that was on her desk *before* she got home from the assembly. And just this morning a journalist who heard somehow about Galileo sent an email to say that she'd like to give us some free publicity in a metroplex magazine.

These offerings—especially the ones that are clearly unrelated to my words at General Assembly 2015—are the gifts of God for the people of God. Or more specifically, for this person of God. I don't usually say that God is directing specific actions for the sake of God's people, making it rain, whatever. But sometimes there's really nothing to say except, "Thank you." To the people God uses, and to God's own Self—thank you. Thank you. Thank you. Thank you. Thank you. Thank you. Thanks be to God.

Excursus: "What Happened When Our Church Went Venmo"

In planting a church for spiritual refugees—especially Bible Belt millennials who experienced the churches of their youth as boring, irrelevant, exclusive, and even painful—I've had to learn a lot of new things. Pastoring traditional congregations for two decades was terrific preparation in some ways, but the difference is never more apparent than when my quirky-as-all-get-out community of belonging in Jesus's name passes the offering plate.

And we do. We announce at the top of each Sunday worship service that the heart-shaped baskets (bought on clearance at World Market) will be coming through later on. We already know that we aren't going to collect a bunch of handwritten checks and neatly folded twenties. When is the last time you met a young adult with a checkbook? Or cash on hand?

Instead, we offer several modes of e-giving, including bank-to-bank electronic fund transfers and a suite of PayPal possibilities. There are iPads in the back of the worship space where givers can slide their debit cards and sign with their fingers. We encourage everybody to pick up a laminated card to put in the basket later. The cards say, "I shared electronically, thanks be to God!" or "I shared thoughts and prayers, thanks be to God!" That way, everybody has something to give. "The gifts of God for the people of God! Thanks be to God!"

But recently a twentysomething in my church wanted to send over five bucks to pay the church for something small. I think we were collecting money for a birthday card. But PayPal takes a chunky fee for every transaction, even for nonprofits, so that's not very efficient. "I wish I could just Venmo it to you," the twentysomething said. And I said, as I often do, "Huh?"

After Venmo was explained to me, I handed over my laptop and said, "Make it so." Fifteen minutes later, Galileo Church had dozens of "friends" on Venmo and had received its first gift—and we had "liked" it and commented by giving our thanks.

See, Venmo is a *social media* app. It's for friends to share money with friends, electronically zapping $$ from one bank account to another. And depending on your privacy settings, anybody who is your friend can see all your Venmo transactions in a continuous feed.

Let's say you and a friend split a pizza; your friend pays; you send your friend a few dollars for your half, along with emojis of pizza and books, at 11 p.m. Now anyone who is friends with you or your study buddy knows that you had a late night cram session and got hungry, and pizza was the remedy. (They won't see the amount you sent or spent.) They can "like" the transaction and comment: "Finals! Ugh!" or "Good work, you two!"

So what happens when the church goes Venmo? We got new givers almost immediately. People who had never given to our church before friended us and sent contributions. And some regular givers moved their giving from a for-fee service to this free-for-now app. That's a 2.9 percent savings on fees that we're glad to have.

But more important than that are the comments the Venmo givers include with their gifts. With every note and emoji, they express what they believe the church is (and should be) spending money on. Consider these comments, taken from Galileo Church's Venmo feed:

"For love and justice"

"So our village can keep providing what our people need"

"Spreading God's love"

"For helping me find my why"

"Cuz I love you"

"Take a stand"

"A church I can call home, finally"

"We keep doin' what we do"

"Those missional priorities, ooh la la!"

"Thank you. So much."

And then there are the ones that communicate best with emojis: rainbows, unicorns, and multi-colored hearts; praying hands and praise hands; kissy lips as a show of affection for a church that loves you back.

This is definitely not your parents' offering plate. Some of these notes respond to specific sermons or liturgies (showing palm tree pics for Palm Sunday, bread and wine for communion). Some acknowledge a habit of regular giving loosely called "tithing." But I am especially affected by the ones that name the church's highest aspirations—justice, mercy, love, compassion, help, hope, belonging.

These are not "designated gifts," like the checks that come with strings attached, for use only in specific programs. Venmo gives Galileo's givers a platform from which to make public their understanding of the reasons for the church's existence. Why does the church need or deserve your generosity?

Why, against the strong current of a greedy, anxious, materialistic culture, should you hand over hard-earned dollars into the church's hands? For what purpose should the church spend these resources, as a good steward of your good gifts? Venmo presents a gold mine of public testimony about what a new generation of adults expects from the ecclesial communities they are helping to build.

There are, of course, questions raised about the public aspect of social media giving. Didn't Jesus criticize those who gave loudly and expected praise for their faux generosity? But the widow who gave her pennies used the same public platform—the treasury box at the temple gate that anyone could observe—and was praised for her selflessness. Galileo's givers are mostly working the gig economy, or working as underpaid teachers or hourly wage laborers. Their mites don't make a lot of noise going in, but they are not ashamed to share according to what they have been given. Thanks be to God!

If Venmo giving raises some questions, it answers others. It obliterates the debate about whether the pastor should be privy to the giving habits of individual givers. We are learning new things about our kids' and grandkids' comfort with living life out loud, transparently, for all the world to see. And we are learning what it means to be in community with people whose generosity we have witnessed. Secrecy about giving is passing away as an ecclesial social norm, and with it the ability to wield influence without investment.

One more factor that I suspect is important in Venmo generosity: immediate and joyful thanks expressed by the church to each giver. Each gift sends a little "ding" to my phone, and it feels important to respond as quickly as I would to a Facebook notification or a text. (The church treasurer helps with this as well.) It's another lesson from church planting: the pace of input and feedback is going to be much faster than that of the yearly, IRS-mandated giving statements that ploddingly reach givers through the U.S. Postal Service.

Most of our millennial givers are not itemizing their tax deductions, so that yearly letter of record is not truly useful to them. We send the letters, of course, but we don't rely on them as our main mode of appreciation. We have come to believe that good gifts, freely given, deserve a quick little celebration of gratitude. With a snappy response and a couple of heart emojis, the church models thanksgiving for all who are watching our social media receipts.

Sharing money via social media apps is just one among myriad ways that new generations are building communities of belonging in Jesus's name and communicating with each other about the church's highest purposes. Venmo is a new wineskin for new wine, and I'm happy to learn all the new things it's teaching me.

What I Asked My Family to Pay

There are lots of things about Galileo that I'm not sure how to write about, but this one is the worst. Under the umbrella of "Things That Were Harder Than I Thought," I want to say what Galileo meant for my family.

That is to say, I want to say what *me* being the Galileo Church planter meant for my family. In so many ways, the fact of Galileo Church has been good for my family. I have two kids who are barely millennials (born 1998 and 2000), until we give their generation an even newer name. Now Church was terrific for them when they were little, with lots of church aunties and uncles to look after them and bring them extra desserts. They got a kick out of their mom (and dad, when Lance and I were in co-ministry together an ice age ago) being "famous," that is, the one who stands up in front and talks when everybody else has to be quiet. Most importantly: they learned to love Jesus in those traditional churches I served.

But Galileo was born in part out of my own understanding that the kind of church that sustained my faith into adulthood would not serve my teenage-into-young-adulthood kids equally well. I have been glad and grateful to see their own experiences and expressions of faith deepen as they came to witness the lives of Galileo's young adults. It matters, I think, that kids see people just a couple of years ahead of them on the path of faith, trying their best and engaging life's hard questions and being faithful companions in community. And my kids have benefitted from a community that celebrates neurodiversity and downright quirkiness. There's certainly no expectation at Galileo that the pastor's kids have to be or behave a certain way.

On the other hand, planting a church is *consuming*. I don't know how else to say it. For the first several years of Galileo's life I could speak of nothing else. I woke up working; I went to bed working. I couldn't sleep at night. I couldn't reliably take a day or an hour off. I was largely absent in the evenings, sometimes missing my family five, six, seven, eight dinners and bedtimes in a row. The rewards were shaky; there were incredible highs when someone would give an indication that their life was *changing! Really changing! For the better!* But the lows were frequent and scary, and my anxiety levels stayed ratcheted up.

But wait, that whole paragraph was about me, and I meant to be saying how this whole thing affected my family. That's just it, see? Galileo was (is) *my* project, my baby, the work I was born for. It felt (feels) like the exact right thing I am supposed to do with the second half of my life. But in pursuing it, I (necessarily?) put myself in the center of our little family universe and assumed the rest of them would orbit around me. Oh, ouch. I am groaning. Wincing. Shrinking from these words, this confession.

I'll check with Lance before I send this into the universe, but I think he'll say it's okay for me to own that Galileo's infancy and toddlerhood were really, really hard on our relationship. It was a tug of war that neither of us could win even if we won, if you see what I mean. I was pulling toward more work, more engagement, more texting, more Facebook, more meetings, more hours, more Saturdays, more evenings, more people, more parties, *more*. Lance was pulling me back toward home, family, dinners at the dining-room table, quiet evenings on the sofa. To me that felt like *less*. To him, that should have been *enough*.

At a particularly low point, just a few months into Galileo official, I attended a small conference for pastor-scholars in Chicago. We were supposed to write a short essay entitled "What Sustains Me in Ministry." I couldn't write mine; I didn't have time to slam out a few hundred words. Worse than that: I couldn't think of anything that sustained me in ministry. Lance and I were fighting. I was leaving for Chicago. I was having a hard time getting any of my colleagues to think I was doing good work. I felt like the whole idea of church planting was impossibly hard. You should see what I wrote. I'll just paste it in here, and let you feel some of that awfulness for yourself.

Excursus: "What Sustains Me in Ministry"
(Written for Association of Disciples Pastors for
Theological Discussion Study Group • October 2013)

I never ignore an assignment; I never miss a deadline. I'm too much of a people-pleaser to do that. I say "yes" to a lot of things and sometimes regret it later, but I never fail to complete what I've been asked to do.

So the fact that I've delayed writing this reflection on vocational susten- nance to the absolute last possible hour—literally, the second leg of the flight to Chicago—is telling. I suppose the easiest way to explain it is that, right this minute, I'm not feeling very sustained in ministry. Not a surprise to me, but it feels like inappropriately rapid self-disclosure to say so to all of you.

You may be aware that I left traditional congregational ministry at the end of May this year and began, on the first day of June, an alt-church plant in the DFW suburb where I live. The new church (in my imagination!) is aimed at "seeking spiritual refugees, rallying spiritual health for all who come, and forti- fying every tender soul for strength to follow Jesus into a life of world-changing service." Mainly we're looking for Millennials who are "spiritual, but not reli- gious"; and LBGTQ people and those who love them; these people don't have church options in our town. They would have to commute to "go to church," if they cared about being part of an institutional church, which they don't. Friendship, yes; church, no.

But if this reflection is to be about me and my sustenance for ministry, I could reiterate the church's mission statement for myself. I feel like a spiritual refugee; I long to rally spiritual health; my tender soul needs fortification to follow Jesus. It's hard to say exactly why I'm in this place of shadow and sorrow, but I have two broad ideas.

First, I have loved the church for so, so long, even when the church did not love me back. My fundamentalist background meant that rejection of my gifts was the norm during childhood, adolescence, and young adulthood. I did not break with the denomination of my youth until well after it had done its damage to my spirit (and my marriage; more on that in a minute). And now I find myself with the Disciples, a fine and healing branch of liberal Protestantism within which I am enjoying a flourishing set of collegial relationships and their appreciation for my vocation—a full embrace, so welcome and needed after so many years of rejection.

But I'm embarrassed to admit that, while I love the DOC (and our similarly situated North American Protestant cousins), the bloom is off the rose. I think the church is in decline in ways that are far beyond what any denominational transformation project can tackle. I'm beginning to think it may be our generation's task to oversee the dismantling of the infrastructure—as well as physical structures—that have been life-giving to generations of Christians, but are now draining the gospel of life and light. And that depresses me.

I hoped that a "next church" R&D project—which is how I think of the new church I'm working on now—would grant me a broad place to stand and breathe, a blank slate with which to recapture my hope and excitement about church as the living, breathing, serving body of Christ in the world. But it turns out—imagine my whiny voice for this sentence—church planting is really *hard*. The last few weeks, indeed, have been kicking my ass. I don't know how to do this, and if there's one thing I loved about two decades of traditional congregational ministry, it's that I felt every single day like I knew how to do what I was supposed to do. I didn't always love the particulars of any given ministerial task, but I loved that sense of competence.

Second in these broad categories of *lack*, is a resurgence of the brittleness of my family life. About twelve years ago, our daughter was diagnosed with autism; and like a lot of couples, my husband and I came to the brink of marital ruin in the wake of that life-altering reality. It was extremely costly to keep it together—lots of therapy, lots of extended family support, a vocational shift for my husband, a painful break from the denomination that was squeezing us like a boa constrictor, and the subsequent loss of friends; and of course, the intensive care of our beautiful daughter and our infant son. We reordered our family life to keep the marriage intact and to provide a healthful environment in which our daughter (and son) could flourish. And she has, they have, mostly.

But here we are a dozen years later, and many of the stresses and sorrows we thought we had put behind us are with us again. My husband is sick of church—any church, new church, old church, Disciples church, my church. He is angry with every North American generation living right now for what has happened to the people of God, and on my worst days, I can match his disappointment. My kids are at the height of their spiritual wonderings and needing guidance from us; plus, autism + adolescence = a^2. My vocational terror (will the new church work? won't it? if it doesn't, what does that mean about church?

about me?) is rendering me less than whole for their sake, all three of them, kids and spouse alike. There is no relief at home from the pressure of ministry. Indeed, it's a risky proposition to share even the positive developments regarding church with my family; I will likely not get from them/him what I'm most hungry for.

So I keep talking to God about it, not in a contemplative or systematic way, but in the haphazard prayers of a person who is mostly lost most of the time. Anne Lamott has famously said that there are only three prayers—"Help," "Thanks," and "Wow!" But I would add a fourth, the one that comes from my heart and lips most often these days: *"What the fuck?"* I believe this to be a biblical prayer; many of the Psalms can be summed up thusly, as a confused and angry servant of God wonders angrily when the promised relief will come.

Too much information? Believe me, if I had something nicer (and probably lesser) to share with you, I would have. But for this moment, this is what it feels like. I'm grateful, sort of, for the assignment to put it into words. May God read these words with you, and find a way to show me the sustaining manna I'm sure God has dropped all around.

Not Everybody Thinks You're Great (January 2016)

There's not much I like more, vocationally speaking, than telling people about Galileo Church. Kazillions of people think it's supercool right up until the moment I've talked too long, taken up more than my share of conversational space, and their eyes glaze over. I've gotten a little better about catching myself before it gets to that point, but here I am, writing a whole entire *book* about Galileo Church. I know what it looks like.

Once in a while I get reminded that not everybody thinks my life project is entirely great. Indeed, some people are superpissed about certain things about Galileo Church, and they find lots of ways to tell me so: comments on our website blog and sermon recordings, comments on our FB posts, emails to our info@ address, that irritating one-star review on Facebook in 2018 that says neither Galileo Church nor its pastor has a moral compass. I actually know that guy. I replied to his one star with this:

Moral compass! Ah, dang it, I knew we forgot something. I guess between lobbying our local school board for LGBTQ+ protections, making peer-to-peer conversation groups around mental un/health, creating gorgeous worship for our gorgeous God and remembering Jesus as a champion of the outcast, and trying to be as no-bullshit as possible in our relationships, our moral compass slipped out of our very full hands. But hey, R, a lot of that stuff is new since you last spent time with us in 2015. Come on over, friend, and see if it still feels true that you're "just not a fan." We get that Galileo Church isn't for everyone, but we'd love for you to experience our current iteration. The members whose moral compass you're reviewing here are mostly people you've never met. Give us a chance to show you who we actually are. Sundays at 5; Tuesdays at 8; lots of times in between. Peace.

The capper, though, is that one time a clergy colleague sent an actual letter in the actual snail mail. I mean, the person literally created a document in a word processor, printed it out, found an envelope and stamp, addressed it to me at home, and put it in the mail. Literally! That's a lot of effort to go through, right? And here's what the literal letter literally said:

Dear Dr. Hayes [*sic*]:

Here's a suggestion or two for you, coming from the pastor of one of those boring, irrelevant, painful and exclusive churches you are asking to support you financially for the coming year.

1. Stop referring to the rest of us as "boring, irrelevant, painful and exclusive." You do not help us with younger people we are desperately trying to minister to when you continually use those terms to refer to us.

2. Stop asking us to support you financially. You have already received a huge amount of money from the TBA, money which the rest of us give (us boring ones). None of us boring congregations have [*sic*] received ANY financial grants from the TBA. You want us to give, not receive. You want to receive, not give!

3. Put the Disciples Mission fund and the TBA back in your 2016 budget. I see in your website you are eliminating denominational support entirely.

4. In your seminar at Ministers Week, please explain to the rest of us how you can justify asking us to support your budget, **when you do not support the Disciples mission in any way.**

5. It is cool to offer beer to people who will come to your activity, but think what you do to recovering alcoholics.

6. And tell me how I explain to my teen-age daughter, who looks at your website, how you defend using language like "No Bullshit!" in your promotion. She wonders. Is that what "being cool" requires?

You might be surprised how often the six suggestions above are brought up when your fellow Disciple pastors get together, when you're not there, of course. A little awareness of the struggles the rest of us are going through would be appropriate. I have to remind you, **you are not the center of the universe!**

Sincerely, one of your boring, irrelevant and exclusive fellow pastors.

Coming back to this letter three years after receiving it, I have such a swirl of feelings, including my sincere disappointment that my last name, which is just four letters long and not hard to find in lots of places, is so often spelled wrong in tense situations. Also, I wish the writer would employ the Oxford comma.

I'm also truly appalled that a clergy colleague would write an anonymous letter; haven't many of us suffered the cruelty of anonymous missives slipped under our office doors in traditional churches? Haven't we longed for the chance to have an honest conversation with a parishioner who's mad enough and misdirected enough to criticize our shoes or our bad breath or our old-ass car in an unsigned note? Yeah, all of those examples are real ones, not for me, necessarily, but for colleagues who are friends of mine.

But three years later, I'm more mellow than the hot, righteous indignation I felt when I first received this letter. I hear the anguish in my colleague's voice; it's the anguish many of us feel when we consider that the institution we have invested our lives in is fading away. Galileo Church can't make that happen, but our presence can make it more obvious, perhaps just by the contrast in my own enthusiasm for my work, for the beautiful things that keep happening among these beautiful people, and the low-level, baseline anxiety that many of my colleagues suffer in their daily work of *not letting it die on their watch*. I have felt that. I have felt that so deeply that I dreamed alternative careers while sitting at my Now Church desk: long-haul trucker, bank teller, back to the librarianship that got me through grad school. I remember that feeling, and it helps me find enough grace for my anonymous letter writer.

Besides, they weren't entirely wrong about any of those points. We had indeed dropped denominational support from our congregational budget because we had lost a huge amount of denominational support a few months prior and were wondering how to keep going. We got frugal pretty quick.

At the time, though, receiving that letter really sucked. The second half of 2015 had been hella hard, and I wasn't sure Galileo Church, my family, or myself were going to survive in our present circumstances. I had depended on the idea that I had supportive and well-wishing clergy colleagues, and here was this person saying they were all talking about me behind my back. And yeah, as the letter writer knew, I had accepted an invitation to speak at Ministers Week at Brite Divinity School in early February 2016, about—guess what?—Galileo Church, and how amazing it is. The letter writer couldn't know that I had fallen into a depressive hole that I didn't know how I was going to climb out of. The letter dug me in a little deeper—it's never just one thing, right?— especially with all that it implied about how other people talked about what I was pouring my life into. It was like sprawling on the floor of the BBQ restaurant all over again, only this time I was a blubbering mess, and no voice of God was making it okay. More on that in a minute.

This is what I decided to do. I prepared a kick-ass talk for Ministers Week all about how beautiful it is when God brings broken people together for healing. I rubbed a palmful of vasoconstricting medicine on my face to keep it from flaring with the bright red patches of rosacea that betray my anxiety every time. I carried the letter with me up to the podium in the big room where a hundred or so of my colleagues were assembled. I held it up, saying, "Before I get started this afternoon, I'd like to thank the person who recently took the time and effort to send me some helpful suggestions for my new church-planting endeavor. This person is a colleague of ours and likely understands how very hard this church-planting work is and wants to help. However, the writer forgot to sign the letter or otherwise leave me any way to be in touch for face-to-face conversation. The letter did indicate the writer's interest in attending this talk, though. So if you're here, please know how much I'd like to speak with you. Thanks again for reaching out." And then I went on with my talk. *Heap* those burning coals.

Nope, I never did receive any acknowledgement from the actual human who wrote the letter. What I got instead were hugs and handshakes from dozens of colleagues who are also my friends, who sometimes ask probing questions about Galileo and even offer criticisms, all in the hope of seeing it, and me, succeed and flourish. I'm happy for conversations that help me think better, see more clearly, and even (gasp!) change my mind about the next right move. Well, maybe *happy* is too strong. But if I'm gonna dish it out, I have to be ready to take it, yeah?

And I like to think I'm gentler now with colleagues like the letter writer, now that I'm out of that depressive hole, now that Galileo can see beyond the next liturgical season, now that the days aren't filled with panic about money and rental space. I hope that's true. I hope there's a way for us all to be clear-eyed about what's coming next in North American church life, and not blame each other for it. Seems to me we're going to need each other more than ever in years to come.

Also, H-A-Y-S. No "e." Thank you.

I Wanted to Crash (December 2015)

In early 2015 I asked my doctor for help with sleep and got a scrip for a sedative: Temazepam, just a few itty-bitty milligrams. I wanted to feel a little less panicky, a little less exhausted, a little less plagued by nightmares that came when I was fully awake at three in the morning and wouldn't let me catch another wink before it was time to bound out of bed and start the frantic pace of work again. The work I loved, but still. I was so tired.

I want to say what all that anxiety and exhaustion was about, but it's hard. It's hard for me to admit that while so many amazing things were happening all around me, while the reign of God was taking shape in the lives of all the amazing people God had sent to Galileo Church, like we were actually gonna *be* a church and not just an idea I had one time, I was suffering. I wasn't *only* suffering; there were hours and hours and days and days of pure joy. When I say I love my work, I mean it. But that doesn't mean the work isn't hard. Don't read that in a whiny voice. I'm doing my best to be matter of fact.

Someone asked me recently how I deal with being the one who hears so many stories of trauma. It's true; Galileo Church's people have, on the whole, experienced more trauma than most people, and I hear about a lot of it. The accumulation of other people's damage is surely part of why I felt so heavy in that season. Many times I would hear from someone by email or tweet or text asking for a listening ear, and I would set up a time for that and spend two hours hearing the most god-awful story of pain and suffering, and express deep empathy and offers of tangible help, all the resources Galileo and I could share—only to never see that person again. They didn't need a church; they needed an on-call pastor, a compassionate listener, a friend. So many times.

But I don't actually think it's that particular external heaviness that was getting to me in 2015. I think it was the internal existential terror of realizing that the crazy-ass idea I had, the project I risked my reputation on, the thing I got a whole bunch of people to believe in and give money to, *might actually work*. Like, the people who are coming now are not actually seeing the wobbly, ad hoc nature of the early start-up season. They're seeing a sure-nuff *church actual*, and they're placing hope in it. They're thinking God has smiled on them because they found us. Can I just say, that was terrifying to me? Even right now, I'm shaking as I write it down.

Even so, I think I could have pushed through that terror if circumstances had not conspired to wreck my equilibrium. Three *big things* happened in 2015, all basically concurrently. First, the *big start-up funding* that I received to launch Galileo Church dropped out—from $100,000 in the first year to $85,000 in the second year, and then, in July of 2015, $0. Zero dollars. That's not what I thought was going to happen, and though we figured it out early in the year, the loss of that monthly grant income was catastrophic to our financial bottom line.

And we got evicted for the second time, this time from the Farr Best Theater. Things hadn't been going all that well at the Farr Best, and the eviction prompted a move that turned out to be terrific, but at the moment it was devastating. Suddenly we were seriously homeless, not in that playful "we use quirky borrowed space to do fun church!" kind of way but in that "we seriously don't have anywhere else to go" kind of way. Womp womp.

And my family moved out of the Hampton Drive house to the place we now call the Hays-Pape Homestead. This new place is magical, everybody says so, and I almost always agree with them. There are metal bottle trees in the gardens, handlaid mosaics in the bathroom floors, and an intentional blackberry ramble near the little peach orchard. But when we got out here in October 2015 all I could see was a seven-acre tangle of overgrown gardens and several seriously stinky goats and an old house with basic breakdowns of plumbing, electricity, sewage, and *Wi-Fi for fuck's sake* every other day for months and months and months. And just like that, we had lost the Hampton Drive house as a site for some huge percentage of our life together, and it felt all the more like we (the church "we," not the family "we") had no place to go.

I'm telling you, all that stuff was happening *at the same time*. I cannot stress that enough. And through it all Galileo Church kept doing great ministry, starting up new stuff (our It Gets Better group for LGBTQ+ teens and young adults started during that time, for example; and we crowd-funded *Maybe All Is Not Lost*, an album of worship music written for and with Galileo Church, during that same season). We did all that while we found a new place to rent for worship, and my family moved into a new adventure with the goats (and chickens and honeybees and a farm cat), and I figured out how to raise about $100,000 a year to keep Galileo afloat.

I truly believed that getting a good night's sleep, perhaps several in a row, would cure what ailed me. Temazepam and I were good friends through that whole summer into fall. With 15 mg, I could get five hours of sleep, six if I was lucky, with another hour or two of anxious contemplation of all that awaited me with the rising sun. All the things I did not know how to do. All the ideas I would try that would not work. All the people for whom Galileo Church was the last stop, the last try before giving up on faith completely. All of that with me all through the night, with me as soon as I woke up every morning, hours before the alarm was set to wake me.

In December 2015, our friend and co-conspirator Kyle M. graduated from college with a nursing degree. He had worked so hard to get it, and the church had helped with some expenses. It was a huge accomplishment worth celebrating hugely. Kyle threw himself a dinner at a Tex-Mex restaurant and invited me to come. I remember going late; I had some other obligation that kept me from arriving on time. (That was pretty common; I often stacked up appointments and engagements, late to everything but wasting no time in between. How annoying.) I hung out with the group for a while, long enough to drink a margarita, eat some nachos, and join in the accolades for Kyle and his classmates. And I left for home.

It's hard to say exactly what happened on the way home. I don't remember any conscious line of thought that was particularly catastrophic, but as I've said, I always had a running mental inventory of all the things left undone, all the ideas unpursued, all the people untouched. I came around a bend in the highway and saw an overpass ahead in the distance, spanning over the road I was on. I saw that if I didn't straighten out the steering wheel after the curve I would be headed directly for the pylons holding up the overpass, and this seemed like a decent idea. I wondered if I would feel it. I checked to see if there were any other cars nearby, if it was "safe" to crash. I unhooked my seat belt. I kept my foot on the gas.

And then I swerved, away from danger, back to the middle of the lane. I fumbled my seat belt back into place. My vision blurred with tears. My palms and forehead were sweaty. My heart thudded painfully in my chest, and I gasped for breath. The whole thing can't have taken as long as it took you to read these two paragraphs, but my physiology reacted in every possible way.

At home I went directly to Lance. "I am having suicidal ideations," I said as calmly as I could. He blinked a couple of times, taking it in. "What does it feel like?" he asked. We talked, and I said I felt calm enough to go to bed. I pulled out a capsule of my sedative, and Lance said, "Wait." He googled Temazepam, finding suicidal thoughts as one of the possible side effects, and I never took another one. I haven't suffered in exactly that way since that one night. It took some months to feel like I was back to my baseline (low-level, high-functioning depressive; empathic; intermittently joyful) self.

Here's what I am saying: this work that I love with everything I've got has been heavy. There has been tremendous joy in it, the kind of deep-down joy that comes when you're doing exactly what you were meant to do in this world. I still feel that most every day. But I think the weight of, sort of, spending everything—my own energy and giftedness, my privilege as a decent pastor in established churches, my marriage, my family, my house, *everything*—for this project that was (is) inherently *unstable* and *destabilizing* . . . well, one night it just felt like too much to carry, probably exponentially impossible because of the sedative residue built up in my system. And I wanted to crash.

Perhaps it goes without saying that I'm glad I didn't. I'm beyond grateful for Lance's stubborn stand-by-your-person ethic, and for my kids' mature and gracious receipt of the news that I was in need of care. I'm beyond grateful for a strong foundation of Christian theology that doesn't demonize mental illness and emotional distress. I'm embarrassed that it got to that point, but not so embarrassed that I can't own it, especially if it helps you or someone else recognize the weight of whatever it is you're carrying—the heavy, beautiful work that God has called you to, and all that it costs you to pursue that calling, and the circumstances that sometimes collude to bring you to the brink. Don't crash, friend. Get yourself home and ask for help from the ones who love you. And, over time, learn to show yourself the same kindness you keep showing to everyone else.

To Galileo Church's own people reading this, I know, it's the first time I've told you this part. You're probably pissed that I kept it from you. But I kept it to myself because . . . Well, not because I thought you couldn't handle it or that you wouldn't be kind to me in my weakness. But because we keep working, don't we, to make sure that Galileo Church is a leveled-out community where the planter-pastor is not the center of the congregational universe? I didn't know how to tell you how broken I was without turning the conversation back to me. Perhaps I was wrong to withhold it from you. If so, please forgive me; I'm honestly not sure what I think about that decision now. And please know how much strength I have derived from your beautiful expressions of love and faith and hope all along the way, even when you didn't know how badly I needed them. Please give thanks with me for my spouse and my kids, the humans who have consistently nursed me through the hardest parts so I could in turn give my best self to you. For them and for you I give thanks and more thanks. I am so loved. And I feel so much better. No bullshit, now.

Finding Space with Adlai (August 2015 to Present)

While we were at Steven's after our eviction from the Farr Best, the search for worship space grew a little desperate. At our lowest point we considered going back to the fluorescently lit community center. (Gag.) When Chris told me he had been to a bar just outside of town that had a party room in the back and that I should call the manager to check it out, I was skeptical. But I called, and she invited us over. I asked a couple of people if they could check it out for us. They came back with an optimistic report: it could work, except for the antler chandeliers. Maybe we could get them to take those down?

It turns out the antlers were tree branches hung from the ceiling and wrapped in tiny white lights to make honky-tonk chandeliers. The effect was magical. The party room was a former auto-body repair garage made of sheet metal and concrete, with giant garage bay doors on one long side that opened to a narrow parking lot in the back of the restaurant. No one would ever find us back there unless they were looking for us specifically. It felt perfect.

Red's Roadhouse, restaurant in the front and party room in the back, was owned by Adlai, so named in 1952 when Adlai Stevenson ran against Dwight Eisenhower and lost. His parents were, um, hard-core

Democrats. Adlai is not the churchgoing kind, and he tells me often that he doesn't have much use for churches or the people who inhabit them. He didn't even want to rent to a church when his manager first recommended us as a weekly tenant, but then, he said, he looked at our website and figured we were the kind of Christians he could stand to be around. It was about time we got a landlord who saw us for who we were.

That party room became ours for a few hours every Sunday afternoon and evening. We took good care of it, mopping up beer spills from other renters' parties the night before, mostly keeping worshipers out of the main restaurant where a huge bar held thousands of dollars' worth of liquor. Once in a while the Saturday night renters would get into our stuff and take off with our candles or crates or vases or whatever. We became expert at wandering through the dark maze of the silent restaurant to retrieve our cherished things.

Galileo flourished at Red's. Our worship attendance climbed as we felt more and more free to experiment with making beauty for our God Who Is Beautiful. Like the time we talked about the height of ecstatic praise in some of the psalms, and on cue everybody threw a little handful of colorful confetti in the air. We brought leaf blowers from home, opened the garage doors after the service, and blew the confetti out into the parking lot, where the rain melted it away. We sometimes had seventy, seventy-five, even eighty people in worship; but every time we got that high, we plummeted again to fifty-five or sixty. That seemed to be the comfort zone for that space.

So after a while we asked Adlai if we could move into the main restaurant in front. It would be tricky; the restaurant had closed, but he still had Sunday night party rentals in that part, and our being there would restrict access to the restaurant kitchen. He offered us an alternative: how about that big red barn nestled under the interstate? It was currently occupied by a fast-pitch softball pitching coach, but she was leaving anyway. He could outfit it with a stage, add a twenty-ton air conditioner, and we'd be set. We could put a sign on the roof that could be seen from I-20. There was a spacious, separate room we could use for our kids. It might be perfect.

But: we couldn't rent it for the $300 per Sunday we had spent every week of our existence thus far. We'd have to lease it 24/7, on a three-year contract. We gulped, hard. Three years would effectively double the life of our church. And as the sole tenants, we would be responsible for custodial work, that is, cleaning our own floors and toilets. We didn't own a stick of furniture, except for that communion table, the cattle-trough baptistery, and the prayer wall pallets. Not a single chair. How could we?

Oh, but the better question is, How could we *not*? We were stalled out, stuck, in that hidden back room of a defunct restaurant. It was time to move again, this time because we wanted to and because a landlord actually liked us and wanted us to stick around. And it was time to come out to a place where we could be seen by all our neighbors on the busy interstate. The packing was a little less frenzied this time, and it felt good to breathe deeply in the wide-open space of that barn.

We put out a call through social media, and through the office of the local area of our denomination, asking for hand-me-downs. Offers of chairs, tables, benches, pews, pulpits, pianos, organs, and an astonishing painting of a white, blonde, hipster Jesus flashing a peace sign were all offered to us free. (Actually, one pastor who gave us chairs from his church's storage room said, "You can take these chairs, but you also have to take this Jesus painting so I don't have to hang it back up in my church. Make it disappear." *Shhh*.) We borrowed every available pickup truck and began filling our new space. (White, blonde, hipster Jesus did not make the cut, for #reasons.)

So this is our space now: a small, elevated stage with music stands and stools for preaching, singing, praying, and karaoke when a party calls for it. Our fence-wood and metal-pipe communion table, down on the floor, as close to the people as it can be. The cattle-trough baptistery over to one side, encased now in weathered wood, looking like a rustic hot tub, in front of an arrangement of custom shelves Mark made to hold our precious, junky communion dishes. On the other side of the stage, the expanded prayer wall, Lance having constructed more über-pallets so we would have more room for our supplications, with the counter-height tables Missy made for writing our prayers on those cards.

There are lots of mismatched chairs, with mismatched end tables interspersed in the rows so you have a place for your coffee (or your beer, we don't judge). In the back, but connected, is the toddler corral so we can see and hear the babies, and they can see and hear us. The kids have a spacious room for their Sunday afternoon kids-only G-group. Best of all, there's a quiet room, a small, separate space with sofas and soft lights just in case somebody needs to escape from the activity of worship or needs a nap more than they need a sermon. We've hung some shade cloth outside, and got some money to build a nice playground set for the kids. Kat designated a flowerpot for cigarette butts, so we're keeping it clean. And yes, there is a big, gay sign on top of the Big Red Barn, GALILEOCHURCH.ORG in rainbow colors that sparkle in the sun, which can indeed be seen from I-20. We're not hiding anymore, and that feels right. The Big Red Barn is kinda perfect. Except for the rats in the attic, where we store our quirky collection of stuff, but Mark is taking care of those. One rat at a time.

The BRB has two bathrooms, and one of our first move-in tasks was the removal of the gender-specific signs. We worried over what to replace them with—how do you symbolize a truly gender-neutral space without words? It came to me in a flash, maybe by the power of the Spirit, that we didn't need to say *who* could go through those doors. We only needed to say *what* was behind those doors. We ordered two signs with plain drawings of toilets on them. *Voilà!*

The hour or two before worship is always a little nutty in the BRB. We have a sound system to check, a reflection station to set up, candles to light, toilet paper to replace, bread and wine (usually grape juice, honestly; we are our parents' children) to set out. There's a weekly team working on all that, using a checklist system so that we almost never forget anything. (Except for that one time I was gone and nobody filled the communion dishes, and they had to press pause on the whole service while Ryan ran to the kids' room and grabbed the animal crackers.) I will confess to still experiencing a tinge of panic every Sunday afternoon that maybe this is the week no one will come. But when people begin to come in the door, I relax. As I've said, I like to watch them walking in, blinking back the brightness of outdoors in the contrast of the low light inside, the muscles of their neck and shoulders relaxing as they take a deep breath and remember again what it feels like to be safe and free and loved.

Okay, I take it back. I wouldn't trade traditional church space for all the searching, all the false starts, both the evictions, the smoky-meat smell in my hair, the sheet-metal buildings that Adlai collects. The sense of movement, of being light on our feet, of making church wherever we show up, the Spirit building us into a shelter for each other—these are the gifts of God for the people of God. Thanks be to God.

Top Ten Awfullest Memories of Galileo Church's First Five Years

10. We repeatedly scheduled intergenerational roller-skating parties at Arlington Skatium, even though every time someone forty years or older was seriously injured.

9. We invited a Tulsa band to play for us in worship. An ice storm hit the Metroplex on Sunday. Most churches canceled evening activities, but we were stubborn. The band members were just about matched by the number of worshipers who actually showed up. We had to put them up overnight because they couldn't get back to Tulsa. Roads were literally closed for days.

8. We pursued the potential renovation of an old Fina gas station for longer than was reasonable. Finally, a kindly architectural firm told us it would cost a quarter-million dollars to make it habitable, not including EPA-mandated cleanup. Yeesh.

7. That payroll thing with the IRS. I know I've talked about it a lot, but it still haunts me.

6. Three times, we scheduled sing-along events with beer—Beer & Hymns, Hymns & Libations, whatever. Three times it was pretty much a bust, with the third time the worst of all. The hymns were great, the beer was fine, but it just wasn't our jam.

5. There was that minute when everybody thought it would be a good idea to bring their dog to worship.

4. That time Jennie and I, checking out a space to rent, set off the burglar alarms when the agent didn't show up to let us in and we went in anyway. When we figured out the police were on their way, we ran for it.

3. The Walk of Shame: on our first Wild Goose trip, Joel and Lance went to a nearby town to get ice and groceries, carrying it all to our campsite in a new Styrofoam cooler with "Walmart" printed on the side. Neither Styrofoam nor Walmart is real big at Wild Goose.

2. For Pentecost 2014 we scheduled ourselves into a frenzy. It was the #firsttime for people to join the co-conspiracy in worship. We premiered Paul Demer's new album *Canvas of Sky* with his full band and tons of guests, throwing a postworship record release party complete with a cookout. At the last minute we added on a wedding for a sweet couple who had never been to our church before and who never came back after—long story. It was probably not the first time we had said yes to too many things. It was definitely not the last.

1. Rats, rat traps, rat relocation, rat-eaten candles, rat shit in our communion dishes. Rats.

CHAPTER 7

#Adulting

We Are Not as Cute as We Used to Be

Refined by Fire

The stories of Galileo's infancy are invigorating. For a couple of years, every day seemed to crackle with threat and possibility. Adrenaline and caffeine were the physiological fuel for my work. Every small success was cause for celebration; every small failure taught us something we needed to know.

Then came the toddler years. No longer an adorable infant, our clumsiness was pronounced as we made our way up the learning curve. Small successes were simply necessary daily output; we knew small failures could compound into bigger ones and had to be dealt with seriously.

In our kindergarten years (because it may take us a couple of tries to graduate to first grade) we have turned toward the tasks of scaling up our tiny-church processes, tying off loose ends from previous, unfinished work, and correcting mistakes we had previously let ride. Things have gotten more systematic; we have written several more policies and shored up job descriptions; we have routinized aspects of our previously organic life together. A couple of us who remember Year One fondly have been heard to sigh, "It's not quite as fun as it used to be." We're not seriously wishing we could go back; we're just indulging in the nostalgic fantasy of turning away from present difficulties we didn't have before. I mean, of course we didn't have our present difficulties before; we were just a baby. Growing up introduces complexity and complication. That's how life works.

But moving into a more mature institutional phase has its particular joys too. For one thing, there is so much more room in our infrastructure for all the people who are not here yet. We have learned how to scoot over, institutionally, and make room for newcomers. That means writing stuff down that we used to be sure that "everybody" knew. It means developing a curriculum, and a delivery system for it, that teaches newcomers what Galileo Church imagines itself to be and how their presence among us will necessarily change us. It requires intentional, timely, and honest evaluation of what we've just done. It relies on better and better financial record keeping and projection, which after all this time we are finally getting a handle on.

For another thing, we are more useful now than we were before. Like a kid who has learned to empty the dishwasher, we know how to do stuff that is good for the world. We're not quite so much building the airplane while we're flying it, anymore, so there's more energy for flying and less terror of crashing.

But growing pains are real. I can't tell the stories of our big-kid, kindergarten self without first pointing to the dumpsterful of ashes over there. The fire was dangerous and almost burned us up, but in the end it was for our refinement. Here's what happened.

Dumpster Fire, Part One

Content consideration: nonspecific recollection of sexual assault of a minor child.

This was the first time we had an honest-to-God church fight. Not like our fun fights over what flavor of margaritas to have at our next party. But a real one, about God, about what God wants for and from us, about how to be God's people right here. I've been through those before in traditional church, lots of times. But this was the first one, for me, with the lighter fluid of Facebook squirted on the flame.

It was the very beginning of 2017, during our move in to the Big Red Barn. I really thought he was our problem to solve. I was wrong.

I got a call from a guy who says, basically, "I want to come to Galileo Church. Can we meet and talk about it?" And there was a time in our early life together when I would have jumped on it. "Yes! Coffee? Beer? This afternoon? Tomorrow night? What's your pleasure?"

But three years into our life together, I wasn't quite so eager. I'd had so many coffees and beers with people who never ended up coming to church—they just scratched that itch by meeting with a pastor to talk about spiritual things. So I said, "Come on over for worship a couple of times and see what we're about. Then if you want to get together, we can."

He said, "I can't come to worship until we meet. I'm on the sex-offender registry and have to have the pastor's permission to attend church." Ah. Okay. We set up an appointment.

This paunchy senior citizen with rough hands and work boots met me at the coffee shop. The smell of cigarette smoke was overpowering, permeating even the envelope he handed me with his paperwork in it. He wanted me to see the documents concerning his arrest and jail term and parole terms. He wanted to tell me his story.

"I was raised at [a fundagelical church] in this town. I knew I felt a certain way about boys, but I knew it was wrong. So I got married to a woman who said we could make it work, and we had kids, and I just pushed it down. We were okay.

"And then the Internet came. And I couldn't get away from it—liking guys the way I did. Online I could get a date with a stranger. We could meet up, and then never see each other again. My wife didn't have to know. I knew it was wrong, but I wasn't hurting anyone.

"Then one day I showed up at the address the guy gave me, and when he came to the door, I knew he wasn't twenty-one like he said. I should have left right then, but I didn't. I knew he wasn't twenty-one, but I didn't know he was fourteen. I didn't know. His sister came home and caught us. She called the police. I got arrested. I went to jail. It was in the paper. My church kicked me out. My wife kicked me out. I live at the feed store that my daddy left me, in the back.

"I'm off parole in a couple of months. Part of my reentry program is to find some social connections. I found your church online at the library; I can't have Internet at my residence. It seems like your church is good to people like me. But if you have kids there, I have to have permission, and the church has to make a plan for me. You can talk to my parole officer and my counselor. Their numbers are in my file, and I gave them permission to talk with you."

Over the next couple of days I talked to the parole officer, who verified that the guy was following reentry protocol and that church membership is recommended for people coming off this kind of arrest. She verified his story about the assault of the minor child he met online and the older sister coming home. I talked to his therapist, a specialist in rehabilitation of sex offenders. He said that over many months in therapy, this guy had taken several tests to determine whether he's a pedophile. He is not. The therapist said, "Most churches won't even talk to our clients. I'm so glad yours is considering. We can help you write a plan that puts good boundaries in place, but I'm telling you, this guy is not interested in hurting anyone. He knows what he did and how wrong it was. I don't see him reoffending."

I talked with a few of our church leaders privately, asking for their discernment. I brought all that information and discernment to Galileo's missional logistics team. I said, "We do justice for LGBTQ+ people, and this feels like a justice issue to me. In a sense, it's the church that did this, pushing this man's sexuality to the edges where he ends up seeking connection through sex with strangers. We can make this work. We can offer mercy to him in a transparent, no bullshit way. Can't we?" And for a minute, it felt like that's what we were going to do. It felt right, just for a minute.

But I had not yet considered all that needed to be considered. Mainly, this: that many people at Galileo Church suffered sexual assault and abuse as children. The number of those cases that I know about is larger than the number in traditional churches I have served, not because (in my considered opinion) there's more of it in my church but because there's more safety to talk about it in my church and because we offer more chances for people to process their experiences theologically, in light of God and God's reign. And I had not considered that some people who have experienced sexual trauma can be retraumatized by the presence of a perpetrator, even one with a sympathetic (to me) story, even one who got caught and paid the price, even one who bears little resemblance to the one who actually hurt them. I did not understand what this man's presence would or could mean to some in my church, how emotionally expensive and dangerous it would be for them to perpetually process his presence in a place that was supposed to be a safe haven, a refuge for their battered spirits.

Word got out, as it does. Not because people are gossipy but because secrets are impossible to keep, and secrecy is not how we operate anyway. But when news travels by unofficial channels, it gets twisted, and then people are (mostly inadvertently) saying things that are far from true. This one became, in short order, "Katie has invited a pedophile to be part of our church."

So we backed up and started the conversation over again, most especially with co-conspirators and friends of the church whose perspective as survivors we needed to hear. I listened more—to more stories of sexual abuse and trauma. I received waves of people's hurt and heartache and the genuine feelings of betrayal that some people experienced when they heard an approximation of what we were about to do. I reached out to colleagues for counsel. I got a better perspective, learned so much, felt the Spirit changing my mind. And so I wrote a letter. Isn't that what you do, when you feel the Spirit changing your mind?

Excursus: Dumpster Fire: The Letter

February 17, 2017

To the members of the Missional Logistics Team, the Spiritual Care Team, and my coworkers, those who are called and gifted by the Spirit for the good work that God has begun in our church:

Grace to you, and peace, through God our Parent and the Lord Jesus Christ.

I can't tell you how many times I have given thanks for each of you in the last several weeks. Your engagement in the ongoing conversation about the extent of God's welcome, and our ability to embody it in the specific case of R, has been heartening. Even as we disagreed—most of us experiencing serious disagreement within our own hearts about which way to lean—we remained engaged with each other and found avenues for honest expression of emotion, values, hunches, aspirations, and confusion. I hope you experienced these weeks as I did—as a period of significant confirmation that we are not playing around at this "seeking and sheltering spiritual refugees" thing.

As I often say, "I am not the boss of this." But over the last several days I have come to some blessed clarity concerning my own discernment about R and Galileo. I offer these points to you for your consideration, so that I may ask for your prayerful agreement with a new course of action.

1. A clergy colleague helped me see that there was some arrogance in my own assumption that Galileo is a super-church that can withstand anything, and that we are especially equipped to handle truly difficult things like welcoming R. He helped me realize that I had not done adequate research, meaning that I had not trusted that there are other Christians nearby who know how to do what we don't know how to do.

(In fairness, this was reiterated to me by both the parole officer and the counselor. It felt, for real, like we alone were willing; and by being willing, we had to find a way to be able.)

With very little research, through a friend, I found a brand-new non-profit organization called Redemption Bridge. It's a pilot project in Tarrant County that will be implemented across Texas in years to come. Its sole focus is reintegration of criminal offenders, adult and juvenile, with help for job placement, housing, counseling, and—ta dah!—faith community placement. It turns out that R's problem is not a new problem, and we are far from the first church to muddle through it, and there are Christians around us who are further down this road than we are. Imagine that.

2. It also became clear to me that I had not seriously considered what R's experience at Galileo might be like—that indeed, it might be psychologically dangerous for him here. With our ethos of transparency, disclosure, no bullshit, etc., he could become the recipient of anger, rage, and grief from many in our number who remember their own abuse or assault/s. Or, if any of those folks left because of his presence here, he would receive our own grief over lost friendship. The unintended consequence of our welcome might be to set him up as a target. My sense about him is that he is not strong enough to receive that, and that the impossibility of protection would cause him harm.

3. In Christian ethics we often use the principle of "one and only one" to describe how we "weight" each person in a dilemma of conflicting interests. In a conflict, each party counts as "one and only one," with no one counting

more because they give more money, say; or counting less because they are a baby, for example. Every human counts as one and only one.

And that's the principle some of us have been using to consider R's need for welcome: that if "all are welcome," then everyone within the "all" should count as one and only one. Nobody's welcome (an abuse survivor, for example) should preclude someone else's welcome (a penitent sex offender, for example).

I agree that that's the right starting point. But it's also the case, in Christian ethics, that we are asked to acknowledge the reality of "special relations" in our weighting of human beings. I have an obligation to my spouse, for example, that is greater than my obligation to all the other humans in the world. In my personal, ethical math, Lance counts as more than one.

So within Galileo, we have co-conspirators and friends who are "ours"— people with whom we share life at various levels. And in covenant (whether the explicit covenant of co-conspiracy or the implicit pledge of safety for those wounded souls who have already washed up on our shores) we have created "special relations" with a number of people whose psyches cannot bear a persistent, personified reminder of their trauma. I might wish for each of them that spiritual and emotional healing would lead to an unbreakable, inviolable sense of self—but I can't and don't love anyone less for confessing that this is not their reality.

And so I am persuaded that my special relations with the beloveds currently constitutive of Galileo Church preclude weighting R's need for welcome equally with their need for safety.

In conclusion: though I am not the boss of this, I have taken a couple of steps that you should know about.

1. With just a few phone calls, starting with Redemption Bridge, I found a compassionate and wise pastor whose church is not only willing to welcome R but whose church has broad experience in this work. I have shared her information with R and expect to hear soon that he has met with her and formulated a plan for his integration in her church.

2. I talked at length with Aaron, and asked him to share with his G-group that it's likely we will not be asking them to help us integrate R into Galileo. It seemed necessary to alert that group as to my own thinking before they met last night to continue working out the details of their willingness to help. We

should consider how we might thank them for that willingness; their strength has been and will be a remarkable gift to our church.

3. I talked with Dick Lord, our Area Shepherd, and asked if he could come to a worship service soon and take us through a litany of confession and absolution. He was very encouraging to me and agreed that this would be a good next step. It feels to him, as it does to many of us, that this is a turning point for Galileo Church. We're sort of growing up—realizing that we are far from perfect, really just people doing our very best to honor the God who made us and knows us and loves us. Dick and I agreed that we might remember this season as "when the glitter rubbed off of Galileo." I hope you like that image as much as I do. It seems to us, as I think it does to many of you, that sharing this new knowledge with the whole church would be valuable. "But speaking the truth in love, we must grow up in every way into him who is the head, into Christ, from whom the whole body, joined and knit together by every ligament with which it is equipped, as each part is working properly, promotes the body's growth in building itself up in love."

I hope we'll be able to discuss this at next week's Missional Logistics Team meeting, scheduled for 6:30 on Wednesday 2/22. Those meetings are always open; if there are members of the Spiritual Care Team who would like to join us, you are most welcome.

If this letter upsets you or pleases you, relieves you or disturbs you, I would be happy to receive your feedback. It is important to me that we keep the conversation open for as long as necessary, until each of us can rest well in the sure knowledge that God has helped us, as God has helped R, with a strong arm and a mighty hand.

With prayers of thanksgiving for your steadfast work on behalf of this church that we love,

peace—Katie

Dumpster Fire, Part Deux

That was a pretty great letter, huh? I would love to report that after sending that, everyone was fine, and we all lived happily ever after.

But that is not what happened.

Having decided *not* to invite R to Galileo Church and instead appreciating a sister church's ability to welcome him fully, we made plans to hold a worship service in which we, the church's servant-leaders, told the story of what happened and asked for forgiveness. We felt especially heartbroken that Galileo's promise of welcome for all people, even and especially the ones that have been turned away by traditional churches, had hit its limit. We wanted to clear the air and practice transparency, telling the church what had happened and how it signaled turning a corner for us all.

I wrote a litany of confession and absolution that included a space where I would narrate the entire story, protecting everyone's privacy but telling the whole truth about what happened. Dick Lord, our area shepherd (a retired pastor, a mentor-caregiver assigned to us by our denominational governance, and a gift to Galileo, whose name the MLT members practiced saying out loud, over and over, because we were so juvenile at times that we found it funny, no disrespect to Dick, but you find it funny too, don't you?), would come to worship and lead the litany.

In preparation for that worship service, understanding better about what it means to have compassion for people whose hurts are invisible and in the past, but still so tender, I used Facebook to issue a "trigger warning." Here's what I wrote in Galileo's Facebook group (with a bounded membership of people who are actually "with" Galileo in some sense rather than on our public page) on a Thursday in advance of Sunday worship:

So, at 5 p.m. on Sunday 3/19, we will do all the things that make us feel terrific. And we will do one thing that will make us feel like crap.

The church servant-leaders (Missional Logistics Team, Spiritual Care Team, pastoral staff) need to tell you about a situation we've been dealing with. It weighs, like, 14 tons. It's resolved, and it's okay, and in some ways it does not change our life together at all. We could keep it private, and it would probably fade away . . . but that's not really how we do, is it? And frankly, we could use your help in getting back to a place of peace.

Here's the thing: if you are triggered by the mention of sexual assault, which NOBODY AMONG THE CHURCH LEADERS OR IN OUR CHURCH HAS DONE THAT WE KNOW OF, the story we need to share could be hard for you. Please don't automatically assume that you can't come on Sunday, though. Just know that we know that some stories are hard to hear, and harder for some than for others. We are praying for you constantly. Constantly. Constantly. Right now, while I'm typing, prayers for you are happening.

And we, your church servant-leaders, would love it so much if you were also praying for us. You are, right?

Peace to you. Grace to you, and peace, from God our Parent and our Lord Jesus Christ.

Aaaaaaand *that* is when the shit hit the fan.

Dumpster Fire: Shit Hits Fan

It's quite impossible for me to describe what happened next with any measure of objectivity. All I can report with any accuracy is my own state of mind: I kept trying really hard to do it right, and while many people appreciated the effort, some people felt like it was too wrong to be repaired. My heart ached for all of us, all around. My stomach hurt. My head spun.

Mainly, at this point, a few people were too hurt and angry to receive the Facebook post. My intent really did not matter at that point. It just seemed shitty to them that this awful reality in their own lives would not simply lie down and that their pastor kept bringing it up in ways that exacerbated the pain. Comments on the post I had written came in, many of them appreciative and prayerful, but several of them angry. Beloved spiritual refugees who thought they had found safe harbor on our shores accused me of baiting them and using their pain to entice people to come to worship and—worst of all—endangering their children and being an untrustworthy person and pastor.

I detest arguing on social media and follow a strict practice of inviting people into face-to-face conversation whenever I can. It seemed especially important in this case not to go on defense, publicly, against people who were truly wounded, even if their original wounds were not from us. So I kept thanking people for their comments, inviting conversation, and reaching out with phone calls to all that I could. (To be exact, there were four individuals in two couples who were especially and publicly angry, and one of those people was willing to take my call.) I asked the church leaders, no matter what they were feeling, to stay out of the online conflict. It was so hard not to defend the work of all those weeks, all those meetings, all those prayers. But we managed to let it lie.

The night of the service came. The whole worship service was about the reality that sometimes we can't do all that God asks us to do. We can't welcome every single one. We can't forgive everyone who hurts us. We can't take adequate care of the people we've been given. Our church is so human; we are so human; being human is so hard. Sometimes we can't do what's good or right or beautiful; we can only choose the "least worst" option from among several bad options. And then we shared this litany:

Litany of Confession and Absolution

Galileo Church Pastoral Staff,
Missional Logistics Team,
and Spiritual Care Team
March 19, 2017

Kaytee B: In January of this year, right around the time we were moving into the Big Red Barn, Katie H. brought a question to the Missional Logistics Team. Broadly stated, the question was, "When we say that 'all are welcome,' is anybody excluded from the 'all'?"

Nathan: Specifically, a person we did not know had asked permission to come to Galileo Church, and we didn't know how to answer. It seemed at first that the answer would obviously be "yes," based on our theology of God's abundant mercy and wide welcome, and based on our stated mission of seeking and sheltering spiritual refugees. This person was definitely a spiritual refugee.

Kaytee B: But it quickly became clear that welcoming this person into the shelter of this place, this community, would have consequences we had to consider carefully. After many meetings and much prayer, and not a few tears, in consultation with the Spiritual Care Team, our Youngster Czar, and one of our G-groups who might have helped with the concrete details of the welcome, we decided to tell him "no." We were and are shocked and saddened by our own decision, and yet we feel it was the least-worst thing to do.

Nathan: We're here tonight, members of the Missional Logistics Team, the Spiritual Care Team, and the church's pastoral staff, to confess what happened in the name of transparency. It feels like a turning point, in a way, as Galileo Church grows into "real church" with "real church problems." We want you to know what happened, and we want to ask God's forgiveness for the ways our church is not a perfect embodiment of the reign of God.

Kaytee B: Rev. Dick Lord is here because he is our congregational shepherd, appointed by the Trinity-Brazos Area of the Southwest Region of the Christian Church (Disciples of Christ). In other words, he prays for us and advises us when we need help. He'll assist with our litany of confession and absolution. But first, Katie H. will tell us more about what happened.

Katie H: [tell the story]

Katie H: Members of the MLT and the SCT and the pastoral staff, please join me in this litany of confession.

Kaytee B: Our church is not yet four years old,
               but God has called us to do great things.
               We have learned to say "yes"
               to projects and possibilities
               that sometimes take our breath away.

Nathan: Sometimes in our MLT meetings
               we feel almost invincible, like a super-church
               with super-powers. Like we can't fail.

Malcolm: And that feels good,
                because we spent so much time
                in the early years worrying that
                we would not survive another season.

Allison: But when we hit this wall,
                when we met this obstacle,
                we found that we could not
                get over or around it. It would not move,
                and we were stuck.

Susan: So we had to face the reality
                that we are not a super-church.
                We are just a church, filled with
                regular people and led by regular people.

Aisling: We had to admit that we
                could not do for this person
                what we had done for so many before.
                We could not welcome him.

Corina: And this feels like a failure
                of Galileo Church's highest ideals.
                It feels like we can't really say,
                "All are welcome at the table of our Lord."
                Because in this case, we had to say
                "All" does not include that one.

Ryan: As the Youngster Czar I believe
                that we made the least-worst decision.
                For the sake of the families and kids
                who are already here,
                and for the sake of the families and kids
                who will come to us in the future.

Travis: The Spiritual Care Team believes
that we made the least-worst decision.
For the sake of each courageous person
who has endured violation and violence
and comes to Galileo Church
seeking shelter and solace.

Jay: The Missional Logistics Team believes
that we made the least-worst decision.
For the sake of the good and great work
that God has called us to keep doing.

Katie H: But it feels shitty, you know?
Shitty. Because we're sure
that Jesus loves this guy, and
would've added him to his traveling band
of disciples, and would've counted him
among the blessed of God. But we could not.

Harmony: Additionally, we are embarrassed
at how quickly we believed that
no other church in our vicinity
would be able to receive this person.
We imagined that we were
unique in our virtue
and alone in our valor.

Jenny: We forgot for a while that Galileo Church
is part of the larger body of Christ.
We are surrounded by followers of Jesus
who have experience and wisdom
with exactly this situation,
and we almost forgot to seek them out.

Aaron: And we confess our deep relief
at finding a church nearby

that is ready to receive
the one that we did not.

Missy: This is one of those decisions
            where nobody is happy.
            Some in our church will be disappointed
            that we were not more courageous
            and more faithful to the gospel
            of reconciliation and love.

Francine: Some in our church will be hurt and angry
            that we even considered saying yes,
            even though we decided to say no.
            You'll think we are unwise,
            or inconsiderate of your suffering.

Kyle: So we are also confessing
            our fear that our church is not
            strong enough to bear the weight
            of this awful moment.

Ros: But we would not keep it from you.
            We are asking you to help us
            bear what has happened.
            Your leaders need your help.

Katie H: So there is our confession.
            First, that we as the servant-leaders
            of Galileo Church could not embody
            the welcome as we imagined we could.
            Second, that we did not more quickly
            reach out for help from the wider church.
            Third, that we are fearful about
            what this means for our church—
            about what it looks like to move on from here—
            and that we need your help.

We are asking you, the whole church,
to hear our confession and to pray for us,
and for each other,
and for the one we turned away,
and for each person who wonders
whether God's people,
and specifically whether Galileo Church,
can make room for them
at the table of our Lord.

Rev. Lord: Servant-leaders of Galileo Christian Church,
we have heard your confession.
And God has heard your many prayers
over all these weeks
as you have wrestled
with this question.
You have taken your work very seriously.
If you have not been granted peace
around your decision,
you are at least blessed
with the knowledge that the
larger body of Christ
has made a welcome space
for this man you could not welcome.
Now you are asking your whole church
to help you deal with the feelings
that come from that decision.
No church is perfect. Scripture says,
"If we say that we have no sin,
we deceive ourselves,
and the truth is not in us;
but if we confess our sins,
God is faithful and just to forgive our sins,
and cleanse us from all unrighteousness."
And now I invite you to share
the confessional prayer from

the *Book of Common Prayer,*
an old prayer that Christians
around the world use for repentance.

ALL: Most merciful God,
we confess that we have sinned against thee
in thought, word, and deed,
by what we have done,
and by what we have left undone.
We have not loved thee with our whole heart;
we have not loved our neighbors as ourselves.
We are truly sorry and we earnestly repent.
For the sake of thy Son Jesus Christ,
have mercy on us and forgive us;
that we may delight in thy will,
and walk in thy ways,
to the glory of thy Name. Amen.

Rev. Lord: Almighty God have mercy on you,
forgive you all your sins
through our Lord Jesus Christ,
strengthen you in all goodness,
and by the power of the Holy Spirit
keep you in eternal life. Amen.

Paul: *Invite the MLT and SCT to sit down. Invite everybody to sing "Hands and Feet" (The Brilliance).*

That night was the last time that some of our beloveds came to Galileo Church. One woman, as she hurriedly left after worship, shouted over her shoulder to me, "Rot, Katie!" A few people were so traumatized by the public meanness on Facebook and IRL that they stopped coming around, unwilling to risk relationship in a community that could turn on each other that way. An entire family full of beloveds, lots of kids included, walked away and didn't come back because the parents felt we were not taking their children's vulnerability seriously. Others were deeply disappointed in our church's refusal to welcome R as just another spiritual refugee, one who so needed community. It was a sad and sleepless time, for me and I know for many others at Galileo Church. The glitter was indeed all scraped off; we were just a church, doing life together, messing it up, messing it up more the more we tried to fix it. Blech.

Dumpster Fire: Under All That Glitter

I still grieve all that we lost in that season early in 2017—the people, the innocence, our clarity at the communion table about the correlation between God's welcome for all and our welcome for all. But it turns out there was goodness under all that shit-splattered glitter, goodness just waiting to be uncovered.

We started referring to the whole episode as "the dumpster fire" (Kaytee B gets full credit for that one), from the conversation about welcoming R or not all the way to the FB fight and the painful worship service. It's great nomenclature because it doesn't depend on your point of view. Everybody on every side could agree that the dumpster was on fire. And dumpster fires are contained. They don't burn down the city because the dumpster keeps the flames in check. We felt like a conflict that could have been catastrophic didn't do as much damage as it might have, and we were grateful.

So, good things that came out of the dumpster fire. First, the church leaders resolved not to let the conflict rest without exploring whether we had learned anything, systemically speaking, about Galileo Church and how it does or doesn't work. Indeed, with just a little analysis we could see that many of the people who were most distressed and angry about our process (not the decision itself but how we got there and how we communicated it with the church) were not strongly connected to the life of the whole church. They were tangentially connected to distant G-groups that we were pretty sure were not working all that well.

That is to say, we had G-groups that were doing their own version of "togetherness," without much emphasis on Christian discipleship and mostly without guidance or oversight from the church's leaders or pastor. Yes, I'm saying we had weekly G-groups meeting in homes whose facilitators and members almost never attended worship or had any other contact with Galileo Church, and our pastor (me!) never visited them. In our effort to decentralize authority, to trust the church to be the church, we left some of our G-groups drifting in outer space, too far from our gravitational field to trust that we had their best interests at heart.

The church leaders held a long, working retreat over the summer and wrestled through what it would take to shore up our relational infrastructure. We knew that G-groups would have to be supported (better or *at all*) as they carried out the intended mission of the whole church. We wrote a letter to the church to say we were suspending the whole G-group system for a couple of months and rebooting it in the fall in new and life-giving ways. The system still isn't perfect—we're all still just human beings here—but those groups are way more supported and connected and accountable now than they were before. Thanks be to God.

Second, I want to persuade you that there was real growth in the church through all this mess, not just systemically but spiritually. Lots of us had to evaluate what it really *meant*, all these promises of transparency and no bullshit and welcome and togetherness. How much responsibility did we have for each other? How possible was it to really do church in a way that makes us stronger, not more scared and cynical? Did we have it in us, and could the structure we had built bear the weight of our mistake making, learning, and relational repair? *Was God, the Creator and Sustainer of the universe, really with us?* Or was this whole thing on our shoulders alone?

There were lots of conversations in those days about all of that. Remi (they/them/theirs), a young adult whose involvement with Galileo had been deepening over several seasons, was particularly troubled. Remi is one of those all-in people, the true believers who don't hold anything back once they commit. Church conflict is especially hard on people like that. Recently, when they applied for a college scholarship based on a commitment to pursue ministry in our denomination, they wrote about the dumpster fire and how much it hurt to watch some of our ideals go up in smoke.

I said to Katie H, "I think at some point I might have imagined that every Sunday, here at Galileo, God was getting everything God wants. I guess this event is showing me that we're just not there yet." Katie asked if I would be willing to share that insight with our congregation. I agreed. Before leaving from that meeting, I walked all around our worship space and prayed. For everyone who had sat in those seats and heard R's story, for everyone outside who would never find us, for our leaders to find peace with their decision. Upon hearing the story, I had thought I would never want to do that work. In the days that followed, I found that I did not want to do anything else.

The following Sunday, I shared my insights with our church at the communion table. I explained how selfish it was of me, to imagine that on all God's green earth, this little barn was where God was getting every single thing God wants. I affirmed that it is still true, as it always has been, that all are welcome at the Table of our Lord, and that at our little piece of that table, we welcome as many as we can. That talk was a turning point in our community, from surviving the changes in our church identity to thriving in them. The role I played in that transition affirmed my call to ministry, and I've been chasing that goal ever since.

So, yeah, we made it through! Attendance dipped for a while, and we grieved the beloveds who wouldn't return, and we processed and processed and processed until we felt we had wrung every last drop of learning out of the whole thing. Nietzsche was right: we came through it stronger.

Even people who have come around since the dumpster fire of '17 understand that it was a galvanizing time for Galileo Church. I don't often quote chapter and verse to verify my experiences, but this one is too good to pass up: we were *refined* by that dumpster fire, as the good book says in 1 Peter 1:7. If there were easier ways to do it, we'd have surely chosen them. But I think we can mostly agree that we're glad it happened. And so, so, so glad it's over.

Till next time.

Excursus: Closing the Learning Loop
(A Pastoral Letter to the Church, June 2017)

Dearly beloved,

We hope that this letter finds you strong in the strength that God supplies, purposeful in your discipleship of Jesus, and enjoying the comfort and communion of the Holy Spirit.

This letter is long, we know. If you don't have time to read it all, please skip to page 3, "G-Groups: a new plan"; and also read page 6, "What to do now."

Background re: Infrastructure

It's been about ten days since the servant-leaders of Galileo Church (that's the Missional Logistics Team, the Spiritual Care Team, and the pastoral staff, plus a few of our littlest kids) gathered for twelve hours (twelve hours! in a row!) to consider how our church might best accomplish all that God has entrusted us to do and be.

It remains our deep commitment to let God show us new things about how God is working in us. We are (mostly) unafraid of disruptive change as long as it serves our reason for being: *to seek and shelter spiritual refugees, rally spiritual health for all who come, and fortify every tender soul with strength to follow Jesus into a life of world-changing service.*

You are probably aware that earlier this year we got some strong clues that our infrastructure (which is how we connect people to each other) was not as strong as we thought. That is to say, our ways of connection for the sake of Christian friendship were not (always) promoting strong relationships. Strong relationships would give us a common sense of purpose, could withstand the healthy expression of incommensurable points of view, would promote deepening discipleship of Jesus for every individual, and would build up trust in and among the whole church.

Some parts of our infrastructure were doing that, *but not all the parts, all the time.* So the servant-leaders convened to talk about infrastructure—in other words, where the metaphorical "house" of Galileo is strong, and where it's not strong enough. This is especially important because we believe that we will, someday, absolutely go through situations that are as hard as the one we faced together in the winter/spring of 2017. We have a chance now to make some changes that could be vital to our continued survival for the sake of the gospel we exist to share and the refugees who are not here yet, and we're grateful for that chance.

G-Groups: Form Follows Function

As you likely know, Galileo has one large gathering each week for worship (Sundays at 5 p.m.), and many small gatherings that happen throughout the week at taco bars and coffee shops, in the Big Red Barn, and in people's homes. These small gatherings were the particular focus of our working retreat, during which we discerned two main purposes for G-groups.

1. G-groups are Communities of Care in which we honor each other's stories. By practicing habits of listening, narrating, and truth-telling, we learn to trust each other. We share mutual vulnerability. We take turns. We tell our stories. We pray for each other. We allow each person to be exactly who they are, without judgment, without expectation. There is little time for noisy chit-chat; G-groups are more likely to clear the clutter that fills our heads so much of the time. Like Jesus, we take risks in listening and speaking (and being quiet together) so that we can meet people where they are. We each expect that we, in turn, will be met and seen and appreciated and loved.

2. G-groups are Communities of Learning in which we deepen our discipleship of Jesus. Together we learn (or relearn) the One Big Story that God has been telling for a long time. We read the Bible. We join in conversation with Scripture, with each other, with authors we respect, with our servant-leaders, with our Lead Evangelist. We come with soft hearts and open minds. We want to know what God wants, so we can *want* what God wants. We look to Jesus as the fullest expression of God's logic (*logos*, "Word," see John 1:14) among us. We do not expect to ever finish this work, but we hope to keep moving closer to the Center all the time. This is rehabilitative work for many of us who originally learned this One Big Story in a way that diminishes and hurts us or our neighbors. This rehabilitative theological exploration takes time, and we're lucky to be doing it together.

G-Groups: Shared Expectations

The servant-leaders recognize, however, that G-groups have been operating without a shared set of expectations about how G-groups should function to best accomplish the dual purposes of Care and Learning. It is time to be explicit about what we believe G-groups need to successfully achieve those purposes.

1. G-groups need leadership support. Those who lead G-groups need training, curriculum choices, and ongoing connection with other servant-leaders for counsel and relief. Leaders should usually not also be group hosts; it's too hard to be in two roles at the same time.

2. G-groups need shared hosting. Those who host G-groups (in their home, or at a public location) need support in this work, and occasional rest from it. G-groupers (people who come to G-groups, obv!) can share the responsibilities of set-up, clean-up, meal preparation, and attendance reporting. Each G-group needs a system for taking turns, in part to prevent host burnout; and the church should provide teaching about how to participate as a helpful partner in a G-group.

3. G-groups need consistent attendance in a right-sized group. G-groups work best when G-groupers are consistent, and when the groups are right-sized. About a dozen adults is the maximum number for most groups. We know that every person can't come every time, but prioritizing attendance is import-ant for the group's sense of safety-in-belonging. And that safety-in-belonging is essential for the Care and Learning that are the groups' dual purposes.

4. G-groups need to prioritize Care and Learning in the way they spend their time. Without setting a rigorous, uniform schedule for all G-groups, we want to communicate the expectation that eating and drinking, checking in, praying, and engaging biblical-theological learning are essential components of each week's G-group meeting.

5. G-groups need to connect G-groupers to and within Galileo Church. It is our high hope that G-groups will be conduits of close connection with the whole body of Galileo Church. Galileo is forming (and reforming) a the-ology, ethos, ethic, and whole-church relational web, and it feels important that everyone who enters Galileo at any point, including G-groups, be able to participate in our life together. That is not to say that every person in every G-group should always be present for Sunday worship and other expressions of our life together. But it is an express desire that G-groups intentionally draw near to the heart of the larger church, rather than drifting toward an isolated existence apart from the larger church.

G-Groups: A New Plan

Here is a plan that we hope will form G-groups that are strong Communities of Care and Learning, while addressing the shared expectations for leaders, hosts, G-groupers, schedules, and whole-church connection.

1. We're scheduling quarterly turnover. G-groups will follow a standard-ized, quarterly schedule together. New quarters start each December, March, June, and September. G-groups will meet for 10 weeks, and we'll take a church-wide Sabbath rest from G-groups for 3 weeks.

2. Leaders and hosts will vary from quarter to quarter. Indeed, we hope to recruit enough new leaders and hosts that no one will host or lead a G-group more than three quarters of the year—two would be even better. Leaders will receive training and support, and shared hosting responsibilities will be com-municated to all G-groupers.

3. G-groupers will sign up for G-groups every quarter. G-groupers prom-ise to prioritize attendance for 10 weeks. G-groups that currently hold more than a dozen adults will divide in ways that we hope are natural and freeing. If you are currently in a G-group that you love, you can (mostly) stay with that group, understanding that it may divide into smaller groups, change its weekly schedule, meet at someone else's home, and have a different leader.

(This means that we will no longer publish a long list of all the G-groups and invite people to go to whichever one they like; that system has contributed to overcrowding and inconsistency of attendance, hurting the possibility of those groups engaging in Care and Learning. The G-group leaders and hosts, the Spiritual Care Team, and the Lead Evangelist [*moi!*] will work to make sure G-groups are balanced and beautiful. If we mess that up, let us know, and we'll work together to fix it.)

4. Newcomers to Galileo will be offered a G-group just for them: Galileo 101. We hope that new G-groups will grow from this shared experience, with leaders and hosts drawn from among those who have been around a little longer.

5. The Lead Evangelist (*moi!*) will travel to each G-group on a rotation. I'll be available to answer questions about the church, or to talk about the biblical-theological foundations for our life together, or just to get to know each of you better. We imagine that G-groups might send me a question that they'd like to explore, so that I can prepare a discussion around your questions.

6. Curriculum and scheduling will be . . . well, not standardized, but delib-erate. We ask that each G-group choose from Bible study, book study, G-grou-per autobiographies, or other curriculum that supports Galileo's mission and missional priorities; and that each G-group report to the servant-leaders their ten-week plan each quarter.

7. Some G-groups will remain open—i.e. come when you can, any time, no

sign-up required—and constant—i.e. no quarterly rotation or Sabbath breaks. Open G-groups include:

- *G-Sunday*, Sundays at 3 p.m. at the Big Red Barn. (Formerly called Sunday School for Grown-Ups.)
- *G-Kids and G-Youth*, Sundays at 3 p.m. at the Big Red Barn.
- *G-Coffee*, Sundays at 3 p.m. at McDonalds next to the Big Red Barn.
- *Bible & Beer*, Tuesdays at 8 p.m. at Fuzzy's in Mansfield.
- *G-Study*, whenever its leaders select a new book and set up a schedule for reading and conversation, at AB Coffee in Mansfield.

Working Groups of Servant-Leaders

The servant-leaders still have work to do to implement the plan we've outlined. We're forming five working groups that will meet during July and August, bringing back their ideas and plans to joint meetings of the Missional Logistics Team and Spiritual Care Team.

1. Working Group for G-group Leadership Development and Curriculum Support. How do we train leaders for G-groups (separate from hosts) who can lead check-ins, Bible studies, book studies, and prayers; and help make connections for pastoral care? Members include Ryan (staff), Allison (MLT), Nathan (MLT), Melina (SCT), Laura Jean (ordination candidate).

2. Working Group to Develop Shared Hosting Handbook. Can we (a) recruit and train hosts that are not already hosting, and (b) collect and produce resources for the sharing of host responsibilities in G-groups? i.e. recipes, food purchase ideas, meal service recommendations, clean-up ideas, reimbursement instructions, timing guidelines. Members include Missy (MLT), Susan (MLT), Francine (SCT), Kaytee (SCT), Aisling (MLT), Eleanor (ordination candidate).

3. Working Group to Schedule Leaders/Hosts/Locations. Our new quarterly schedule will start September 2017. We'll recruit leaders and hosts, map locations, and give instruction to the whole church about what's about to happen. Harmony (SCT), Katie Jane (MLT), Mark (MLT), Missy (MLT), Francine (SCT), Tyler (ordination candidate).

4. Working Group to Reimagine Spiritual Care Team. What is the role of the SCT in the overall Galileo infrastructure? What is the relationship of SCT members to G-groups, including and especially G-groups that are not the primary group for any SCT member? Melina, Kaytee, Harmony, Travis, Francine (all SCT), Jenny (ordination candidate).

5. Working Group to Plan Integration of Newcomers. What is the best structure, within a quarterly G-group structure, for getting newcomers connected in G-groups? How do we teach Galileo 101 without insisting, "this is the way we've always done it"? How do we form new groups so that we're not packing existing groups with more people? Kimberly (MLT), Astreia (MLT), Corina (MLT), Ashley (ordination candidate).

What to Do Now

Galileo's servant-leaders hope for three things—nope, four:

1. *That we will be engaged together in prayer for our church's infrastructure, as it is the framework for all that we are called to do and be together, and we need God's help and each other's cooperation to make it work. Pray your thanksgiving for the G-group leaders and hosts who have opened their hearts and their homes to so many for so long. Pray God's help for our working groups, for future hosts and leaders, for G-groupers across our whole church who depend on this infrastructure for companionship on their journey.*

2. *That all G-groups (except the Open G-groups as described above) will take a Sabbath rest in July and August of this year. In other words, don't meet as a group. Invite each other to dinner, go bowling together, get ice cream with church friends, whatever . . . but let your group leaders and hosts, and all of our best intentions, relax and breathe for a while.*

3. *That each Galileo person (G-person?) will prayerfully consider whether you might be a good leader or host for a G-group—not forever, but for one quarter at a time, with plenty of training and support. If you're wondering whether this might be a good fit for you, please let me know and I'll talk and pray through it with you.*

4. *That our church will be ready for a September G-group Restart with new configurations, new hosts and leaders, and new expectations for how we can be Communities of Care and Learning for each other.*

We continually give thanks that God has called us into community with each of you, and that the Spirit of the living Christ is helping us live into the future of God's imagining. Please let us know what this letter means to you. May God lead us more and more deeply into Communities of Care and Learning, for God's own sake, and for the sake of the world God loves, and for the sake of the people who are not here yet.

grace and peace,

Katie,

with the Missional Logistics Team, the Spiritual Care Team,

and the pastoral staff of Galileo Church

A Christian University: We Didn't Pick This Fight (Early 2018)

Picture this: a conserving Christian university hires a talented, smart, experienced, het-cis couple to serve as its co-chaplains. Their hiring is announced in the school paper, with a link to their home church, which happens to be named after a Renaissance era mathematician. Alumni of the university click the link, read about Galileo Church, and freak out because we are so queer and so everything that is wrong with the world, the way they see it. Alumni calls to the administration of the university result in the couple not having the job, though they had quit their jobs here and sold their home in preparation to move. We grieve and rage with them, but we don't talk about it at all because of #legalstuff. And because it's their story to tell, and they're not vindictive people.

But a few days after that all goes down, we are alerted that an alumnus of the university has declared open hostility for the way the school handled the situation. He wishes that instead of the couple disappearing from the school's landscape, the school would instead state its unequivocal rejection of their hiring because of their queer-affirming theology. He makes a website; he puts up a Facebook page; he publishes his screed against the liberalizing of his alma mater. And then he brings Galileo Church into it.

To prove how awful we are, in an open letter published online, he pulls text from our own website. He's kind of grossed out by our whole aesthetic and ethos, and he's sure our theology is bankrupt. The best stuff is gleaned from our own writing: "In addition to its 'missional' priority on LGBTQ+ activism, the Galileo Church website describes the church aesthetics [*sic*] as 'unironic super-gay.'" Which is so true. But it's a lot to have your entire church denounced repeatedly as un-Christian, theologically and morally bankrupt, in public.

We were, um, pretty angry about all of that. First of all, for our friends who lost their dream job, and, second, for getting dragged into a fight we did not start and did not want. We called a meeting of church leaders and anybody else who wanted to talk about it and figure out what to do.

Our anger at first led us to imagine how we could counter the angry man's attack. How could we make him look and feel foolish and small? How could we use our wide social media audience to poke fun at his small-minded homophobia and trans phobia? How, indeed, could we provoke even more back-and-forth with him, certain as we were that we would come out of such a conflict smelling sweet? We wanted vindication. We might not have asked for the fight, but now that we were in it, we intended to win.

But.

But (1) how much of that agenda could we pursue in the name of Jesus our brother, who, "when he was abused . . . did not return abuse; when he suffered . . . did not threaten" (1 Peter 2:23)? And (2) though our friends were seriously hurt, were they actually asking us to pick up swords to fight for them?

(1) Not much.

(2) No.

So—still in the same meeting—we took another swing at it. "Who," I asked, "is actually getting hurt, here? Our friends are going to be fine, they've assured me. And Galileo Church is actually fine; this guy hasn't done anything but quote us back to ourselves. We *are* unironic supergay, whatever the hell that means. So no harm done."

But.

But many of us in that room could remember being eighteen, nineteen, twenty years old, away from home at college or elsewhere, trying to work out our identity. We could remember adults in our families, in our churches, in our Christian universities, who did not help us live into our whole selves, who actively prevented us from living into our whole selves. We could remember the devastating realization that who we were was not ever going to be acceptable to God (or so we believed at the time). We could remember being dangerously confused, dangerously heartsick, as we tried to grow up into the persons God imagined us to be. We remembered imagining that God did not love us or want us as we were. We knew that the real hurt in this fight would be, probably already was, the collateral damage to the queer students of said Christian university.

So we decided, as we often do for the hardest stuff, to write a pastoral letter. Hey, it's the way the early church got through a lot of hard stuff, right? We wanted to add our public voice to the clamor, hoping that our song of liberation and acceptance in the name of Christ would rise above the noisy critics' kvetching. We wanted to tell those precious not-quite adults that we were mentally telegraphing buckets of love their way, buckets and buckets of the very love that God had poured out for us. I got busy writing.

We posted the letter to our website on February 15 and linked to it from all our platforms. It got shared half a billion times or so. (JK. I lost count.) We sent it to the school paper at the university and the local newspaper in that town. We hoped beyond hope it would make its way to the students who needed it most, and within forty-eight hours, it had.

My phone rang with a call from an area code I did not recognize. It turns out, the then-president of the semi-official LGBTQ+ students' group at the university is from Hawaii. She said, "We got your letter. It is amazing. We are so grateful. We are crying actual tears over here. We are sharing your words with each other. It's like an *epistle*, just for us!"

In the weeks to come, that student group would read our letter aloud in their alternative chapel service. Another student would recite it as part of a performance of *The Vagina Monologues* in that city. The student group invited me to preach at their chapel service, an invitation I was happy to accept. Until, that is, the angry alum found an announcement of that intention in our newsletter and published it on his website. That's when the university told the student group to disinvite me, saying I wasn't on the approved speakers list. The administration actually made that young woman call me herself and tell me to stay home. Unbelievable.

Here's the really weird thing about all of this: the angry alumni and Galileo Church are actually on the same side of this triangulation with the university. We too wish this school and all Christian institutions, including congregations, would get clear about their policies regarding LGBTQ+ inclusion. As it is, the vaguery of "all are welcome" in many churches, and the admissions policies of Christian institutions that are not explicit about their beliefs concerning LGBTQ+ identities, are full of potential harm for LGBTQ+ persons who erroneously trust that the church or school has their best interest at heart.

We've been especially appreciative of a new nonprofit called Church Clarity (churchclarity.org), the whole purpose of which is to press all Christian institutions to be explicit in either their full inclusion of or their restrictions on LGBTQ+ persons. #Clarityisreasonable is their mandate, and we agree. Clarity is coming at the particular university in question. The school administration has doubled down on policies that seek to regulate the expression of lesbian or gay identity. And I believe that Galileo Church's public, pastoral presence to current students there sends a loud, clear message to those who come next: *this is not a safe place to be queer*. It is survivable, but it's not an environment for the flourishing every human being deserves. We republish our letter every so often just to let everybody know it's still true: "God's *love*, rather than God's judgment, is the force that powers the entire exquisite, expanding universe." You are so loved. Yes, you.

Excursus: To the Dearly Beloved Queer People of the University (February 2018)

To the dearly beloved queer children of God, especially those connected with [a certain Christian university];

From the co-conspirators and friends of Galileo Church, a gathering of God's faithful in the suburbs of Fort Worth;

Grace to you, and peace, from God our Mother-Father and our brother-Savior Jesus.

We hope this letter finds you feeling strong in the strength of God's power; but we fear that may not be the case. Your identity, wherever you fall on the LGBTQ+ rainbow, has been under assault during this last little while. It's likely that your school and church communities don't feel like safe places for you right now.

That's why we're writing to you. **We have news for you,** and we're hoping you'll receive it as the best news you've ever heard: *God's love is real, and God's love is for you, and God's love is worth it.* (We'll say more about "worth it" in a minute.)

Just so you know, there are lots of people at Galileo Church who come from the same theological background that you do. Yeah, we've got a lot of former CofC-ers in our number. (A bunch of Baptists, too, and you might find this hard to believe, but *there's not that much difference.* At least, not in the way those groups have historically thought about LGBTQ+ people.) We were Christians who thought we knew that God likes and approves of some people more than others; and that God dislikes and disapproves of the way some of us feel in our hearts, in our bones, in our spirits. Some of us tried for years (and prayed, and prayed, and prayed) to become other than we are. Some of us even tried to hurt ourselves to get rid of the constant pain of thinking God didn't want us.

And then we found out the truth: that **God's *love*, rather than God's judgment, is the force that powers the entire exquisite, expanding universe;** and God's love is *not* meted out in stingy little portions to some people and withheld completely from others. God knows exactly who each of us is, and God is so *extra* that God loves us like a freakin' waterfall of love, just as God made us. And God, as you no doubt know, **made some of us QUEER.** And fabulous. And glittery. And gorgeous. And did we mention fabulous?

So, listen, there are a couple of things we would really like you to hear from us, as sort of sub-points to the main point about God's love for you.

1. You are not an issue or a problem or a pawn in a theological or institutional debate. You are a human being, made *imago Dei*—in the very image of God. You don't have to sit still and react politely when people all around you are debating your right to exist here in all the fullness of your LGBTQ+ identity. You can argue, or ask a friend to stick up for you, or leave, or curse a blue streak and *then* leave. Any of those paths is honorable.

If you have the strength right now to remind people that *you exist*, you splendidly queer Christian, that's great. If you don't, **give yourself a break**. Please take it from people who have known the existential exhaustion of having to defend their right to breathe the air we are all sharing: sometimes you *can't even*, and that's okay. Because we've got your back! (Better than that— Jesus has your back! See sub-point #2.)

2. You do not have to feel grateful to us, or any of your friends or family, for "accepting" you. One thing we have learned is, without queer people, the church is not the church. Jesus lived and died outside of the religious estab-lishment because of his preference for people just like you—debated, belittled, marginalized, rejected. And Jesus showed us the very heart of God, so . . . *voilà*, *God's very heart is for you.*

(Indeed, in the gospels, Jesus's ire is only ever aimed at Very Religious People who keep trying to box other people out of the blessings God has in mind for all people, or step on people whose defenses are not strong. Ever notice that?)

So there are tons of "allies" at Galileo Church—straight people, cisgender people—who really don't want to be congratulated for "welcoming" LGBTQ+ people. Mainly, they feel grateful that there are any LGBTQ+ people who will give them a chance, and give Galileo Church a chance. Because let's face it, the straight-cis church has not often been worthy of your trust. At Galileo the allies finally figured out that Jesus was hanging out on the margins of society, outside the religious establishment, with people just like you, the whole entire time. So **if the allies want Jesus, they gotta stand with you.** See?

3. Back on that thing about God's love being *worth it*—we get that you might not be thinking that's true right now. It has cost you dearly to stay in a place, among people, who can't be trusted to love you completely. And be-cause many of those people carry the name "Christian," you may be ready to throw in the towel on your own Christian faith. We get that. We seriously do. Some of us have barely hung on to our faith by our fingernails.

But we want you to hear us say, from over here in a very safe, very brave, "unironic supergay," Jesus-loving church, that God's love is tooooootally worth it. We don't know anymore how we would live without our #churchfriends. We are so glad we did not give up Jesus to those—well, we'd like to say a certain word here, but this is an open letter—so let's just say we're really glad we didn't give up Jesus to the people who mistakenly thought they owned him. **We have found joy** in our rediscovered, rehabilitated Christian faith. **We wish the same joy for you,** so to reiterate: God's love is real, and for you, and *so gosh-darn worth it.*

Now this letter has gotten long. If you've read this far, thanks. As we wrap it up, **can we ask you for a couple of things?**

a. Can you **share this letter as widely as you can imagine?** It needs to get to people, especially all the dearly beloved queer people of [the univer-sity], who don't yet know that God's love is the realest thing in the world.

Post the link to this letter on Facebook (tag Galileo Church); tweet it out (tag Galileo_Church); Insta a photo of a rainbow-unicorn and tag us again (tag Galileo_Church); rinse; repeat. (And if it works for you, share this letter with people who might share financially in Galileo's mission of "seeking and sheltering spiritual refugees." We want to keep sharing the news about God's Niagara Falls of love, and we're not embarrassed to say, that costs money, and we'd love to have help.)

b. Can you be sure to **talk to someone you trust** if the controversy over your personhood begins to make you feel hopeless or helpless? The world can't afford to lose you. Galileo Church can't bear the thought of missing out on your companionship for this journey. Reach out to us if you need to—we're here, just down I-20, and we want to be of help.

Again, thanks for reading. More than that: thanks for *being*. **You are so loved.** And nothing—no one—will keep us from telling you that, again and again and again. Because "neither height nor depth nor anything else in all creation will be able to separate you from the love of God in Christ Jesus our Lord" (Romans 8:39). Believe it. And stay fabulous.

In the peace of Christ, and in the power of his living Spirit—

The pastoral staff, Missional Logistics Team, and Spiritual Care Team of Galileo Church; and our co-conspirators and friends.

School Board Meetings for Days (Spring 2018 to Present)

She was an elementary school art teacher, and she was getting married. At the beginning of the 2017–2018 school year she told her classes about herself, showing a photo of herself and her betrothed dressed up as Nemo and Dori for Halloween. "She is my fiancée," she told the kids, and when one of the second-graders said, "Ew!" she said, "Don't say 'Ew.' Girls can marry girls, and boys can marry boys, and it hurts their feelings if you say 'Ew.'" A parent complained and got other parents stirred up, and pretty soon the teacher (Teacher of the Year for two years running) was suspended, indefinitely, and sent home with pay. None of this was publicly known for many months because the teacher was warned not to discuss it with anyone.

At least, this is how we think it went down. We're not sure because all those details are tied up in a lawsuit now, the teacher suing the school district Galileo Church was born in.

I started hearing from Galileo Church folks when the teacher's suspension became public in early 2018. Some of them were parents with kids in that school. Some are teachers in the same school district who worried about their own protections under school policy. It took very little investigation to learn that the school district has three policies that govern antidiscrimination, antiharassment, and antibullying, respectively; and that none of the three includes protections for LGBTQ+ employees or students.

We gathered at the Big Red Barn to decide what to do, inviting neighbors and friends, parents and school-district employees, along with activist organization reps. We decided to run on a parallel track to the teacher's lawsuit—parallel, so not crossing or converging—and ask the school board to add "sexual orientation, gender identity, and gender expression" to the lists of protected classes in each of the three existing policies. We looked at examples of this language in the policies of nearby Texas school districts. There are 1,031 school districts in Texas; 11 of those currently have protections for LGBTQ+ persons in their policies. All of those are large cities. The local school district we are working in is not. This town is socially, politically, and religiously conserving. I sometimes say it's a hot crimson dot on a blood-red state map.

All together we call ourselves the Mansfield Equality Coalition, and we attended our first school-board meeting in March 2018. We registered four speakers for the public comments section of the agenda. Each of us had written our five-minute speech from a different perspective: a religious leader (me, wearing a priestly collar), a parent, a school district employee, and a student. There were over fifty speakers registered for public comment that night. Some of them were irrationally hateful. Some of them were ignorant. Some of them expressed amazement that one teacher's private life was such a big deal; couldn't she just keep it to herself? We were proud of our thoughtful, succinct, cogent presentations next to the rants we witnessed.

The dearly beloved queer people from Galileo Church sat through all the comments, enduring the verbal assault. After that #firsttime, we told our beloveds not to come back if it unraveled even one row of their sense of self.

We've had representation and made strongly worded speeches at every school board meeting since March 2018. The policies have not been changed. Attorneys for the school district have warned the board not to amend them while the teacher's lawsuit is still pending. We know this will not be resolved in a hurry. We keep showing up and making our well-prepared speeches to make sure the school board knows they're not off the hook. We have a steady email campaign, sending school board members links to every news report or scientific study that shows again how dangerous it is to leave LGBTQ+ persons unprotected by policy. We imagine becoming even more proactive in seasons to come, inviting traditional media to observe how slowly the bureaucratic machine can be to crank out basic protections for certain kinds of people.

I'm not saying Galileo Church can save gay kids from bullying or gay teachers from firing. My point here is, when we first started, this kind of activism is something we couldn't do, but we are well equipped to it do now. We believe that someday federal law will require protections for LGBTQ+ people in all kinds of public institutions, including schools. We know that it's the small, locally agitative efforts like this one that coalesce into broad-stroke reform at the highest levels. We still believe that the arc of the moral universe is long, but it bends toward justice. As a community-organizing hub for Mansfield Equality Coalition versus "small-town school district," we're bending it.

It's like Dori said: Just keep swimming.

CHAPTER 8

We Are So Glad You've Come

Or: The Work I Was Born For

Just One Week (Early 2018)

In an ordinary week with Galileo Church I do all the normal stuff: hold worship, break bread, kiss some babies, hold a planning meeting or two, have a Diet Coke or a beer or a glass of wine or jalapeño poppers with someone who needs a listening ear, pray, pray some more, write the next sermon in my head and finally on my screen. But there are very few weeks with Galileo Church that are *only* ordinary. Usually, I do all that and more. Like one week at the beginning of March, all of this happened.

- Stephanie texts to say that a West Virginia cousin who had pulled away from her FOO years before has contacted her out of the blue. Stephanie knows her cousin is gay, but her conserving family never speaks of it, and she thinks the cousin must have seen the "Dearly Beloved Queer People of [a certain Christian university]" letter on Stephanie's Facebook page. The cousin wants to visit Stephanie's family in Texas with another MIA cousin who's probably also gay. And Stephanie wants to invite some Galileo people over while they're in town to telegraph her openhearted welcome. Can I recommend some invitees for a low-key dinner? You bet I can. And I'll be delighted to come too.
- Tim, a clergy colleague, writes an email to say that his adult son and his son's partner, both of whom left the church long ago, have been listening to Galileo's sermon podcast, "That's What She Said."

They enjoyed especially the series entitled "Lady Ephesians" in which I compared Ephesians to a drag queen, buxom and gorgeous and completely over the top. Tim and his spouse are going to keep listening also to have a point of faith connection with their son. He'd like to know how he can set up a recurring financial gift to Galileo Church in thanks. I'm humbled and happy to oblige.

- A trans student leader at UTA calls to invite me to keynote a "Faith and Queer Identity" event for undergraduates. "We don't know many faith leaders who would," he says, "but we've heard from past students that Galileo Church's pastor will." He promises me a box lunch for my trouble; will I need vegetarian? I gladly say yes to the engagement, no to vegetarian.

- A gay Galileo co-conspirator who is seriously allergic to worship but fiercely loves his G-group messages through Facebook: "I want to read the Bible, which I know is dangerous on my own, so I want to be equipped with the best Bible I can get. What do you recommend?" I send links for several, with extensive notes about translations and study versus devotional notes. I don't remind him that a few months before he told me he has no use for God or the Bible or any of that crap.

- Tamara, who, for her own reasons, never says two words at worship to anybody, posts an essay in our Facebook group in the middle of the night about how she was kind to someone she hates. She thinks Galileo made her do it. She says how much she doesn't want to be here, doing church, acting Christian. "I've been gone so long," she says. But here she is. After a couple of days I ask if we can publish her essay on our blog. And now it's in this book.

- I meet with Hannah and Eleanor after work, both professionals with busy lives, who have received training and are ready to start our facilitated, peer-to-peer support group for conversation around mental un/health. We decide to call it "Welcome to My Brain" because we like how that conveys the normalcy of all our quirks. There won't be a lot of attendance at W2MB, but they will hold the space and make sure there is room for every soul who needs it. I'm the administrative support for their meaningful ministry.

That's just one week! I could pick almost any week. I happened to scribble down these things as I prepared to exit Galileo temporarily for my writing leave to write this book, leaving myself a little note that would anchor my sense of "why." Why do we do it? Why do people fund it? Why do I want to work all the time? Why is it working? Why do I imagine that long after mainstream Christianity has gone over a cliff in North America, little remnant communities of spiritual refugees will still be sharing the body and blood of Jesus at his table?

You want to know why? Just pick a week at Galileo Church, any week. You'll see.

Mimi on the Beach

I don't dream about the wheat fields and the big farm machinery anymore. There is a new vision for this time that I can show you. But first you have to know the song "Mimi on the Beach." Or maybe you don't. If you don't want a deep dive into 1980s Canadian alt-rock electronica, just skip the next couple of paragraphs.

Jane Siberry, a Canadian songwriter, sang in 1984 about her crush on Mimi, a bold girl who enters the ocean with her surfboard alongside all the boys. The singer is obsessed with the social stratification happening among the kids on the beach ("One girl laughs at skinny guys / Someone else points out a queer"), but even more so with Mimi's intrepid exit from the scene. She waits on the beach, breathless, for Mimi to rise from the water on her pink surfboard. She imagines

> The great leveler is coming . . .
> And he's going to take those mountains
> And shove them into the valleys
> Until there's nothing left except a vast expanse.

Sounds defiantly eschatological, doesn't it?

Remember, our singer isn't the one *doing* the surfing; she's just watching and waiting. She sings my favorite lines monotone in iambic tetrameter: "I stand and scan on the strand of sand / Stand and scan on the strand of sand."

So here's the vision that currently propels my work. I am on the beach, watching. *I stand and scan on the strand of sand.* It's the same posture as the singer, but I'm not looking for strong, capable Mimi; instead, I peer toward the horizon where ships of every kind are passing through the deepest ocean. Cargo ships, sailboats, cruise liners, garbage barges. Once in a while, far more often than I used to understand, one of those boats throws a passenger overboard. Sometimes they throw a whole family into the treacherous waters. I don't much care why they think they did it; just that now there's a desperate, drowning person (or several) flailing in the vast ocean.

I have a fear of natural water (grew up in dry-land farming country and enjoy swimming in chlorinated ponds with concrete bottoms), so even in a vision I don't swim into the ocean to grab them. I know that if I wait, some of those castaways will make their way to my shore. That's how the ocean works. If it doesn't drown you, it tosses you out on the sand eventually. If somebody gets close enough to shore that I can wade in and give them a hand, I do my best.

The castaway on the shore coughs up salt water, vomits out more. I help scrape the muck off their face and arms. They think they are dying. They may be right; I tend to trust people when they tell me how hurt they are. I sit with them there, on the beach, until they feel a little stronger, until they feel a little more alive than dead.

Then I say, "Turn around. You see that stand of trees back there behind us? My beloved friends are there. They have built a shelter for each other in there, and there is room for you. They have plenty to eat and drink, and they will share with you. You can trust them. They will help you back to health. And you do not have to go back into the ocean to swim for your life ever again."

I help the castaway, the lost-but-now-found soul, to their feet. I walk them to the trees, to the comforting shade, away from the burning brightness into the cool darkness of their new home. I introduce them to my beloved friends. Once in a blue moon I tell the story of my own rescue, how this place, these people, saved my one wild and precious life. I have a bite of bread, tip a cup of wine, and then it's back out to the beach for me. *I stand and scan on the strand of sand / stand and scan on the strand of sand.* This is the work I was born for.

How to Write a Book
When You're the Church Founder

Always narrate your church's story to them in ways they can recognize, even when you are not writing a book. Tell them for five years that what is happening here is locally important for our very own lives, but there's a chance it might also be important for people who are not here, people who may never be able to come here. Lots of people want communities of belonging in Jesus's name, and we've found a really good way to do it, so we ought to share, don't you think? They will say yes because they're proud of what we've built together. They want to show it to the whole world, and they trust you to tell the story truthfully and transparently, the best you can. You've been telling it for so long. All you need to do is write it down.

Secure a Pastoral Study Project grant from the Louisville Institute. Let those fine people help you figure out how to tell this story and to whom. Let them suggest, after working with you closely, that perhaps you need to tell the story to yourself first, to figure out what you've actually been doing with your life for the last five years. Let them assure you that this would be a good outcome for their grant money's use. They actually don't care if you ever publish it, though they will be happy for you if you do. And they would like to be acknowledged for their gift if you do.

Ask a sister-friend, someone you've known for twenty-plus years, if she can suspend other parts of her work to fill in for you as Galileo's preacher, liturgy planner, and theologian-in-residence. Tell her you can pay her, but not nearly enough, for all the energy she will spill out for these people you love. Ask her if she will love them too. Tell her you can't guarantee they're ready to hear a black womanist preacher, ready to read the Bible the way she does, ready to see the world through her eyes, but you think they might be, and you trust that she can bring them along. When it turns out that the Rev. Dr. Irie Lynne Session trusts you as much as you trust her, start figuring out how to thank her adequately. You will never figure it out.

Include your sister-friend's story in your last sermon before you go on leave, telling the church not to imagine they're on some kind of vacation because the regular preacher is gone. Tell them the Rev. Dr. Session knows things that you can never know, has things to say that you can never say. Tell them to listen up because you'll want a full report when you get back.

Ask people on the missional logistics team, the spiritual care team, and the pastoral staff to pick up lots and lots and lots of work that you have done previously. Tell them you trust them completely to keep the church afloat in your absence. Then actually do it—trust them. Trust them because they are trustworthy and have shown you that they are capable again and again.

Go home. Do some yoga. Buy an Instant Pot. Find ways to keep from staring at the tyrannical blank screen. Do not write. Feel terrible about not writing. Realize that you are, after five years, seriously tired. Sleep more and more, until you don't want to sleep anymore. Remember what it feels like to be well rested. Think about how it will feel to write a book when you are well rested.

Get dressed, even your shoes, every damn day. Develop a system for keeping your butt in the chair. Poker chips and a timer, if that's what it takes. Imagine the horror of having to tell your church, when the writing leave is over, that you failed to write their story, failed to commit to the virtual page the stories of themselves that you and they have been telling for so long. Guilt is a motivator. Keep your butt in the chair.

Watch your church from a distance. Talk with your sister-friend once in a while; check in with church leaders when it's necessary for your own sense of being needed. Be available if there's an emergency, but remember that almost nothing is an emergency. Watch how, even when there's an emergency, they know what to do. They know how to love each other. They know how to tell the truth. They know how to work it out. They know how to change the plan. They know how to put on a breathtaking Election Eve Eve service of song, prayer, and spoken word called "The World God Wants." They know how to be faithful to God and to each other. Your church knows how to church.

Write it down, these things you have seen, these things you have learned, these things you have become. Tell the truth as best you can. Remember your tendency to lie, because all church planters lie. Don't.

Thanks be to God. *Soli Deo gloria.*

In Their Own Words

For an undergraduate seminar, Remi asked Galileo folks to answer a few questions about their sense of connection to our church. Here are some of the things they said.

> No BS ever right? When my spouse told me we were going to try another church I went, "Cool." She proceeds to tell me that it is LGBTQ friendly. I said, "Cool," but the white cis hetero in me was kinda freaking out. Will they talk to me? Will I have anything in common? Will I trigger someone because I look like someone who bullied them growing up? And that is when I began to tear up a little. This is what my wife [who is African American] felt every time we went on a double date with an all-white couple. This is what LGBTQ people feel when they are trying to be their authentic selves and getting death stares from people walking by. I felt uncomfortable that first Sunday we went, a feeling I have not experienced much in my life. I remember sitting in the back row at Red's trying to hide, and Melissa found us. We already met once at Bible & Beer the Tuesday before, and she remembered our names. I came in to Galileo cautious because for the first time in my life I did not know if I would be accepted. Two years later, I think I can safely say that I am friends with a lot of people at church. The people at Galileo are the most genuine souls I have had the pleasure in meeting in Texas. My Georgia friends were the last time I felt this way. Thank you for welcoming and accepting our crazy crew every Sunday, Galileo. (Sean)

We found Galileo online looking for a church for our kids. My daughter-in-law [who is trans] had discovered her true self, and she and my daughter had decided that her being transgender didn't change their love for each other. We wanted desperately for them to find a community, a church home. It turned out they weren't ready and had their own walk ahead of them. Instead of trying to force our desires and needs on them, we tried Galileo ourselves. I mean, why would we go to a church that wouldn't accept my girls? I had a lot of fear about going to Galileo. My upbringing had taught me to be wary of other churches or belief systems. I was afraid to interpret Scripture or teachings in any other way than that of the Church of Christ. I'm not sure what I was afraid of. But I was very afraid. I had no idea that we were in fact also spiritual refugees!

I was talking to a friend the other day about this very thing. I don't feel required to go to church any more. I don't feel fear I'm going to hell or hurting God if I don't go. I need my family, my family of choice, my support system, my peace. I need it every week, sometimes several times a week. Sometimes it isn't about me; it's about the hug I can give or the smile I can share or even the tear I can shed for someone hurting. There are times I need a rest, and I miss, and I also miss it more than I benefit from the rest. But I know it's good for me to take a break when I need it. It makes me appreciate it more, and I can't wait to be back with my beloveds again.

I have led a responsive reading in worship and it was the hardest thing I've ever done. I grew up in a church where women didn't lead anything in services, so I struggled with the whole thing. Not really that I was doing something wrong, but it was just so abnormal for me. I was terrified to publicly lead in a service like that. At the same time, I was angry that I had let someone tell me all those years that I couldn't.

My favorite ministry at Galileo is how we love the LGBTQ+ community. My heart was always torn between what I was taught and what I truly believed God thought. The pain, the rejection, the hatred in the name of God is something I will never forget seeing and experiencing now with my trans daughter-in-law. I will always do all in my power to show my queer friends and loved ones that I LOVE them with all my heart and so does God. Fuck everyone else! (Kim)

I remember Melina telling me about this strange church at the back of a bar. Melina said they have this cello player that dresses in a skirt and has a long beard, and played the most beautiful music. She happened to visit on a cello Sunday! What made me show up at Galileo was the idea of a church where my trans daughter could feel safe and express her true self. (Mark)

I met Galileo at Tarrant Pride. I had just moved here and was skeptical of everyone. I was a bit late and saw the little float and the walkers— and the T-shirts that said "We are not the center of the universe"—so I knew SCIENCE! But that wasn't enough. There was a booth where it said something about seeking spiritual refugees. I had never heard that term! I literally raised my hand and said, "That is me. God and I are fine, but people and I are NOT. WE are NOT OKAY." I had lived in places where it was dangerous, life-wise, to be gay. I was moving here out of HOPE, so many hopes. I was hoping that I could find a community in which to exist as myself. Any community would do. My secret hope was that I would find a faith community. The sort of bad thing is that when I went to the church the next day, no one out of all the several people I had met was there except for Katie. She remembered me. She said, "It's Melissa, isn't it?" in the communion line. I have always laughed it off as "they were too tired after Pride," but I always make sure I am there the next day just in case.

I have missed a couple of Sundays at Galileo for campaign efforts, but otherwise I am at church unless I am sick. I once was very sick and Katie texted me to give me "permission" to not go to church. She somehow knew that I needed that.

Galileo affects everything, including my family. My daughter found an affirming church in Alabama because of Galileo—long way around but still. Because of Galileo a friend in Alabama was able to reach out for help when her kid came out. About a year after I found Galileo, after communion I went outside and just bawled. I was so overcome with how things happened and how I had found community—I mean, more than that, but that is the best I can do. (Melissa)

I don't get to come to Galileo every week. I've been working in a church, and that greatly limits the Sunday evenings I've been able to attend. That said, every Sunday evening that I have free, I come to Galileo. I love Galileo. Galileo does church right. I take communion some weeks. If I don't take communion, it's typically because my mental health is less than swell, which in some ways seems counterintuitive, but having to interact with people in order to receive communion, even as minimal as that is, can sometimes be hard. I go to the prayer wall to write/read/pray every time that I'm able to make it. There's no face-to-face interaction, but I still get to engage intimately with the community. I love praying for Galileo and its members. I love being in that space. I love standing with the pleases and thank yous of others and offering my own pleases and thank yous into the space as well, trusting that others will stand beside me in my joy and in my sorrow. (Wendy)

The thing that made me originally want to come to Galileo is that it's similar to what the church was like in the New Testament (meeting in homes in small groups, meeting people where they are), and at the same time it's the future of the church. The reason I keep coming is that it has become a big part of my life. The people of Galileo have become like family to me. Galileo has helped me reconnect to my purpose in a lot of ways. (Brandon)

Recently I went through a tragic event with a friend, on a Sunday. I left feeling overwhelmingly sad and shaken to my core and drove straight to Sunday service at Galileo. As I walked up to the door, a few minutes late, I could hear the singing of Stephanie, our worship architect, and it was like my soul exhaled in relief. Church was the only place I wanted to be in that moment. All my life I've heard people say things like that about their church, and I knew it was supposed to be true. It never was for me. I thought it was just me—that maybe I was just too curmudgeonly to let church be of comfort. But that night—my church embraced me, held me up, and cared for my wounds. Not a single person in the room knew what had just happened. Their care was not in reaction to my pain—it's just the same care they offer to everyone who shows up to the Big Red Barn. (Jeana)

I come to church every Sunday that I can with very few exceptions. Sometimes when I come I am world-weary or just tired from staying up late during the weekend. I often feel down about the week to come because it's almost Monday. Worship always helps me feel better about the world. The singing and praying and community that we do during worship remind me that The World God Wants is possible, and indeed real, and that someday it will be on earth as it is in heaven. I always leave worship feeling calm about what is to come because I know that I am not alone, and that God is there for everyone. (Lydia)

I just feel loved, always. I also somehow kind of carry all of you with me all the time. I feel a sense of belonging that I haven't had . . . maybe ever? So yeah. I actually really belong somewhere. And that feeling makes me feel . . . overwhelmed trying to find an adjective to describe it. It's fabulous. And marvelous. Soul comforting. Reassuring. Strengthening. (Ashley)

A fellow Brite student recommended Galileo. She said it was "weird," so I looked it up. I experience connection here. If I'm ever feeling obligation, I find that it turns into connection once I get to G-group or worship or whatnot. When I was attending twelve-step meetings once upon a time, one of the "warnings" was that if you ever want to skip a meeting, you need it more than ever. I find this to be true about Galileo as well. I am a very introverted person. It takes a lot to come out of my cave. I tend to isolate and get into a work-home rut if I'm not careful, and Galileo keeps me from isolating and makes me feel a part of something important. (Eleanor)

I came because I overheard Katie and Aisling and some others discussing supporting trans people during the bathroom bill thing at AB Coffee. I figured out they were some sort of church group. So I asked to find out which one so I could go. Honestly, I have a hard time attending worship some days. It's some sort of odd legacy from my conservative past. I love that Galileo never peer-pressures people into going through the motions. Galileo is a place where I don't have to pretend and where love abounds. (Hannah)